SUNCOAST EMPIRE

D1225615

Other books by Frank A. Cassell

Josie and Salem: An Indiana Love Story (2011)

We Made No Little Plans: A Memoir (2007)

Seeds of Crisis: Public Schooling in Milwaukee Since 1920.
Co-editor, John L. Rury (1993)

The University of Wisconsin-Milwaukee: A Historical Profile.
Co-authors, J. Martin Klotsche and Frederick I. Olson (1992)

*Merchant Congressman in the Young Republic: Samuel Smith of
Maryland, 1752–1839* (1971)

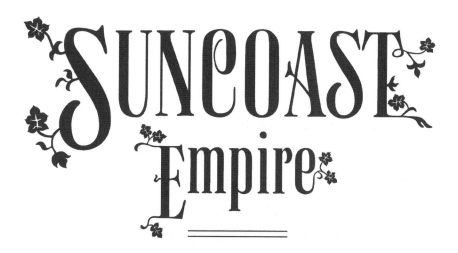

SUNCOAST Empire

*Bertha Honoré Palmer, Her Family,
and the Rise of Sarasota, 1910–1982*

Frank. A. Cassell

Pineapple Press, Inc.
Sarasota, Florida

Copyright © 2017 Frank A. Cassell

All rights reserved. No part of this book may be reproduced in any form or by any means, electronic or mechanical, including photocopying, recording, or by any information storage and retrieval system, without permission in writing from the publisher.

Inquiries should be addressed to:

Pineapple Press, Inc.
P.O. Box 3889
Sarasota, Florida 34230

www.pineapplepress.com

Library of Congress Cataloging-in-Publication Data

Names: Cassell, Frank A., 1941- author.
Title: Suncoast empire : Bertha Honoré Palmer, her family, and the rise of
Sarasota, 1910-1982 / Frank A. Cassell.
Other titles: Bertha Honorâe Palmer, her family, and the rise of Sarasota,
1910-1982
Description: Sarasota, Florida : Pineapple Press, [2017] | Includes
bibliographical references.
Identifiers: LCCN 2016039951 (print) | LCCN 2016045278 (ebook) |
ISBN 9781561649846 (hardback) | ISBN 9781561649853 (pbk.) | ISBN 9781561649877
Subjects: LCSH: Palmer, Bertha Honoré, 1849-1918. | Sarasota
(Fla.)--History--20th century. | Sarasota Bay Region (Fla.)--Biography. |
Palmer family. | Businesswomen--Florida--Sarasota Bay Region--Biography. |
Real estate developers--Florida--Sarasota Bay Region--Biography. |
Agriculture--Florida--Sarasota Bay Region--History--20th century. |
Sarasota (Fla.)--Commerce--History--20th century. | Upper class
women--Florida--Sarasota Bay Region--Biography. | Women--Florida--Sarasota
Bay Region--Biography.
Classification: LCC F319.S35 C37 2017 (print) | LCC F319.S35 (ebook) | DDC
338.092 [B] --dc23
LC record available at https://lccn.loc.gov/2016039951

First Edition

Design by Modern Alchemy LLC
Printed in the USA

Bertha Honoré Palmer.
Chicago History Museum ICH i53159.
Photographer: Matthew J. Steffens.

"And now, Mrs. Davis, in my judgment, the most notable, important, and outstanding and far reaching achievement for Sarasota and the whole Sarasota Bay area, was when the Potter Palmer family came to Sarasota early in 1910."

—A. B. Edwards, first mayor of the City of Sarasota, in an interview with Sarasota County Historian Dottie Davis, July 23, 1958.

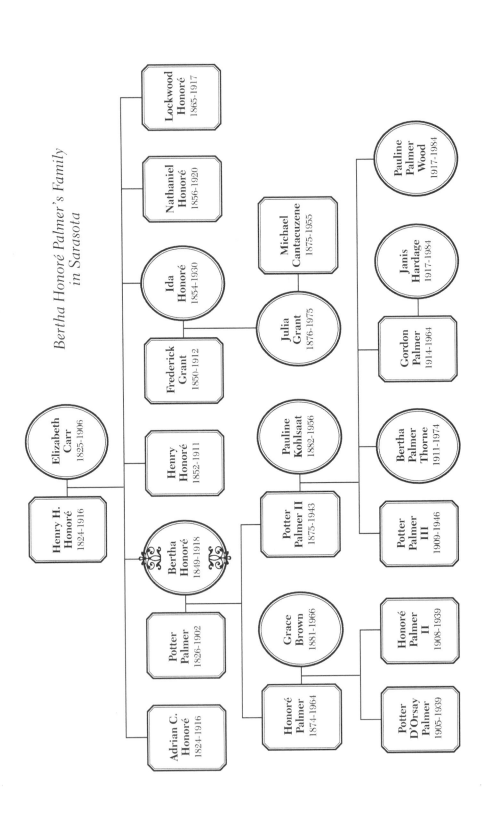

*Bertha Honoré Palmer's Family
in Sarasota*

Henry H. Honoré
1824-1916

Elizabeth Carr
1825-1906

Adrian C. Honoré
1824-1916

Potter Palmer
1826-1902

Bertha Honoré
1849-1918

Henry Honoré
1852-1911

Frederick Grant
1850-1912

Ida Honoré
1854-1930

Nathaniel Honoré
1856-1920

Lockwood Honoré
1865-1917

Julia Grant
1876-1975

Michael Cantacuzene
1875-1955

Honoré Palmer
1874-1964

Grace Brown
1881-1966

Potter Palmer II
1875-1943

Pauline Kohlsaat
1882-1956

Potter D'Orsay Palmer
1905-1939

Honoré Palmer II
1908-1939

Potter Palmer III
1909-1946

Bertha Palmer Thorne
1911-1974

Gordon Palmer
1914-1964

Janis Hardage
1917-1984

Pauline Palmer Wood
1917-1984

CONTENTS

FOREWORD

I first met Mrs. Potter Palmer in the late 1970s, some 60 years after her death. She was introduced to me by my mother, Marguerite E. Cassell, who had a great interest in Chicago's Columbian Exposition of 1893 and the people who made that world's fair one of the grandest ever held. One of those individuals was Bertha Honoré Palmer, President of the Board of Lady Managers of the exposition, spouse of Potter Palmer, who erected the Palmer House Hotel; friend of Jane Addams of Hull House fame; and champion of the principle that women deserve equal pay with men when doing the same work. Bertha and her board made the world's fair a showcase for women's achievements throughout the world and focused attention on the discrimination women confronted in almost every area of life. Many reform groups tried to use the fair to promote their causes, but none succeeded so well as women did, thanks to the leadership of Mrs. Palmer.

My mother's passion for the Columbian Exposition and for Bertha Palmer, who became her personal heroine, eventually persuaded me to help her efforts to understand better the significance of the fair. By 1980 she had collected a great deal of Columbian Exposition memorabilia as well as numerous histories and biographies covering the event and the principal people associated with it. I had by then been a history professor and campus administrator at the University of Wisconsin-Milwaukee for many years. I had written and published a great deal on the origins of the American political party system in the early years of the American Republic. However, administrative responsibilities had hampered my ability to conduct sustained research. In 1980 I found myself free of such duties, at least for a while. I decided to commence a major research project on the world's fair of 1893. That meant, in part, reading Bertha Palmer's official records from the Columbian Exposition as well as many of her personal papers, all located at the Chicago History Museum.

Over the next decade I published articles exploring the impact of the fair on foreign policy, individual states, and national reform movements. My mother co-authored several of these articles, and together we led many tours of the world's fair site in Jackson Park on Chicago's South Side on behalf of the University of Wisconsin Extension. We both strongly supported the proposed 1992 Chicago World's Fair to mark the 500th anniversary of Columbus' voyage of discovery, and I served as a consultant to the organizing committee. However, the idea died on the shoals of Chicago's complex politics. With that, public interest in the history of the Columbian Exposition waned.

Some 14 years later, after I completed a decade as president of the University of Pittsburgh at Greensburg, my wife, Beth, and I retired and moved to Sarasota, Florida. Although I had known some general facts about Bertha's life after the world's fair, I had never examined her final years in any detail. I knew that she had spent most of those years in Florida and died there in 1918. It was not until we arrived in Sarasota that I realized this was where she purchased 140,000 acres, built a great estate, and transformed the agricultural and cattle industries of the region. The memory of Bertha Honoré Palmer is kept alive in Osprey, a town just south of Sarasota, at Historic Spanish Point, which occupies 30 acres of what was once a 350-acre estate Bertha called Osprey Point. Here can be found a small museum and manuscript collection on Bertha's life, particularly in Florida. The site contains a significant representation of the huge gardens Bertha planted around her mansion, called The Oaks—a structure long since torn down. Historic Spanish Point honors not only Bertha Palmer but also the earliest settlers in the Osprey area as well as several thousand years of Native American occupation marked by huge shell middens and burial mounds that Bertha took care not to destroy.

Historic Spanish Point reintroduced me to Bertha Palmer, and in the process raised a number of historical questions that seemingly inevitably drew me into the research that led to this book. From my earlier work I knew Bertha to be the arbiter of Chicago society, whose word was law in terms of social standing and acceptability. She was also a social giant in Bar Harbor, Maine; Newport, Rhode Island; London; and Paris. She had homes in all those locations plus the Isle of Wight. So what was the social leader of Chicago, and friend of kings, queens, and assorted nobility attempting when she established herself on Florida's southwest frontier at the edge of a jungle? Her husband, Potter, had died in

1902, but she brought with her to Florida her two sons and their spouses, several brothers, her father, one aunt, a sister, and her niece, who was born in the White House and married a Russian prince. Once in Florida, what did she actually do? Parts of her experience are well documented, but many important aspects remain a mystery. Her biographer, Ishbel Ross, says she was a great businesswoman. But what exactly did she accomplish to justify such praise? Above all, what was her impact on the development of the Sarasota region between 1910 and 1918?

I believe that Bertha's Florida years represented not merely a coda to her distinguished career before 1910, but a period of personal reinvention during which she achieved a great deal as a real estate investor and as a notable experimentalist in farming and livestock raising. Moreover, her efforts to build an economic empire in southwest Florida attracted both wealthy investors and many middle-class Northerners who bought land, built houses, and established farms and businesses. They became the backbone of the Sarasota community. She quickly grasped the fact that she could not succeed in her business ventures unless she helped make the Sarasota area an attractive one for tourists. She also perceived that few would buy her lands unless they were internally and externally linked by a system of roads, railroads, and deep-water passages along the coastline to facilitate travel and trade. Of necessity she became a driving force in developing infrastructure in Sarasota County and in publicizing the area's natural assets nationally and internationally.

As I studied Bertha Palmer's Florida aspirations, I became more aware of the importance of her family members in managing, developing, advertising, and selling the 140,000 acres of land she had purchased. Among the most influential were her father,

Henry H. Honoré; her brother Adrian; her two sons, Honoré and Potter Palmer Jr; and her niece's husband, Prince Michael Cantacuzene, Count Speransky, of Russia. After Bertha's death in 1918, these men, save for Henry Honoré, who died shortly before his famous daughter, were the leaders of the vast and sprawling economic ventures put together by Bertha and her husband, Potter. Remarkably, the importance of the Palmer family in Sarasota between 1918 and 1982 is little studied or understood. In fact, the family's vast land holdings in Sarasota County gave it great leverage in local matters. The family initiated huge business ventures that made it the largest local employer during the Depression and a vital financial pillar of the community.

Even today the impact of the Palmer family is still apparent, although the great mansions and estates they created no longer exist save for Historic Spanish Point. People living in subdivisions in Palmer Ranch or at The Oaks, the Landings, Eagle Point Club, and dozens of other development communities along the lower reaches of Philippi Creek or around the city of Venice and in the Osprey, Bee Ridge, and Fruitville areas are likely residing on former Palmer lands. Myakka River State Park occupies the site of Bertha's ranch, named Meadowsweet Pastures. And everyone who drives sooner or later passes along such roads as Honoré, Palmer, Potter, D'Orsay, and others honoring the Palmers or those working for them.

I was very fortunate in writing this book to have close at hand the library and archives of the Sarasota County Historical Resources division and its superb staff. At one time or another I received useful tips on local sources from Lorrie Muldowney, Ryan Murphy, and Larry Kelleher. Larry was also invaluable to me as a guide to the photographic and map holdings of Historical

Resources. I owe a special debt of gratitude to former County Historian Jeff LaHurd, who often pointed me in the right direction. He also read the manuscript and made a number of useful suggestions. Executive Director John Mason and staff members Kara Morgan and Garrett Murto at Historic Spanish Point did everything they could to bring relevant documents in their archives to my attention. Staff at the Manatee County Historical Records Library were equally diligent in guiding me through the complexities of land records so that I might better understand Bertha Palmer's acquisition of about one-third of the land in what became Sarasota County. I am very grateful to the patient and knowledgeable archives staff members at the Chicago History Museum, where I spent several weeks exploring that institution's extensive holdings on the Palmer family in Florida. I thank Jim Middleton of Eagle Point Club in Venice, Florida, who provided a wonderful and informative tour of the camp that Bertha Palmer created to attract rich Northerners to the Venice area as a winter retreat. Many of the original buildings remain. I express a very special thanks to the staff at Myakka River State Park. Park Ranger TerranceTorvund, a fellow member of the Sarasota Historical Commission, arranged a fascinating tour of Bertha Palmer's Meadowsweet Pastures ranch house site. He and his colleagues provided a wealth of information on Bertha's cattle raising operation. Finally, I thank June and David Cussen of Pineapple Press for their help and expertise in this project, and Lorin Driggs for her careful and sensitive copyediting.

My spouse, Elizabeth Weber Cassell, was with me every step of the way in the research and writing of this book. She joined me on numerous trips of discovery throughout Sarasota County to establish exactly where the Palmer Empire was located. She typed the manuscript, made editorial changes, and engaged me in many hours of discussions about the significance of the Palmer family to Sarasota County. But all of this was familiar to her for she had done these things many times over during my fifty-year-long career as a historian. The two of us, as part of my research for various books and articles, have walked the battlefields of the French and Indian War, the American Revolution, the War of 1812, and the Civil War. And, of course, she was always a part of my explorations in Jackson Park where Chicago's great White City stood in 1893. More recently we strolled the streets of small southern Indiana towns and along the banks of the White River as we sought to understand the post-Civil War era social structure of the area that gave rise to a remarkable love story. History, in short, has always been an integral part of our 55 years of marriage.

I dedicate this volume to my mother, Marguerite Ellen Cassell, who inspired me to explore the significance of Bertha Palmer and the World's Columbian Exposition. But I also dedicate it to my grandchildren—Grace, Claire, and Jack Grande-Cassell; Jackson Dukes; and Griffin and Conlan Cassell. The last and newest dedicatee is my handsome great grandchild, Kieran Grande-Cassell. It is my hope that at least one of them will become a historian.

Frank A. Cassell
Sarasota, Florida
January 2016

INTRODUCTION

In February of 1910, Mrs. Potter Palmer and members of her family stepped down from their private Pullman car in Sarasota, Florida, after a 34-hour ride from their home in Chicago. One of the best-known women in America, Bertha Palmer was also among the wealthiest. Besides her fabulous home on Chicago's Gold Coast, she had mansions in Paris as well as in London, where she was a member of King Edward VII's inner social circle. In 1893 she had been the president of the Board of Lady Managers at the great Columbian Exposition in Chicago. The creation of the board by federal law marked the first time in American history that the government had granted such official recognition to women. As she famously said, the United States government had "just discovered woman."

In 1900 she was the first American woman appointed by a president and confirmed by the Senate to a government post as a member of the American World's Fair Commission supervising the U.S. exhibits at the Paris World's Fair. Art collector, women's rights advocate, businesswoman, and owner of Chicago's Palmer House Hotel, Bertha now surveyed a frontier community of some 900 citizens, with electricity available only a few hours a day and sewage running down to Sarasota Bay along the middle of Main Street. The town's one hotel was so shabby that a newly built sanitarium was quickly reconfigured to house her party. To the local citizens she must have seemed like a being from a different planet. Yet they also saw her as their economic salvation.

Bertha was accompanied by her older son, Honoré, her father, Henry H. Honoré, and her brother Adrian C. Honoré. Later, other Palmers and Honorés would join them. That February day was the beginning of a seven-decade-long relationship between Bertha and her family and the city of Sarasota and its surrounding areas. The Palmers and Honorés would make a great deal of money from their investments, while the Sarasota region would gain population, a stable economy, an infrastructure of roads, railroads, and new towns, and a modern agricultural industry. Perhaps just as important, Bertha's presence in Sarasota brought national and international attention to the region and spurred yet more migration and investment. In the decades after Bertha's death in 1918, her family initiated additional economic ventures in Sarasota that helped cushion the area from the full effects of the collapse of the Florida land boom and the Great Depression.

This book tells the story of the 72-year-long relationship between a remarkable family and the city and nearby areas. At the heart of this saga is Bertha Palmer herself. She had reached the pinnacle of social success both in America and abroad. Yet she suddenly and with almost no explanation traveled to Florida, purchased 140,000 acres of land, and declared Sarasota to be her new winter home. But she meant her new empire to be much more than a personal fiefdom. She intended to make money from it in as many ways as possible. Her model to some extent was Henry Flagler, who had developed a railroad and luxury hotel empire along Florida's east coast from Jacksonville to Miami and eventually to Key West. She, too, hoped to attract the affluent to buy land along the many miles of scenic coastline she owned in western Florida. Ultimately, however, she made her real mark in raising cattle and developing farmland. Florida was far from the grand balls she had so often attended on two continents. As a very rich woman, she had many choices as to what to do with her life and where to live. Yet at age 61 she elected to spend much of each year on one of America's last frontiers and to create communities out of marshlands, pine forests, and tropical jungles. Her family followed her in this venture, and when she died, they carried on what she had started.

Bertha's family included able, well-educated, and seasoned individuals such as her father, H. H. Honoré, who had accumulated large real estate holdings in several parts of Chicago. He served her as a trusted advisor. Her brother Adrian helped her administer her dead husband's vast real estate empire in Chicago. Both of her sons, Honoré and Potter, were Harvard educated, trained in banking, and active in managing the Palmer House Hotel and other Palmer enterprises. Bertha's niece, Princess Julia Grant Cantacuzene, granddaughter to Ulysses S. Grant and born in the White House, became a writer, a noted anti-Communist, and an influential Washington, D.C., hostess. Julia's husband, Prince Michael Cantacuzene, a high-ranking general in the

Russian army, suffered serious wounds in World War I leading a massive cavalry charge against German troops. Cantacuzene eventually made himself an indispensable part of the Palmer enterprises in Florida during the 1920s, 1930s, and 1940s, as well as an important asset to the Sarasota community. There were, of course, other Palmer family members living or at least wintering in and around Sarasota, including Potter D'Orsay Palmer, eldest son of Honoré Palmer, whose drinking and womanizing caught the attention of the entire nation in the 1930s.

The story of the Palmers in Florida is important for several reasons. First, it adds to the understanding of Bertha Palmer's final years, and shows her capacity to think big, act decisively, and use her wealth and influence effectively. The society queen and social reform advocate excelled as a frontier entrepreneur, just as she had in every other endeavor in her life. Second, the Palmers shaped and influenced Sarasota County and the city over a very long period. The future of the area would likely have been very different if the Palmers had launched their various economic initiatives elsewhere in Florida. The Palmers and Sarasota had a synergistic relationship: Both did well because their interests were so intertwined. Third, besides longevity, the Palmer involvement in the Sarasota area was notable for its breadth and transformative power. The Palmers played critical roles in modernizing farming and cattle raising, improving transportation, spurring population growth, providing banking services, stimulating tourism, increasing citrus production, applying technology, and using engineering to create new land out of marshes. They introduced Sarasota to the power of knowledge and science through their experimental farms that featured the expertise of the state agricultural extension service and the United States Department of Agriculture. They championed cooperative associations of farmers to reduce production and transportation costs and to seek out the best markets for crops. It was, indeed, a remarkable record.

Several historians, including Ishbel Ross, Janet Snyder Matthews, and Linda Mansperger have written about many aspects of Bertha Palmer's experience in Florida. But important parts of that experience, particularly Bertha's role in creating Bee Ridge Farms and Osprey Farms, two of the great Palmer planned agricultural communities, have largely escaped attention. Similarly, some of the Palmer family's contributions to Sarasota between 1918 and 1982 have been referenced by scholars but never addressed in a cohesive manner. Piecing together the entire story of the Palmers in Florida requires a close reading of manuscript letters and business documents located at the Sarasota County Historical Resources division in Sarasota, the Manatee County Clerk of the Court records in Bradenton, Florida, the archives housed at Historic Spanish Point in Osprey, Florida, and the Chicago History Museum. Newspaper accounts, particularly from papers in New York, Chicago, and Sarasota, are essential to understanding what the Palmers were doing with regard to their vast land empire. Fortunately, the fame of the family and the magnitude of their operations guaranteed broad and continuing press coverage both nationally and locally.[1]

Although maps are included in this volume to help the reader understand spatial relationships, a few comments about geography may be useful. The City of Sarasota lies about sixty miles south of Tampa on Florida's west coast and is situated on Sarasota Bay. Sarasota County did not exist before 1921. Prior to that time the area was part of southern Manatee County. The county seat was at Bradentown (now called Bradenton), a few miles north of the City of Sarasota.

There are now two major north-south roadways in Sarasota County: The Tamiami Trail, most of which is also U.S. Route 41, runs close to the water on the west, and Interstate 75 is located a few miles east of the city limits. Between the two are four significant east-west roads. From north to south, they are University Parkway, and Fruitville, Bee Ridge, and Clark Roads. The last three are all important to the story of the Palmer development activities. Bertha Palmer's estate, Osprey Point, was located near the town of Osprey on the south Tamiami Trail, about 12 miles from Sarasota. A few miles farther south is the City of Venice, which owes its name to Bertha Palmer.

Near the interchange of I-75 and Fruitville Road, Palmer Farms once flourished. Bertha's two sons established an 8,000-acre planned agricultural community there in the 1920s. To the south of Clark Road was Honoré Palmer's cattle ranch. Sold after his death in 1964, the developers built a huge housing development called Palmer Ranch. Driving east on Clark Road beyond I-75, a visitor eventually finds the entrance to Myakka River State Park. This was the location of Bertha's 15,000-acre ranch that she called Meadowsweet Pastures. Part of the Air Line Railroad extension from Fruitville to Venice, which Bertha insisted be built as a condition of her initial land purchases, still exists, some of it as a bicycle and hiking path. The old rail line runs through the site of the town of Bee Ridge at the modern intersection of Proctor and McIntosh. The Palmers platted and developed the town in 1912 as the center of Bee Ridge Farms, their first planned agricultural community. Finally, Philippi

Creek runs from the vicinity of the Bobby Jones golf course on Fruitville Road southwest until it empties into Sarasota Bay. The stream was important to the Palmers both because its banks offered valuable development sites and because the waterway itself was part of a massive drainage project constructed to create more arable land for them to sell.

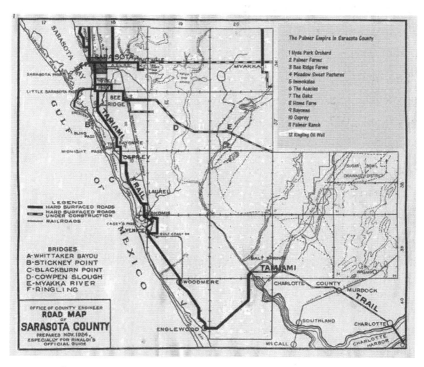

Palmer Empire Map. Adapted from Road Map, Sarasota County, November 1924. *By permission of Sarasota County Historical Resources.*

Notes to Introduction

1. Ishbel Ross, *Silhouette in Diamonds: The Life of Mrs. Potter Palmer* (Harper & Brothers, New York, 1960), 222–254; Janet Snyder Matthews, *Sarasota's Journey to Centennial* (Second Rev. Ed., Sesquicentennial Productions, Inc., Sarasota, 2007), 91–93.

CHAPTER ONE

The Remarkable
Mrs. Potter Palmer

There was little in Bertha Honoré Palmer's life before 1910 to suggest that she would spend her last years as a cattle rancher, citrus grower, and an innovative developer of agricultural communities on the southwest frontier of Florida. Known as the Queen of Chicago Society in the late nineteenth and early twentieth centuries, head of the Board of Lady Managers of the Columbian Exposition, friend of England's King Edward VII, awarded the Legion of Honor by the French government, her likeness sculpted by the famed French artist Auguste Rodin, Bertha Palmer was one of the best-known women of her time. Her contemporaries recognized her as a powerful spokesperson for women's rights, a successful businesswoman, an art collector of some note, a generous patron of many charities, and a strong supporter of Jane Addams and Hull House. Her principal residence was a million-dollar structure on Lake Shore Drive known to Chicagoans as the "Castle." But she also owned or leased estates in Bar Harbor, Maine; Newport, Rhode Island; London; Paris; and the Isle of Wight. She traveled by private rail car or rode in a chauffeured seven-passenger French Cadillac. When she journeyed to and from Europe, she sailed on the largest and most luxurious liners of the day, including the *Lusitania*.[1]

Everything about Mrs. Palmer was newsworthy. Her large collection of jewelry compared favorably to that possessed by European queens. Her gowns, reporters noted, were made in Paris. The weddings of her two sons made the front page of Chicago papers. Every event she attended and every detail of her wardrobe drew the attention of the press in both Chicago and New York. She commanded a large staff of secretaries, stenographers, maids, footmen, and gardeners, as well as a butler, cook, and chauffeur.[2]

When her husband, Potter Palmer, owner of the famed Palmer House Hotel in Chicago, died in 1902, he left a fortune of between eight and ten million dollars. Bertha Palmer could easily have lived out her remaining days in her accustomed ease and luxury. And, indeed, at least for a while, that was perfectly satisfactory to her. However, in 1910 this famous, well-connected, cosmopolitan lady changed her life's direction and ventured south to the land of mosquitoes, alligators, thick jungle, and rough society. The meeting of Bertha Honoré Palmer and the frontier town of Sarasota would prove to be important to all concerned.[3]

The shaping forces in Bertha Palmer's life emerged in her early years. Born on May 22, 1849, in Louisville, Kentucky, to a well-to-do family of French origins, she spoke with a soft Southern accent. From her mother she acquired a strong sense of how a woman behaved and presented herself. Her father, Henry H. Honoré, owned and operated a hardware store. In 1855 Henry, or H. H. as most people called him, moved his family to Chicago to seek out expanded economic opportunities in the great boomtown on the shores of Lake Michigan. He purchased land west of downtown near the modern intersection of Ashland and Jackson in what was then a semi-rural area. He built a large home for his family and sold adjacent lots to other immigrants from Louisville. The area was soon known as the Kentucky Colony. Bertha attended private schools in the city, and she and her sister, Ida, learned early from their mother how to organize, manage, and serve as a charming hostess at the many social functions held at the Honoré mansion.[4]

The Honoré family, which under Bertha's leadership would help lift Sarasota's fortunes a half century later, consisted of H. H. and his wife, Eliza; their two daughters, Bertha and Ida; and four sons, Adrian, Henry, Nathaniel, and Lockwood. In addition, H. H. Honoré's sister Mary Ann was very much part of family life. The Honoré family lived together harmoniously and always demonstrated great personal loyalty to one another.

During the early 1860s H. H. Honoré expanded his land acquisition and development activities. At some point he met one of the most successful businessmen in Chicago, Potter Palmer, who had arrived in the city three years before Honoré. A New Yorker, Palmer had set up a dry goods store on Lake Avenue near the Chicago River, then the downtown business district. What distinguished Palmer as a retail merchant was a series of innovations that made his store popular with the emerging class of women married to successful men. They had money, and they wanted the latest fashions in household goods and clothes. At a time when it was difficult for unaccompanied women to be out in public, Palmer made it easy, safe, and comfortable for women to shop at his store. He began extending credit, allowed customers to return goods they were unhappy with, and personally traveled to New York and Europe to find the products his largely female clientele desired. During the Civil War Palmer also made a great deal of money providing cotton fabric to the United States government for uniforms. Overwork and stress forced Palmer in 1865 to bring in Marshall Field and Levi Leiter as partners to run the store while he sailed for Europe to repair his health. Later he sold out to these two men.[5]

While developing his store Palmer began investing in real estate. It was this decision that led to his association with H. H. Honoré. Although they never became partners, the two men

Potter Palmer. *Chicago History Museum ICH i26498. Photographer unknown.*

undoubtedly shared a great deal of information on the real estate business in the city. They also became social friends. It was during a visit to the Honoré mansion in 1862 that Potter Palmer met 13-year-old Bertha Honoré, his junior by 23 years. The story is often told that Palmer was so entranced with Bertha's beauty and poise that he swore he would marry her when she was old enough. After that, whenever Bertha and her mother shopped at his store, he personally escorted them and presented the wares for their inspection.[6]

Bertha completed her basic education in Chicago in 1865. Her parents then sent her to the Convent of the Visitation at Georgetown outside Washington to receive more advanced instruction. She graduated in 1867, having earned many school prizes for her singing and for playing the harp and piano. Additionally, she won honors in history, geography, chemistry, botany, philosophy, literature, and several other subjects. She certainly had mastered all of the womanly and social skills thought proper at the time, but she had also shown herself to be extremely bright, thoughtful, and disciplined.[7]

Bertha returned to Chicago to make her social debut in the fall of 1867. Potter Palmer, his health refreshed and his real estate investments prospering, now set about seriously wooing Bertha. He was already a close friend of her parents and a business associate of her father. Finally, in August of 1870, the 21-year-old Bertha and the 44-year-old Potter were wed in her parent's new home on Michigan Avenue. The plan was for the couple to live in the bridal suite of the not-yet-completed Palmer House Hotel, Potter's latest venture that was part of his bold initiative to make State Street rather than Lake Street the main business district in the city.[8]

The new Mrs. Potter Palmer, the wife of a millionaire, was now ready to begin a life filled with promise and achievement. Already socially well established, she now was thrust into the top ranks of the expanding Chicago social world dominated by dozens of new-made rich men and their wives, all anxious to achieve the status to which they felt entitled by reason of their wealth. Bertha Palmer had all the qualities needed to become ultimately the unquestioned leader of this elite group. Besides Potter's fortune, she possessed faultless style, intellect, and—as time would show—tough-mindedness and political acumen. She also looked the part. A petite woman at 5´5˝, she had wavy, thick brown hair that would turn prematurely gray. She possessed a calm manner and a low voice that would come to express power. Friends described her eyes as very expressive and bright, even piercing. Pictures of the older Bertha show her boldly staring into the camera. A wonderful complexion together with a well-proportioned figure made her, in the minds of many, the very expression of ideal American womanhood and beauty.[9]

At the very beginning of the marriage, the entire edifice of Potter Palmer's wealth seemed to disappear within 27 hours. That was the time it took for the great Chicago Fire of 1871 to burn itself out. As it happened Potter was not in Chicago when the disaster occurred. Vast stretches of Chicago lay in smoldering ruins, including the new Palmer House and all the rest of Potter's State Street properties. Bertha, not yet having moved into the Palmer House, was living in a home just outside the city and saw the smoke and flames. She opened her door to her family and other homeless refugees. When Potter finally reached the city he saw that the work of a lifetime had been destroyed, and he pondered abandoning Chicago. But his young wife refused to let him give in, reminding him that Chicago more than ever needed its leading men to spur the recovery effort.[10]

And the city did recover with incredible speed. Aid flowed in from other cities and new men came to Chicago, sensing that careers could be made out of the catastrophe. As for Potter, he boarded a train for St. Louis and approached the Connecticut Mutual Life Company, which loaned him $1,700,000 on his personal credit, a staggering amount at the time. With these funds Potter commenced rebuilding the Palmer House and his other State Street properties.[11] In 1874 Bertha and Potter finally moved into their quarters in the rebuilt Palmer House Hotel. That year their first son, Honoré, was born, and a year later Potter Jr. made his appearance. Meanwhile, Bertha's sister, Ida, had followed her sister and become a student at the Convent of the Visitation. A few years after her return to Chicago, Ida attended, at her sister's invitation, a private dinner party at the Palmer House. Other dinner guests included Civil War hero General Philip Sheridan and members of his staff. One officer caught her eye: Colonel Frederick Dent Grant, eldest son of President Ulysses S. Grant. Fred and Ida seem to have fallen in love instantly at the affair. In short order both sets of parents approved a marriage, which was held in the Honoré home on October 20, 1874, to huge public interest. As the bride and groom stood before an altar erected in the parlor, three couples stood behind them: President and Mrs. Grant, H. H. and Eliza Honoré, and Bertha and Potter Palmer. Everyone seemed to admire the diamond tiara Ida wore, Bertha's wedding gift to her sister. For Bertha the marriage opened new doors to influence. She often visited Ida, who now lived in the White House while Fred served with General Custer and the Seventh Cavalry in the West. Bertha developed close ties to the

Grants, and they often invited her to stand with them in White House reception lines. The fact that she was a Democrat did not seem to bother the Republican president.[12]

In 1876, as Ida prepared to deliver her first child, the U.S. Army granted Fred Grant leave from the Seventh Cavalry to return to Washington to be with his wife. The baby, President Grant's first grandchild, Julia Dent Grant, was born in the White House. She would grow up to be a Russian princess and much involved in life in Sarasota, Florida, as well as national politics. That same year was, of course, the year of Custer's defeat and the slaughter of his command. Baby Julia had likely saved her father's life; thanks to her he was nowhere near the killing grounds at the Little Big Horn.[13]

Bertha and Potter, by all accounts, had a happy and mutually satisfying marriage. They lived in a splendid suite in Chicago's greatest hotel. The Palmer House was considered the place to stay in Chicago for those who could afford the cost. Bertha, called Cissie by her husband, helped plan the artistic scheme for the great public rooms of the hotel. Already she was an object of public attention and frequently mentioned in the newspapers. She cut quite a figure, apparently, as she passed through the vestibule of the hotel wearing the latest Paris gown and a stylish hat on her way to her coach. Although her duties as a mother took up much of her time, she gradually became more and more involved in the life of the city and in philanthropy. She helped form the Fortnightly Club, which attracted other wives of newly rich men to discussions of literature as well as the issues of the day. In the early 1880s Bertha delivered a paper on "The Obligations of Wealth." Her friend Ellen Martin Henrotin once spoke on "The Social Status of European and American Women." Henrotin, married to the president of the Chicago Stock Exchange, deeply influenced Bertha. She spent her life as a champion of social reform. It was she who persuaded Bertha to join the Chicago Women's Club. Unlike the Fortnightly Club, this organization represented a broad range of women in the city. Its 500 members included married and unmarried women, professional women, housewives, and social leaders such as Bertha. The Women's Club was part of a broad movement in post-Civil War America in which women organized to seek civic improvements as well as self-improvement. Among other activities, the club's members held literary meetings, read papers on public issues, and attended lectures. Over the years the Women's Club took up such problems as the treatment of children in the judicial system and the terrible conditions for women in the county insane asylum. The club members pressured political leaders at every opportunity to do more for women and children.[14]

It was as a member of the Chicago Women's Club that Bertha met Jane Addams, who, with Ellen Gates Starr, had established a settlement house on Chicago's West Side where huge immigrant populations lived. Founded in 1869, Hull House sought to help these newcomers adapt and become a part of American society. It provided language training, day care services, general education, and many other services to the immigrants. The Chicago Women's Club and Bertha Palmer personally provided resources to support Jane Addams and her work.[15]

Bertha's social and political ideas continued to mature. She became more and more interested in finding practical ways to help working women and their children. In her mind, most women who worked did so because their husbands failed to provide properly for their families. Alcoholism accounted for much of this, and Bertha came to support the goals of the Women's Temperance Union as a way to remedy the situation, even though she personally was not a teetotaler. Whatever the reasons, she argued publicly, many women found themselves forced to work outside the home to feed their children. They often labored in sweatshop conditions and suffered pay discrimination. Bertha became an early supporter of equal pay for equal work, and even helped women millinery workers form a union, which did succeed in improving their working conditions. Later she held illustrated lectures at her house to educate her rich friends about the plight of women workers.[16]

In these and other ways Bertha Palmer showed that she cared deeply about the condition of women and children in American society. She also demonstrated a certain independence of thought and action that likely surprised her social peers at times. But there were clear limits to her idealism. She abhorred extremism and shunned the suffragists and their movement to obtain the vote for women. To her the suffragists were unwomanly in their behavior, and their goal not nearly as important as alleviating the daily stress of women and children. These divisions within the women's movement would confront her a few years later when she assumed the post of president of the World's Fair Board of Lady Managers.[17]

In 1882 Potter Palmer decided to build a mansion suitable for his exalted position in Chicago society. Always the entrepreneur, he intended to make his new home the basis of another real estate masterstroke, similar to his State Street initiative. At a time when the rich and powerful men of Chicago lived on the South Side along Prairie Avenue or in mansions on South Michigan Avenue, Potter decided to create an entirely new enclave for the wealthy, one that he would own and develop. He selected a barren, sandy, marshy wasteland north of the business district and along Lake Michigan. There he created North Lake Shore Drive, which soon would be nicknamed the Gold Coast. He assumed that his name and reputation would cause his friends and business associates to invest in North Lake Shore Drive property just as they had followed his lead in the State Street venture. His own new mansion was to be the chief advertisement for the enterprise. It took extensive and costly work to drain and level his new property. He and Bertha hired two well-known Chicago architects, Henry Codman and Charles S. Frost, to design a grand mansion estimated to cost $90,000, a princely sum at the time.[18]

As the project went forward, Bertha asked for changes and additions to the architects' original plan. She also insisted on costly furnishings and decorations. When the price of the mansion reached one million dollars, Potter stopped counting. In truth he could not deny Bertha anything she really desired. When finished, it was the finest home in Chicago, and Palmer was able to sell off all the other lots he owned in the area at a substantial profit. From now on, the Palmer Castle stood figuratively and literally at the very center of Chicago society.[19]

It took three years to complete work on the Castle, a massive structure of granite and limestone that featured an 80-foot-high tower with a spiral staircase. It was rumored that Potter often withdrew to the tower during his wife's frequent social occasions. The core of the mansion was three stories high. Each room in the home was decorated in a different style and adorned with appropriate rugs and furniture. There was the entryway, with a marble mosaic floor and a stairway with newel posts that bore the Honoré coat of arms. Visitors were stunned by the opulence

The Palmer residence in Chicago, popularly dubbed the "Castle."
Chicago History Museum ICH i26497.

as they were led through the drawing room, the music room, the dining room, the ballroom, and the library. Bertha's bedroom on the second floor, not open to the public, was decorated in the Moorish style, with ebony and gold as the predominate colors. It had a carved ceiling, and oriental rugs graced the oak floors. In her dressing room there was a swan-shaped sunken tub.[20]

The Castle was the place from which Bertha ruled Chicago society. She entertained frequently, with formal dinners often scheduled several times a week. To be invited to one of her dinners signaled acceptance and standing in Chicago society. Not to be invited was a stinging rebuke to the social pretensions of matrons Bertha judged unworthy. When Bertha arranged for an annual post-Christmas Charity Ball at the Auditorium Theater on South Michigan Avenue, her invitation list became the definitive roster of high society in Chicago. She was not a woman to be crossed.

By the late 1880s, as Bertha entered her forties, she seemed to be at the peak of her power and influence. She had retained her youthful beauty and feminine charm. She sustained her contacts with the Washington scene through the Grants. She earned praise as a philanthropist, a fighter for women's rights, and a reformer interested in addressing some of the many social problems American society faced because of urbanization, immigration, and industrialization. She occupied the very center of Chicago society, yet she maintained relations with a wide variety of people, including labor leaders, working women, and even a few suffragists. Her family, all of whom she cared about passionately, were doing quite well in their own lives. Sons Honoré and Potter would soon enter St. Mark's School in Massachusetts in preparation for attending Harvard. Her sister Ida was happily married to Frederick Grant, a rising star in the United States Army. One of her brothers, Nathaniel, would before long win election as a circuit court judge in Cook County. Another brother, Adrian, had graduated from the University of Chicago and become an attorney. He helped manage H. H. Honoré's real estate investments. Her husband, Potter, continued to prosper as a hotel proprietor and real estate developer. He served as a member of the South Park Commission, where he championed linking Jackson Park to Washington Park by means of a one-mile-long strip of parkland to be called the Midway. All of these areas would be important in 1893 when the World's Columbian Exposition opened its gates.[21]

Potter, who had no family other than Bertha, loved her intensely and freely let her spend his money. The Castle was one result, and so was her huge wardrobe, purchased at the great stores of Chicago, New York, and Paris. Another evidence of his largesse was jewelry mostly purchased in London and Paris. Bertha always looked resplendent in her diamonds and pearls. Potter himself estimated she was wearing $200,000 worth of jewelry at one of her social events at the Castle. He said it with pride in his voice. But Palmer did more for Bertha than keep her in fancy clothes and exquisite gems. He enjoyed talking with her in the evening about his world of business, of the deals he made, or how he outfoxed a competitor. When, years later, people congratulated her on her effectiveness as a businesswoman in Florida, she noted that these conversations with Potter constituted the only business education experience in her life.[22]

Both Bertha and Potter devoted themselves to supporting cultural institutions in Chicago. Like their fellow members of the social elite, they desired to move beyond Chicago's rough and tumble frontier image to one that was far more genteel and civilized. They were all tired of New York's sneering at Chicago's pretensions to cultural merit. The Palmers and their friends understood that great museums, particularly art museums, must be a vital part of Chicago's strategy. Thus they supported the Chicago Art Institute and its predecessor institutions. Potter had bought art for years in New York and Europe. By the late 1880s Bertha took an increasing interest in art collecting and eventually became deeply absorbed in the world of art, particularly in Paris. In purchasing art, Potter had relied on Chicagoan Sara Tyson Hallowell. Beginning in 1873 Hallowell organized art displays at the annual Illinois Interstate Industrial Exposition held along Chicago's lakefront. She also advised several other wealthy Chicagoans besides Potter on their purchases of art. She was especially interested in introducing Chicagoans to more recent genres of French art such as the Barbizon School and the Impressionists. Bertha also trusted Hallowell, who later introduced her to the Paris art dealer Paul Durand Ruel and the American Impressionist Mary Cassatt, who lived in the French capital. Before long the Palmers acquired a respectable art collection, large enough to persuade Bertha that new space had to be added to the Castle to house and display the precious paintings.[23]

Despite Bertha's many accomplishments and her unique standing in Chicago society, she soon achieved even greater fame and broad international recognition. What really made Bertha Honoré Palmer a figure of historical importance was her association with the 1893 World's Columbian Exposition, the greatest and most influential world's fair of the age. It was by no means a foregone conclusion that Chicago would host a fair celebrating the four-hundredth anniversary of Christopher Columbus' discovery of the New World. Indeed, there was a lengthy public relations and political battle involving Washington, D.C., New York, and St. Louis, as well as Chicago, all of whom sought the glory and the profits of hosting this great event. Congress would make the decision, and each of the four cities organized aggressive lobbying efforts. Mudslinging and brash bragging were the common elements in each of the four city's campaigns. New York newspapers, for example, christened Chicago "the windy city," not because of its weather but for its braggadocio. [24]

Chicago women actively contributed to the city's efforts to win the right to host the fair. A women's auxiliary organized to raise money for the effort. With years of organizational and fundraising experience obtained through participation in women's civic, reform, and literary clubs, the members of the auxiliary proved able allies to the exclusively male group appointed by the mayor to lobby for the fair. But those women were very much like Bertha Palmer: rich, well connected, and no friends of what they saw as extreme feminism. Their agenda was to insist that there be a women's building erected on the fairgrounds, that the material and intellectual achievements of women be displayed and recognized, and that there be space allocated for women to hold conferences on issues they cared about.[25]

Both in Chicago and around the United States another group of women also organized to take control of women's activities at the exposition. They called themselves the Isabellas, after Queen Isabella, who financed Columbus' voyage of discovery. Made up of lawyers, doctors, and other women in professional positions, the Isabellas strongly advocated women's suffrage and other initiatives to free women from male domination. Like the auxiliary, they wanted women represented at the fair and a building dedicated to women's exhibits and meetings. They also argued for a huge statue of Queen Isabella on the fairgrounds in recognition of her role in the discovery of America. Above all, they wanted Congress to name the Isabellas specifically as the sole representatives of all women at the Columbian Exposition. Thus, months before Bertha emerged as the leader of the women's division of the world's fair, a major contest commenced to determine who would represent women and how the political, social, and economic aspirations of women would be portrayed at what promised to be the greatest international exposition of the nineteenth century.[26]

On April 25, 1890, despite the furious opposition of New York's representatives and senators, President Benjamin Harrison signed into law a world's fair act that named Chicago as the site.

The law provided for the establishment of a national commission to oversee many aspects of planning and managing the exposition. Confusingly, there was also an Illinois corporation that controlled the millions of dollars raised by the Chicagoans to pay the costs of building the exposition. Congress and the President failed to address fully the responsibilities assigned to each group, thus creating a potentially disastrous bureaucratic mess.

The world's fair law also provided for a first in the nation's history: a federally appointed group of women charged with carrying out federal policy. There was to be the Board of Lady Managers, with 117 members and an equal number of alternates plus nine additional women from Chicago. The mere creation of the board was a huge step forward for women. They had been given a precedent-setting opportunity to show their capacity to lead, to organize, and to manage a highly complex government enterprise intended to demonstrate women's contributions to all facets of human endeavor. Everything the board did would be carefully observed, and there were many critics hoping it would fail.[27]

By late summer of 1890, the World's Fair National Commission began soliciting the names of nominees to the Board of Lady Managers from political leaders in the states and territories. Both the Chicago-based auxiliary and the Isabellas worked hard to get their candidates named. Bertha was one of the nine special managers appointed from Chicago.

In its final form the membership of the Board of Lady Managers had a majority of women more closely aligned with the views of the auxiliary than with those of the Isabellas. However, the Isabella managers were still intent on controlling both the board and the Women's Division of the Columbian Exposition. But women's groups other than the Isabellas expressed displeasure with the board's membership. Women labor activists complained that not a single woman factory worker appeared on the roster. Black women were equally outraged at their total exclusion from the board.[28]

At the first meeting of the Board of Lady Managers held in Chicago on November 20, 1890, Mary Cantrill from Kentucky and a member of the Southern caucus within the board rose to nominate her friend and fellow Kentuckian, Bertha Honoré Palmer, for the post of president of the Board of Lady Managers. The only possible challenger, Mary Logan of the Isabellas, refused to accept nomination, thus clearing the way for Bertha's unanimous election as the most important woman associated with the Columbian Exposition. An Isabella, Phoebe Couzins of St. Louis, won election as secretary.[29]

Bertha Palmer emerged from the world's fair experience as one of the best-known women in the world, but her path to that distinction proved difficult. She and her supporters had to fight hard to push back the Isabella threat, which only ended when Bertha and the board dismissed Phoebe Couzins as secretary. Couzins had brought the board's work to a halt by refusing to fulfill her responsibilities as secretary. The World's Fair National Commission approved the dismissal action at Bertha's urging. Couzins, a lawyer, then took her case to court, where she eventually lost. There would be more confrontations with the Isabellas, but all were successfully defused. Bertha and the large majority of Lady Managers backing her were now free to develop the Women's Department as they wished. The outcome of this lengthy battle clearly established her as a tough and politically savvy woman who would not tolerate challenges to her authority.[30]

Bertha, who had excellent political connections with the National Commission, the Illinois World's Fair Corporation, and Congress, led a successful fight to obtain funds from World's Fair authorities to build a women's building on the fairgrounds. She was determined to make the structure entirely an expression of what women had achieved. Everything about it highlighted the talents of women, beginning with the design. Working with Daniel Burnham, the man in charge of actually building the fair and an eminent architect in his own right, Bertha arranged for a national competition open only to women architects. Sophia G. Hayden, the first female graduated from the architecture program at the Massachusetts Institute of Technology, submitted the winning design. Although one of the smaller worlds' fair buildings, the Women's Building fit well with the neoclassical architectural style that characterized almost all the principal structures at Jackson Park. The pavilion rose on the western shore of the waterway surrounding Wooded Island and could be reached by land or by one of the many gondolas and electric boats that darted about the canals and lagoons of the exposition. It stood two stories high, with a rooftop garden added at Bertha's suggestion. Its main hall soared to a height of seventy feet. In the tympanums at either end of the hall appeared two huge murals by women artists personally recruited by Bertha: Mary MacMonnies' *Modern Woman* and Mary Cassatt's *Primitive Woman*. The rooms of the Women's Building contained libraries full of books written by women, inventions patented by women, sculptures by women, and an amazing array of sewing, knitting, lace work, and embroidery—some the work of European royalty. Almost every day women visitors to the fair could attend lectures at the

Women's Building, World's Columbian Exposition. *Chicago History Museum ICHi53308. Creator: C. D. Arnold.*

Women's Building on an astonishing array of topics, including women's reform issues.[31]

In addition to the Women's Building, the Board of Lady Mangers raised money to erect a women's hotel near the fairgrounds where unattached females could obtain room and board at a very modest rate. Bertha opened the Castle for another fundraising event to build the Children's Building next to the Women's Building. In part this structure served as a day care center, allowing mothers to enjoy better their visit to the fair. However, the building also had an educational purpose, for it contained a demonstration kindergarten, a German idea for educating young children that would soon be widely adopted in America.[32]

In organizing the Women's Division, Bertha reached out to women's groups in all parts of the United States. Her idea was to have state governments appoint some women to their World's Fair committees and charge them to put together displays of women's work for the state buildings being erected at the north end of the fairgrounds around the Palace of Fine Arts. She called upon the lady managers of each state and territory to approach their legislators and ask for their support. In Illinois she personally testified before the state legislative committee considering the matter and won the members over with her poise and her persuasive arguments. Illinois appropriated $80,000 for the use of women appointed to the state's committee. Many other states followed suit. Spurred by these women serving on world's fair state commissions, local women's clubs in cities, towns, and villages across the nation soon collected and organized exhibits for display in their state buildings or in the Women's Building. It was the greatest compilation of women's work in American history, irrefutable evidence of how far the nation's women had come in terms of achievement in a wide variety of fields, organizational capacity, and effective participation in civic affairs.[33]

Just as she had a broader vision for how the Columbian Exposition could boost the cause of women nationally, Bertha Palmer also wanted to help women in the rest of the world and in so doing create an international women's movement. The fair, after all, was an international event, and she did not want the rest of the world's women ignored. There were few ways open to Bertha and the Board of Lady Managers to attract overseas support for their work. The law creating the world's fair made no reference to the board approaching other governments, and the State Department offered only limited help. Typically, Bertha took the matter into her own hands. Accompanied by her husband and members of the Illinois World's Fair Corporation seeking exhibits for the major buildings of the fair, Bertha sailed for Europe in 1892.

Bertha's first stop was London, where she took tea with Queen Victoria's daughter, Princess Christiana. Despite serious differences between the two women over the proper role of women, the princess did agree to lead a British commission of women to organize displays for the Women's Building. With consummate tact Bertha arranged for a few suffragists and Women's Christian Temperance Union supporters to join a largely conservative group of aristocrats as members of the commission. In Paris Bertha, who spoke perfect French, found more enthusiastic support. The French president's wife, Madame Carnot, said she would head the French women's world's fair group. Bertha managed to persuade an impressive array of powerful French women to join the effort. Finally, she met and charmed Jules Rothe, Minister of Commerce, who helped arrange the official establishment of the French women's commission and an appropriation to carry forward its work.[34]

During the Paris visit, the Palmers purchased a great number of Impressionist paintings with the help of Sara Hallowell, their art advisor. It was at this time that Bertha commissioned Mary MacMonnies and Mary Cassatt to paint the two principal murals in the Women's Building. She and Potter met and dined with many of the Impressionists whose work they were purchasing. They even traveled to Claude Monet's estate and gardens at Giverny, west of Paris. Sometime during their Paris sojourn, the Palmers spent time with the famous sculptor Auguste Rodin, creator of *The Kiss* and *The Thinker*. Rodin was hoping the Palmers would purchase some of his work, and persuaded her to pose for a bust. It is unclear if she did pose, and there is no record that she commissioned such a work. Nevertheless, Rodin did sculpt her likeness. The bust now resides in the Musée Rodin in Paris. She was the only American woman he ever sculpted.[35]

After Paris, Bertha and Potter traveled to Vienna where Ida's husband, Frederick Dent Grant, was American Minister. Ida's daughter Julia, always a great favorite of her aunt, was now 15 years old and could speak German fluently. The Palmers, thanks to their family connections, were especially well treated and invited to great balls and royal entertainments. But at that time the United States and Austria were engaged in a trade dispute so serious that Fred felt he could not raise Bertha's request for the establishment of an Austrian women's world's fair commission with the government. Ida, however, helped by introducing her sister to influential noblewomen who agreed to form a commission. Before sailing for home, the Palmers met with Queen Marie Henriette of Belgium and Queen Margherita of Italy who both pledged their support and agreed to head their national commissions. By the time Bertha returned to Chicago she had done much to advance the interests of the exposition and the Women's Division. She had also made quite an impression on European society as the representative American woman. She was beautiful, fashionable, poised, intelligent, and well organized. She had tact and charm and always knew a great deal about the people she met. Men liked her business-like approach when she made presentations. Before she was finished, Bertha Palmer, by personal visits or letters, had obtained commitments to create national women's commissions from 41 countries, including far distant Japan where the empress took a personal interest.[36]

Bertha was much more than the chief executive of the Women's Division; she was also its public face and principal spokesperson. Among her many talents was oratory, for she had a gift for expressing complicated ideas in powerful language. At the dedication of the exposition on October 21, 1892, held in the not yet finished but impressively huge Manufacturers and Liberal Arts Building, she was among a group of leaders invited to speak. Few of the 75,000 in attendance heard any of the speakers, since it was before the general use of microphones. Even the 5,000-voice choir that performed was nearly inaudible to those at the far end of structure. Bertha's speech probably ranked as the most important one given that day, for it dealt with ideas and values instead of self-congratulation as most of the others did. She minced no words on the importance of the Board of Lady Managers: "Even more important than the discovery of Columbus . . . is the fact that the General Government just discovered woman." She explained that no such organization as the Board of Lady Managers had ever existed before in the United States: "It is official, acting under government authority and sustained by government funds. It is so far-reaching that it encircles the globe." The board's major concern, she continued, would be "the formation of a public sentiment which will favor woman's industrial equality and her receiving just compensation for services rendered." To do this, Bertha promised, the board would put together exhibits that showed the value of women's work to industry, science, and the arts.[37]

Seven months later, on May 1, 1893, President Grover Cleveland stood in the Court of Honor and signaled the grand opening of the Columbian Exposition by pressing a gold telegraph key. Flags then rose to the top of their poles, the great fountains sprayed plumes of water, and the powerful engines in the vast Machinery Building thundered to life. Afterwards the president dined with world's fair leaders in the Administration Building. He sat across from Bertha Palmer, who excused herself early to preside at the official opening of the Women's Building. There, thousands of people crowded into the central room. Among them were representatives of many of the foreign commissions Bertha helped establish. There were also many women members of state world's fair committees as well as the Board of Lady Managers. By now women in America and abroad realized the importance of what Bertha and her board had accomplished, and there was great enthusiasm that day as those lucky enough to be there saluted their leaders and proudly admired the Women's Building.[38]

Bertha praised all of them but referred to the many internal and external challenges the board had confronted. Again she returned to the larger importance of what had been achieved. The core of her speech once more dealt with the issue of wage equality for women and the persistent and irrational biases against women forced to work because of absent or drunken husbands. "Of all existing forms of injustice," she said, "there is none so cruel and inconsistent as is the position in which women are placed with regard to self-maintenance—the calm ignoring of their rights and responsibilities which has gone on for centuries." Things are tough enough for men in industrial jobs, she argued, and far worse for women who face hostile public attitudes by working outside the home. Employers used this prejudice to pay women less than men for comparable work, thus profiting at their expense. Bertha then went on to demolish foolish sentimental arguments about women mounted on pedestals and that taking care of her family was the only proper job of a woman. Bertha asserted that many women had no other choice to keep their families clothed, fed, and housed than by working. And by working they enjoyed a new sense of independence once freed from being helpless and dependent. "Having the full use of their faculties, they rejoice in exercising them." Thus, from beginning to end, Bertha Palmer consistently articulated that women were more powerful when they were organized; that huge technological changes had placed women in difficult circumstances where they faced discrimination; and that working women not only supported their families but found self-reliance, independence, and the possibility of choices in life. It was a set of messages that clearly resonated with women, who made the Women's Building one of the most popular structures at the Columbian Exposition.[39]

Given her background and her official position, it should not be surprising that Bertha hosted a seemingly endless series of lunches, teas, dinners, and musicales at the Castle during the six-month run of fair. She called herself the "nation's chief hostess," and with considerable justification. Visiting dignitaries from around the nation and the world swarmed to Chicago. Many would have stayed at the magnificent Palmer House Hotel or perhaps the Auditorium Theater Hotel on South Michigan. But an invitation to one of Bertha's events was the best way to gain public notice of one's importance. Bertha's ability to match visiting dignitaries with her friends and allies at receptions held at the Castle strengthened her position as head of high society in Chicago. However, in June of 1893, a month after the opening of the exposition, she faced a totally unexpected challenge.

A social high point of the world's fair was to be the visit of the Infanta Eulalia of the Spanish royal family, who traveled to Chicago to boost the world's fair exhibits of her nation. Bertha took the Infanta's visit very seriously and did everything in her power to make sure Eulalia, a well-known grouch, would be happy and satisfied. Bertha selected one of the most impressive suites at the Palmer House for the visitor and sent her own silverware and gold plate for the Infanta's use. The day of the planned reception at the Castle, the Infanta visited the fairgrounds at Jackson Park. At one point she shocked everyone by lighting a cigarette, a very surprising act for any cultured woman in that age. When told that Mrs. Palmer would be her hostess that evening, Eulalia referred to her as an "innkeeper's wife." Still she went to the Castle that night, although clearly unhappy with being there. She ignored the people Bertha introduced to her, including Vice President of the United States Adlai Stevenson, General Nelson Miles, Marshall Field, George Pullman, Julia Ward Howe, and a host of politicians and international dignitaries. In less than an hour the Infanta angrily left the mansion before dinner was served. The rest of her brief visit to Chicago and the Columbian Exposition was filled with similar examples of her bad manners. Newspapers in America made much of the encounter. For the most part Bertha was praised for her dignified handling of the situation, but she was angry enough to complain to the U.S. State Department about Eulalia's behavior. Strangely, a decade or so later the two women reconciled and actually became friends. Nonetheless, it was probably Bertha's worst moment on the very public stage she occupied.[40]

In October of 1893 the great Columbian Exposition, Chicago's White City, closed after six spectacular months. Fires soon destroyed most of the great structures during the ensuing winter, including the Women's Building and the Children's Building. The Manufacturers and Liberal Arts Building, the biggest structure in the world at the time, burned to the ground in a single hour. But the exposition was as much an idea as it was a physical reality. Twenty-seven million people had visited the fair and been influenced by its design and neoclassical architecture. Daniel Burnham, the builder of the fair, emerged as America's preeminent urban planner, whose designs shaped Washington D.C., Chicago, and other cities. The City Beautiful Movement took hold across America, as towns and cities tried to copy the neoclassical look of the world's fair. Railroad stations, banks, city halls, and county courthouses borrowed freely from the world fair's architectural vocabulary. Chicago itself emerged from the fair a changed metropolis, more self-confident, and now firmly established on the map of the world's great cities.[41]

The fair made Bertha Palmer an international celebrity. She became a heroine to millions of women for her effective and forthright advocacy of women's rights and achievements. Her name and face were familiar to newspaper readers from Tokyo to London, Berlin, Paris, Vienna, and St. Petersburg. She had forcefully demonstrated that a woman could manage a major enterprise, handle the challenges of diplomacy, influence governments, and yet never compromise her role as a lady. Few men had ever faced the challenges she did as president of the Board of Lady Managers; even fewer could compete with her graceful exercise of power.[42]

After the fair, Bertha's control of the Chicago social scene became more absolute than ever before. She continued to run the annual Charity Ball and to support her favorite causes and organizations. To many she seemed more distant personally, more self-assured, and more authoritative. She now had a staff of 27 at the Castle, and no one outside her family could see her without an appointment. Her sons entered Harvard, and her sister's family remained in Vienna. In the middle 1890s the Palmer family summered at Bar Harbor, Maine. Bertha was no longer as passionate about buying and selling art, but took an interest in collecting oriental porcelain figures. By 1896 it seemed apparent that her dazzling social life, her reputation earned as the president of the Board of Lady Managers, and her frequent trips to Europe did not entirely satisfy her restless ambition.[43]

A diplomatic opening as U.S. Minister to Germany offered a possible new adventure for Bertha and Potter. She had met many American ambassadors during her travels and thought their lives interesting. Although Potter had no particular credentials for the appointment, many ministers were businessmen and political party loyalists rather than professional diplomats. Bertha mounted a major campaign on Palmer's behalf beginning with Vice President Adlai Stevenson of Illinois. Her correspondence for this period testifies to the amount of work she put into the campaign and the wide range of contacts she possessed. Besides her Chicago connections, she called on people she had worked with during the world's fair to support Potter's cause. Always astute at public relations, Bertha persuaded newspaper publishers to print favorable articles. In the end she had to endure a rare defeat. The German post went to a State Department insider.[44]

Although disappointed, Bertha quickly moved on to other activities. She and Potter sailed for Russia to attend the coronation of Czar Nicholas II. She was well treated in St. Petersburg by the Russians who had represented their country at the Columbian Exposition. The Palmers returned to Chicago in time for the 1896 Democratic Convention. Bertha, an avid Democrat, heard William Jennings Bryan, the party's nominee for President, deliver his famous "Cross of Gold" speech advocating free coinage of silver. She attended every session of the convention, held a reception at the Castle for the delegates, and socialized with the Bryans. She did not, however, publicly endorse Bryan's controversial position on the free coinage of silver. But as women could not vote or hold office, Bertha had no chance to translate her political skills and passion into electoral politics. Something else, some new challenge, was needed.[45]

Bertha finally decided that she would win social acceptance from the notoriously insular and, at least from the Chicago perspective, downright snooty New York rich. Her battleground would be Newport, Rhode Island, the summer home of New York City's elite, led by the redoubtable Mrs. John Jacob Astor. Bertha was an outsider, and perhaps worse from the New York point of view, a Chicagoan. She did have beauty and money as well as Paris gowns and jewels. She certainly was known for her role at the Columbian Exposition, and her extensive political and social contacts in Europe could not be ignored. Her first foray at Newport took place in the summer of 1896. She rented one of the grand "cottages," called Arleigh, and threw a spectacular party marking the coming out of her niece, Julia Grant. In 1898 she managed to organize an event in which the future kings of Belgium and Italy were honored. This achievement, due to her world's fair contact with the queens of Belgium and Italy, did impress the New Yorkers. So, too, did her jewels and the gorgeous trappings of the Palmers' coach and four.[46]

That year, 1898, was a war year, as Spain and the United States clashed over their rival imperial interests. Bertha joined Mrs. Astor and other Newport matrons sewing items of clothing needed by the American troops marshalling in Tampa prior to the invasion of Cuba. Frederick Dent Grant now served as military governor of Puerto Rico, and Ida joined him there. Julia remained under the wing of her aunt, who kept her well-dressed and appropriately decked out in jewelry. But there was a problem. Potter Palmer's health had worsened since 1896, and by the fall of 1898 Bertha and the doctors felt he could not possibly go through a Chicago winter. Bertha packed up her husband, her two sons who had just graduated from Harvard, and Julia, and sailed for Europe.

Potter's poor health was not helped by the overseas adventure. Eventually the family made its way to Egypt in an effort to find a climate that would help Potter recover, but nothing seemed to work. Bertha cut short the Egyptian trip, and the group sailed back to Italy and Rome. While there Julia, Honoré, and Potter Jr., attended parties with a group of young diplomats and military attachés. One of them, Prince Michael Cantacuzene, Count Speransky, took an instant interest in the beautiful Julia. She learned from him that he was a Russian noble with huge land holdings as well as a cavalry officer on detached duty because of injuries suffered in a horse show accident. When Bertha and her family moved on to Cannes in southern France, the passionate Cantacuzene was not far behind. Within two weeks he proposed, and Julia, the granddaughter of an American president and war hero, accepted.[47]

In her own telling of the story, Julia made clear that she confided everything to her Aunt Bertha. It would have been impossible for the matter to have gone so far without Bertha's consent, if not active approval. Moreover, Julia badly needed Bertha to assure her parents in Puerto Rico that this was a good match. As for the prince, he needed to persuade his family that Julia was a worthy spouse for him despite the fact that her father could not afford a dowry on his army salary. Presumably, the fact that the rich and famous Bertha Palmer was Julia's aunt helped the Cantacuzenes accept the marriage. In any case, both families blessed the proposed wedding, which was to be held at Newport, where Bertha had rented the Astor cottage, Beaulieu. Before leaving Europe, the family stopped in Paris, where Bertha purchased Julia's trousseau. The wedding plans and preparations attracted international attention, but not all of it was friendly. Mrs. Grant, widow of the former president, received many letters protesting Julia's wedding to a foreigner.[48]

The storybook wedding took place in September of 1899. Actually there were two services, one Russian Orthodox and the other in an Episcopal church a day later. Julia sparkled in a simple but elegant white gown. The prince wore his full regimental white uniform with high black boots and a golden-colored helmet topped by a silver eagle. The newlyweds soon left for Russia where Julia, already a veteran of royal court life, was presented to the royal family. Julia's wedding closed out Bertha Palmer's decades-long social career, at least in the United States. Although she would host occasional and always memorable dinner parties for visiting American presidents or foreign dignitaries at the Castle, she never again led society in Chicago or at Newport as she had in the past. That did not mean she was any less the Queen of Chicago Society, for no one dared compete with her for that role.[49]

In 1900 Bertha suddenly found yet another challenge that gave her a chance to shine when President McKinley nominated her for an appointment as the only female member of the National Commission representing the United States at the Paris exposition of that year. Some senators opposed the appointment based on her gender, as did a few French officials. But the Senate did approve her appointment, which was, of course, another step forward for American women. Bertha was an excellent choice. She was of French ancestry and spoke the language fluently. She had traveled to France many times and knew most of the key government officials and their wives. Her Columbian Exposition service, both as an administrator and as a hostess, enhanced her value to her fellow commissioners. She made it her business to keep American women visible at the fair by arranging appointments for them on the award juries in the different divisions of the fair. She even managed to have Jane Addams named to a position in the fair's administration. Much like her experiences at the Chicago fair, Bertha had to deal with antagonistic American women who were jealous of her official post and of the preference she was shown. Mostly, however, the fair for Bertha was a long round of teas, dinners, and balls. She, of course, was known as a great hostess, and her own events did not disappoint. She renewed acquaintances with many wealthy and powerful individuals that she had met before in Chicago, Newport, Bar Harbor, and the many parts of Europe she had visited. Among these were the King of Greece, Queen Henriette of Belgium, and the Prince of Wales, the future Edward VII, who at 51 still appeared youthful and energetic. Bertha charmed reporters and government officials alike. Potter did not even try to keep up with his wife even though his health had somewhat improved. In April of 1901 Bertha received word that the French government had bestowed on her the Legion of Honor because of her contributions to the

Paris world's fair. She was but the third woman to receive this designation. The other two were Florence Nightingale and the artist Rosa Bonheur.[50]

In that same year Bertha's life took a strange turn when her oldest son, Honoré, decided that he would run for a seat on the Chicago City Council, and she agreed to be his *de facto* campaign manager. Honoré was now 27 years old, very well educated, widely traveled, and comfortable in any social situation, from exclusive men's clubs to the fanciest of balls. He knew national and world leaders. He even had some work experience in a bank and assisting his father run his real estate empire. However, he had never participated in a political campaign, knew little of Chicago's notoriously rough-and-tumble politics, and possessed scant knowledge of the men who cast votes in his district. Beyond all these shortcomings, he was a Democrat like his mother in a solidly Republican area. The newspapers saw Honoré as "red meat" for their political reporters and cartoonists. But everyone failed to realize in the beginning that his mother, who could not even vote for him, was a very tough adversary who had money, contacts, and enviable organizational skills. Nor did they appreciate that Honoré had some of his mother's steeliness of purpose and her legendary ability to outwork everyone else.[51]

The newspapers covered the race almost daily from start to finish. On March 12 the *Chicago Tribune* reported Honoré had shown up at a dance at Turner Hall where he gave a campaign speech and then asked a beautiful blonde in a blue gown to be his dance partner. Later a dozen Democratic campaign workers dressed as clowns carried him about on their shoulders. Night after night he patrolled the bars of his ward accompanied by political bosses who introduced him around. Early in the campaign he was attacked by a University of Chicago political scientist who said that if elected he would be a mere tool of those bosses. Honoré responded that his financial independence made it possible for him to battle entrenched corruption. He came out with a new campaign slogan: "It is no crime to be rich." The Palmer family influence quickly became apparent as wealthy old-line Republicans like Franklin McVeigh started showing up at bars they had likely not entered before to endorse Honoré. In what must have been a memorable scene, Bertha threw open the Castle for a reception for all of the Democratic campaign workers. It can safely be said that few if any of them had ever seen the inside of the mansion before. The newspapers slowly came to appreciate Honoré's tenacity. April 2 was Election Day, and reporters noted that Honoré was up before dawn visiting polling stations and meeting people on the street. By his side as always was Jimmy Quinn, the leader of the Democratic Party in the Seventh Ward. In the end, Palmer family money and contacts combined with Honoré's surprising campaign abilities carried the day. Honoré wrote out a victory statement, which the *Chicago InterOcean* duly reported had carefully been gone over by his mother before he issued it.[52]

Honoré won re-election in 1902 and served a total of two years as a member of the City Council. He seems neither to have disgraced himself nor done well enough to seek a larger political post. The Palmers' world changed fundamentally on May 8, 1902, when Potter Palmer senior died at the age of 76 after years of declining health. His wealth was estimated at between 8 and 12 million dollars. Since almost all his worth was in the Palmer House and other real estate, the total value of his holdings tended to fluctuate. His will divided his estate into two parts. Half went outright to Bertha, while the other half went into a trust for his two sons. Potter's will named Bertha and her brother, Adrian C. Honoré, as joint trustees. Bertha arranged for Potter's body to be temporarily interred at Graceland Cemetery on Chicago's north side, where nearly all of the city's elite in the late nineteenth and early twentieth century found their final resting places. She soon started planning for a large and impressive burial area for Palmer family members.[53]

In the aftermath of Potter's death, the Palmer and Honoré families pulled even closer together. That part of the Potter Palmer bequest put into trusteeship was managed through the Palmer Estate Company, incorporated in Illinois. Bertha, her father H. H. Honoré, her brother Adrian, and her two sons all took a hand in managing the real estate empire. In subsequent years the company began purchasing properties across the country. These included a manufacturing firm in Chicago, mining interests in Mexico, oil and gas lands in Louisiana, orchards in Oregon, and a ranch in Colorado.

There were a number of other changes in Bertha Palmer's life after her husband's death. Honoré, his political career over, married Grace Greenway Brown of Baltimore in 1903 in a London ceremony. Grace was one of three Brown sisters, all considered great beauties. Their father had been a prominent businessman in Maryland. One of Grace's sisters had married Stanley Field, nephew of Marshall Field. The two couples would later occupy adjacent mansions along Sarasota Bay. In 1906 Bertha's beloved mother passed away, a great blow to all the Honorés. Then, in 1908, Potter Palmer Jr. became engaged to Chicagoan Pauline Kohlsaat, daughter of newspaper magnate Herman H. Kohlsaat. Bertha rushed home from Europe to be at the wedding, where

Honoré served as his brother's best man.[54]

After 1902 Bertha entertained far less than she had in the past and spent relatively little time in Chicago living in the Castle. Increasingly she focused on Europe, a place she knew well from the numerous visits she had made there with Potter. Her world's fair experience meant she had many friends and acquaintances in all the major countries. She knew most of the kings and queens personally, as she did members of the nobility. Her niece, Julia Cantacuzene, kept in close touch with her from the Russian capital at St. Petersburg, relating the latest news from the Czar's court. Among the signs of her new interest in Europe, particularly London and Paris, were a series of real estate transactions. Bertha leased Hampton House in London, an estate on the Isle of Wight, and a townhouse in Paris at 6 Rue Fabert. She became a fixture at grand balls, dinners, operas, plays, musical performances, and at the Ascot races. There was much newspaper speculation about a possible second marriage for her; a number of titled men she had been seen with were discussed as possible husbands. Bertha forcefully denied all rumors and made it clear she had no such plans.[55]

In 1907 Bertha Palmer took on her last great social challenge by becoming part of King Edward VII's Marlborough Circle. The son of Queen Victoria, Edward was far more gregarious and sociable than his mother. He also had a liking for American women, of whom there were many in London who had wed penurious peers of the realm in need of an infusion of American cash. Bertha had known Edward before he was king and was friendly with his wife, Queen Alexandra. With their royal nods, she moved into the king's inner group of friends. Her high status became clear to all when the king invited her to a royal ball under the classification of distinguished foreigner, a title usually reserved for ambassadors.[56]

Being part of the king's circle meant Bertha spent the social season in London giving and attending sumptuous dinners. In the summer the group adjourned to Biarritz, a tourist town on the southwest coast of France. Bertha was among those who played golf with the king and dined with him at his invitation. He seemed to appreciate her ability to carry on dinner conversations on serious issues as well as the doings of the rich and famous. Never more than eight persons attended these intimate royal dinners. Through these events Bertha became familiar with all of the king's chief advisors as well as important bankers and merchants.

For Bertha and other women in the king's circle, it was expected that they should be grand hostesses organizing the great dinners and social events during the social season that would be the talk of London. That sort of thing came naturally to a woman who dominated Chicago's social scene and won acceptance at Newport. Hampton House, a two-story structure featuring a grand entrance hall and ballroom, was her base of operations. Decorated in French style and boasting a large rear garden, Hampton House was perfectly adapted to stage a seemingly endless series of teas, dinners, balls, recitals, and garden parties.[57]

Bertha's greatest triumph was to attract the king to her home for a private performance of the opera *Salome* by Richard Strauss. She had paid the entire cast to come to Hampton House to perform at a reception she was hosting, even though censors had closed down the production in several European cities because of its portrayal of the *Dance of the Seven Veils*. Through 1909 Bertha continued this whirlwind, if banal, life as a kind of royal courtier. Few could claim greater success than she as a social leader on two continents. Her principal qualities of beauty, wealth, intelligence, and style carried her from one social triumph to the next. But the Edwardian era was coming to an end. Edward's health faltered and he died in the spring of 1910. His successor, George V, and Queen Mary made it clear that a new era was beginning, and American hostesses would not be as important in the new reign.[58]

Bertha was back in the Castle when word reached her from her sources in London that the king was quite ill. It was January, deep winter in Chicago, and she had to know that at age 61 she faced the same question she had in 1893 and 1902: "What shall I do with my life?" In broad terms, her choices were more of the same or something quite different. She could continue to be the social arbiter of Chicago while being recognized as a famous hostess in Europe, or she could seek out new challenges in some other field. As the wife of Potter Palmer and daughter of H. H. Honoré, Bertha certainly had learned from them a great deal about real estate development. As co-trustee of Potter's estate, she had been party to a number of real estate transactions in Chicago and across the country. Perhaps she saw herself becoming a major figure in the real estate business. Or perhaps the Castle was cold and drafty and the winds of Lake Michigan harsh and uncomfortable. Whatever was going on in her mind, she was drawn to an ad in the *Chicago Sunday Tribune* of January 23, 1910, which spoke of land-acquisition and citrus-growing opportunities near the town of Sarasota on the shores of Sarasota Bay on the west coast of sunny and warm Florida. She reached for her telephone and called her father.[59]

Notes For Chapter 1

1. Janet Snyder Matthews and Linda Mansberger, *Mrs. Potter Palmer—Legendary Lady of Sarasota* (Gulf Coast Heritage Association, Osprey, Florida, 1999), 7, 14.

2. Ross, *Silhouette in Diamonds*, 40–66.

3. Ibid., 182–183.

4. Ibid., 14–17; Jeanne Madeline Weimann, *The Fair Ladies* (Academy. Chicago, 1981), 10.

5. Ross, *Silhouette in Diamonds*, 18.

6. Kalmbach, *Jewel of the Gold Coast: Mrs. Potter Palmer's Chicago* (Chicago, Ampersand, Inc., 2009), 41–44.

7. Ross, *Silhouette in Diamonds*, 19–20, 24–25; Weimann, *The Fair Women*, 7–9.

8. Ross, *Silhouette in Diamonds*, 24; Kalmbach, *Jewel of the Gold Coast*,

9. Ross, *Silhouette in Diamonds*, 40–41, Kalmbach, *Jewel of the Gold Coast*, 11–12.

10. Ross, *Silhouette in Diamonds*, 1–10; Weimann, *The Fair Women*, 12.

11. Ross, *Silhouette in Diamonds*, 8.

12. Ibid., 40–46; *Chicago Tribune*, Dec. 20,1874; Weimann, *The Fair Women*, 12; *Chicago Tribune*, Dec. 20, 1874; Kalmbach, *Jewel of the Gold Coast*, 20–21.

13. Ross *Silhouette in Diamonds*, 48.

14. Weimann, *The Fair Women*, 13–14; Margo Hobbs, "Bertha Honoré Palmer's Philanthropy in the Arts." M. A. Thesis, The School of the Art Institute, 1992, Rollins Coakley Collection, Sarasota County Historical Resources, 1, 11.

15. Weimann, *The Fair Women*, 16.

16. Ibid. 5; Ross, *Silhouette in Diamonds*, 47; Hobbs, "Bertha Honoré Palmer's Philanthropy in the Arts," 13–15.

17. Kalmbach, *Jewel of the Gold Coast*, 33.

18. Ross, *Silhouette in Diamonds*, 51–53; Kalmbach, *Jewel of the Gold Coast*, 23–24.

19. Ross, *Silhouette in Diamonds*, 55.

20. Ibid., 55; Weimann, *The Fair Women*,17; Kalmbach, *Jewel of the Gold Coast*, 30–33, 36–39.

21. Weimann, *The Fair Women*, 15–16; Ross *Silhouette in Diamonds*, 56; Kalmbach, *Jewel of the Gold Coast*, 30–33, 36–39.

22. Kalmbach, *Jewel of the Gold Coast*, 30, 36–39.

23. Ross, *Silhouette in Diamonds*, 47; Hobbs, "Bertha Honoré Palmer's Philanthropy in the Arts," 2–3; Kalmbach, *Jewel of the Gold Coast*, 59–62.

24. Frank A. Cassell and Marguerite E. Cassell, "The White City in Peril: Leadership and the World's Columbian Exposition," *Chicago History* (XII, Fall 1983), 10–27; Weimann, *The Fair Women*, 22–25.

25. Weimann, *The Fair Women*, 5–29.

26. Ibid., 28–30.

27. Ibid., 33–42.

28. Ibid., 43.

29. Ibid., 47.

30. Ibid., 55–70.

31. Ibid., 52–55, 143-149.

32. Ibid., 331-333; Ross *Silhouette in Diamonds*, 78-79.

33. Weimann, *The Fair Women*, 105; Ross, *Silhouette in Diamonds*, 60.

34. Weimann, *The Fair Women*, 06–107; Ross, *Silhouette in Diamonds*, 59–60.

35. Ross, *Silhouette in Diamonds*, 62–63; Program Book, Musée de Rodin (Paris). In 1906 Rodin sculpted a bust of Bertha Palmer, which is on display at the museum. Coakley Collection, Sarasota County Historical Resources.

36. Weimann, *The Fair Women*, 139; Ross, *Silhouette in Diamonds*, 61

37. Weimann, *The Fair Women*, 223; *Addresses and Reports of Mrs. Potter Palmer, President of the Board of Lady Managers, World's Columbian Commission* (Chicago: Rand, Mc-Nally & Co., 1894), 159; *Chicago Tribune*, Oct. 22, 1892; Ross, *Silhouette in Diamonds*, 80.

38. *Chicago Tribune*, May 2, 1893; *Chicago InterOcean*, May 2, 1893. Harlow Higginbotham, *Final Report of the President to the Board of Directors of the World's Columbian Exposition* (Chicago, 1898), 209–213; Thomas Palmer, *Report of the President of the World's Columbian Exposition* (Columbian Exposition Records, Manuscripts Division Chicago History Museum).

39. Weimann, *The Fair Women*, 255–256; *Chicago Tribune*, May 2, 1893; *Chicago Inter-Ocean*, May 2, 1893; Mary Kavanaugh Oldham Eagle, *Congress of Women Held in the Women's Building, World's Columbian Exposition* (Chicago 1893), 25–29, 131–141; Kalmbach, *Jewel of the Gold Coast*, 33.

40. Ross, *Silhouette in Diamonds*, 83–100; *Chicago InterOcean*, June 10, 1893; *Chicago Tribune* Oct. 13, 1893; Kalmbach, *Jewel of the Gold Coast*, 33.

41. Thomas S. Hines, *Burnham of Chicago: Architect and Planner* (Chicago: University of Chicago Press, 1974), 125–216; Charles Mulford Robinson, *Modern Civic Art or the City Made Beautiful* (New York and London, 1916), *passim*; Harvey Kantor, "The City Made Beautiful in New York," *New York Historical Society Quarterly*, LVII (April 1973), 149–171.

42. See Frank A. Cassell, "A Confusion of Voices: Reform Movements and the World's Columbian Exposition of 1893," in Alan D. Corré, ed., *The Quest for Social Justice, II: The Morris Fromkin Memorial Lectures, 1981–1990*. (The Golda Meir Library, the University of Wisconsin-Milwaukee, 1992), 59-76; Ross, *Silhouette in Diamonds*, 100.

43. Ross, *Silhouette in Diamonds*, 100–115.

44. Ibid., 121–122.

45. Ibid., 122–123.; Kalmbach, *Jewel of the Gold Coast*, 81.

46. Ross, *Silhouette in Diamonds*, 125–137; *New York Times*, Aug. 1, 1896, July 23, 1898, Aug. 11, 1898.

47. Ross, *Silhouette in Diamonds*, 135–140.

48. Ibid., 141–143; Princess Julia Cantacuzene, *Revolutionary Days*, edited by Teresa Evans (Chicago: The Lakeside Press, 1999), xvii–xviii.

49. Ross, *Silhouette in Diamonds*, 144; Cantacuzene, *Revolutionary Days*, xviii.

50. Ross, *Silhouette in Diamonds*, 164–177; Kalmbach, *Jewel of the Gold Coast*, 81; *New York Times*, Feb. 13, 1900.

51. Ross, *Silhouette in Diamonds*, 178–181.

52. Ibid., 181; *Chicago Tribune*, March 12 and 14; April 2, 1901; *Chicago InterOcean*, April 3, 1901; *Chicago American*, May 5, 1902.

53. Ross, *Silhouette in Diamonds*, 182–183; *New York Times*, May 5, 1902.

54. Ross, *Silhouette in Diamonds*, 183–189; Marriage Records of Parish of St. George (London), August 20, 1903, record of marriage of Honoré Palmer and Grace Brown, Coakley Collection, Sarasota County Historical Resources; *New York Times*, July 22, and 25, 1908; *Chicago Tribune*, July 27, 1908.

55. Ross, *Silhouette in Diamonds*, 190–196.

56. Ibid., 197–210; Kalmbach, *Jewel of the Gold Coast*, 81–82.

57. Ross, *Silhouette in Diamonds*, 211–219.

58. Ibid., 220–221.

59. *Chicago Sunday Tribune*, January 23, 1910.

CHAPTER TWO

Building an Empire

T
he man who had placed the advertisement for lands in and around Sarasota was Joseph H. Lord. Originally from Maine, Lord was the largest landowner in the Sarasota area in 1910. His holdings exceeded 100,000 acres and included some of the most valuable lots in the town. He came to Chicago in hopes that he could find buyers for his Florida properties among the Northerners enduring another Chicago winter. He leased offices in the Marquette Building in the Loop area of the city. As it happened, Bertha's father, H. H. Honoré, also ran his own real estate empire from that location. After receiving Bertha's call, H. H. strolled over to Lord's office to get acquainted. His daughter wanted his advice on Lord's reliability and the wisdom of investing in Florida land. Whatever was said at the meeting, H. H. was impressed enough to urge Bertha to invite Lord to the Castle for a chat. Bertha, too, was impressed by the big Floridian, whose enthusiasm for Sarasota stirred her interest.[1]

Things now moved quickly. Within a few days Bertha had arranged for her father, her brother Adrian, her son Honoré, and several members of her staff to travel by private Pullman car to Sarasota. They left Chicago on February 8 for a trip that would take most of two days and transport her between two worlds that could hardly have been more different. There is no definitive information on what Bertha knew of Florida as her train chugged south. But as she was always careful in her business dealings, it is very unlikely that she began this trip without first reading everything she could find that was pertinent.[2]

The Florida of 1910 was truly a frontier state. Its total population was around 753,000, less than that of the city of Chicago. Phosphate mining, fishing, citrus growing, and beef ranching were its principal industries. Much of the southern half of the state was virtually empty of people, and a great deal of the land was too low and wet to sustain farming. Bertha would surely have known of two men whose personal drive and ambition had transformed the east coast of Florida and much of the upper west coast as far south as Tampa into economically successful zones. Henry Flagler, one of the founders of the Standard Oil Corporation, had spent nearly thirty years creating an "American Riviera" from St. Augustine to Miami. He built the Florida East Coast Railway, running from Jacksonville to St. Augustine to West Palm Beach to Palm Beach and finally to Miami in 1896. Along the way he built great hotels for the rich who could now escape winters in New York, Philadelphia, or Boston for the pleasure grounds of Florida. In 1910 Flagler was engaged in building his last and greatest project. The Florida Overseas Railroad started in Miami and stretched across the arc of keys that ended in Key West, the state's largest city at the time, and the deep-water American port closest to the eastern terminus of the as yet unfinished Panama Canal. Flagler's achievement was certainly one of the great engineering triumphs of the age.

Bertha also likely knew a great deal about another New Yorker, Henry Plant, who also used railroads and hotels as development tools, but on the other side of the peninsula from Flagler's operations. Plant was sometimes a rival, occasionally a business associate, but always a friend of Flagler. His rail system ran from Georgia to Jacksonville, and ultimately to Tampa. When his railroad reached Tampa in 1884, Plant erected the Tampa Bay Hotel, the grandest on Florida's west coast and costing $2.5 million. It still stands today on the campus of the University of Tampa. Plant died in 1899, but he more than anyone created Tampa and opened the way for future development along Florida's Gulf coast. Plant's railroad empire did not long survive his passing. When Bertha arrived in Sarasota she was riding on the Seaboard Air Line Railroad, a successor to Plant's line.[3]

By the time the Palmers and Honorés reached Sarasota, its 962 citizens were in a high state of excitement. J. H. Lord had wired his partner, Arthur B. Edwards, about the visit and word spread quickly through the community. Since Lord could not reach Sarasota for some days, it was up to Edwards to welcome Bertha and her family and begin the process of persuading her to invest some of her millions in local real estate. The slightly built Edwards could hardly have been more of a contrast to the burly, six-foot-five, college-educated Lord. He was a local boy born north of Sarasota in 1874. His parents died when he was but 15 years old, and from that point he was on his own. Energetic and enterprising, Edwards had gone into real estate and insurance and distinguished himself as one of Sarasota's biggest boosters.

J. H. Lord, who sold Bertha Palmer thousands of acres of land around Sarasota.
By permission of Sarasota County Historical Resources.

In 1910 he was just at the beginning of a long career of political and business leadership in the area.[4]

Edwards understood that his first problem was to find suitable quarters for the visiting millionaires. The only hotel, the Belle Haven Inn, was located near the foot of Main Street close to the waters of Sarasota Bay. Unfortunately, the building had been neglected, and Edwards deemed it unsuitable for such distinguished guests. Nearby, however, was a much newer structure housing a sanitarium. It was owned by an Englishman, Dr. Jack Halton, who settled in the Sarasota community in 1905. After some hurried discussions, the patients were moved out and appropriate furniture installed. With this makeover, the sanitarium, at least temporarily, became a hotel for a very select clientele.[5]

No one in Sarasota, of course, had ever met Bertha Palmer, or for that matter, anyone remotely as famous as the fabled Queen

A. B. Edwards, Lord's partner in 1910. He later became mayor of Sarasota.
By permission of Sarasota County Historical Resources.

of Chicago Society. From the pages of Sarasota's one newspaper, the *Sarasota Times,* written and published weekly by Mr. and Mrs. Cornelius Van Santvoord Wilson, they knew quite a bit about Bertha and her family and her ties to presidents, kings, queens, and assorted nobility. They certainly knew she was very rich. What they could not know was what kind of a person she was and how she treated other people. A. B. Edwards commented years later that he wondered if she would be "snooty." In fact, she proved to be quite the opposite. Edwards recalled that from their first meeting at the Sarasota railroad station she was always cordial and kind. She even won local hearts by describing their all-too-obviously run-down village as "refreshingly quaint."[6]

The relationship between Edwards and Bertha proved to be important. If he found her approachable, she seemed drawn to his personal story and his ability to talk about the relatively short history of Sarasota from his own experience. Over several days of touring the area and during evenings spent chatting at the Halton Sanitarium, Bertha and her family heard much from Edwards about this little town at the end of the railroad track on the edge of a jungle.

Edwards undoubtedly told the Chicagoans of his memories as a boy coming across strangers in the woods south of his home, men who turned out to be surveyors for the Florida Mortgage and Investment Company. They were laying out a town in 1884 in preparation for the arrival of a colony of settlers from Scotland. There was no one living in the area they were laying out; it was entirely untouched Florida scrubland or jungle filled with many forms of palms, shrubs, and some pine trees. A year later the Scots colonists arrived expecting to find a fully functioning town, but discovered a wilderness instead. They had been promised much in return for their investment in the company, and were both angry and deeply disappointed. Local settlers provided shelter for the newcomers and tried hard to help them out by teaching them basic skills, such as fishing in the waters of Sarasota Bay where fish were so plentiful that they had been known literally to flop into fishermen's boats. Despite this neighborly assistance, most of the Scots soon migrated north to cities where they had relatives or friends.[7]

It was a catastrophe, but out of the disaster, Sarasota was born. The turning point was the arrival in the spring of 1886 of John Hamilton Gillespie, a former soldier and son of Sir John Gillespie, head of the Florida Mortgage and Investment Company. Young Gillespie had been born in 1852, studied law in Edinburgh, was a member of the Royal Company of Archers, Queen's Bodyguard for Scotland, and had served in Australia. He represented his father and was, in fact, the operating chief of the Florida Mortgage and Land Company in America. Even though few colonists remained, Gillespie threw himself into organizing, settling, and selling company lands, which included Sarasota and 50,000 acres around the town in what was then Manatee County. He proved to be a dynamic leader. Thanks to him, streets were built, a hotel erected, a part of Sarasota Bay dredged, a town cemetery—Rosewood—established, and the area's first golf course created. Gillespie served as mayor for six years after the town incorporated in 1903. That was also the year the Seaboard Air Line Railroad reached Sarasota. A short branch of the railroad ran from the downtown station to a pier on which several fish processing factories were located. This constituted one of the most important industries in the town. Gillespie had done much to turn his father's dreams of an American colony into a reality. Unfortunately, he was powerless to address the economic downturn known as the Panic of 1907. The national economic collapse hit Florida and Sarasota very hard. The enthusiasm generated by Gillespie's programs dissipated quickly, and the town went into decline. Out of necessity Gillespie sold all of the Florida Mortgage and Investment Company lands outside the town of Sarasota, and J. H. Lord was the buyer. Now the whole area was in a bad state and Lord was offering to sell the land to Bertha at cut-rate prices.[8]

Edwards' stories gave Bertha a pretty clear picture of Sarasota's history and contemporary problems. But she likely was also affected by his obvious passion for his native land. She and her family joined Edwards for a cruise along the shores of Sarasota Bay and the wooded keys that shielded the mainland from great storms. She fished, and was immediately successful in the area

Bertha Palmer and members of her family in 1911 in Sarasota, Florida.
Chicago History Museum ICH i12038. Photographer unknown.

known as Big Pass. She enjoyed the warmth of the sun, the spar-
kling white sands of the beaches, and the glorious colors of the
sea and the jungle. At some point she compared the beauty of
the bay quite positively with one of her favorite European desti-
nations, the Bay of Naples. It was a quote used by the Sarasota
Board of Trade for decades to attract visitors.[9]

On one of her cruises with Edwards and her father, the boat
entered Little Sarasota Bay just south of the main bay. Edwards
suddenly remembered something remarkable. He told her that
not far away there was an unusual sight, a cabbage palm and a
live oak that had grown together and seemed to be a single plant.
Bertha was entranced and asked to see this phenomenon. The
boat docked at a dilapidated wharf. Ignoring her father's protest
that she was risking injury, Bertha pulled up her skirts, stepped

out of the craft, and marched inland to see the romantic trees. While she enjoyed the trees, she was even more affected by the natural beauty of the entire area. The views of the bay, the green shorelines of the keys, the white beaches, and the turquoise shade of the sea powerfully attracted her. At that moment she decided that this would be the site of her winter home; and, of course, she had the money to make her whims reality. The next day she returned and tried but failed to persuade the owner to reduce his asking price. She paid $11,000 for 13 acres that would constitute the core of her planned estate. Eventually, the acreage would grow to nearly 350 acres.[10]

Shortly after the purchase, Joseph Lord finally arrived from Chicago and took over showing the Palmers and Honorés the land he was prepared to sell them. An important juncture had been reached. Bertha had initially decided to create a great estate for herself. Rather than develop the land for sale to others, she intended to buy enough to build a personal retreat reflecting her life and interests. Soon Lord appealed to the business instincts of the visitors, all of whom were experienced and successful in buying, developing, and selling land. Lord was trying to persuade them to invest in his Florida properties with the aim of reselling them to others for a profit. There is little evidence that Bertha came to Florida with this prospect in mind. However, by the end of her visit, which she extended from three to eleven days, Bertha was very much alive to the business opportunities she saw in purchasing and developing land around Sarasota.[11]

While Bertha returned to Chicago and then sailed for Europe, the wheels of the Palmer-Honoré enterprise continued to turn. By April her son Honoré and his family were back in Sarasota Bay, living on a luxurious houseboat for a few weeks. Sometime in this period a soil specialist hired by Bertha investigated the lands she was thinking of purchasing. His report no longer exists, but it undoubtedly mentioned that the Sarasota area possessed only limited high ground suitable for year-round habitation and planting. The shoreline was relatively high and well drained, as were ridge lands created by ancient oceans. These included Bee Ridge, Tatum Ridge, and Lockwood Ridge. The ridges, however, would require both irrigation and drainage to ensure successful farms and groves. Much of the remaining land was low and very wet or even covered by water during the long rainy season. Only extensive and expensive drainage projects could turn this property into profitable farms, although some of it served as grazing land for cattle during part of the year.[12]

While Bertha and her family were not particularly knowledgeable about soils and farming, they knew that land could be reshaped if enough technology and effort were applied. Potter Palmer had demonstrated this when he created Chicago's Gold Coast out of sandy scrubland along Lake Michigan. The great Columbian Exposition occupied over 700 acres of Chicago's Jackson Park. That area had also been mostly wasteland. Thanks to modern machinery, it had been drained, graded, shaped, and sodded to provide a memorable setting for the White City of 1893. Since then new mechanized devices made large-scale land reclamation a more economical option.

On May 12, 1910, the *Sarasota Times* announced that Bertha had purchased 37,000 acres of land south of the town of Sarasota from J. H. Lord. This was but the beginning. The Manatee County land records reveal numerous purchases of property by Bertha and members of her family. Before long, the family owned over 80,000 acres. These acquisitions in 1910 were part of a rational plan of development. The properties stretched along Sarasota Bay at least from the mouth of Philippi Creek all the way to an area that would become the community of Venice. A great swath of Palmer lands stretched east along the modern roads of Bee Ridge, Proctor, and Clark, well past today's Interstate 75 corridor. Yet another vast expanse ran north and east from the current intersection of Honoré Avenue and Bee Ridge Road past Fruitville Road. At its peak the Palmer holdings covered 218 square miles of Manatee County. When Sarasota County was formed in 1921, the Palmer and Honoré interests owned between a fourth and a third of the county's land.[13]

The size and sweep of Bertha's purchases startled the Sarasotans, who were not used to thinking in such grand terms. They were further amazed by the news that Bertha had arranged with officials of the Seaboard Air Line Railroad Company to extend its tracks 20 miles from Sarasota through the small village of Fruitville and then straight south to a new terminus that Bertha had named Venice. Why the railroad agreed to build the extension is unclear. At the time there were few people living in the area and limited agricultural production.[14]

Most of the land the extension would serve now belonged to Bertha. It is a measure of her thinking and planning that she insisted on the extension as a condition of her land purchase. She knew that there was no possibility of developing that property without rail connections to move people and products between her proposed empire and Northern cities and towns. In this she was supported by other local landowners such as the Knight family, who quickly realized that they, too, would benefit economically if the spur were built. Bertha and her neighbors all donated land to the railroad as an encouragement to begin the project.

Even so, there were unspecified complications and continuing negotiations. Some thought the railroad finally came to an agreement when Bertha threatened to build the extension herself. What is known is that top railroad executives went to Chicago and met with Palmer representatives. When they returned it was clear that some kind of a deal had been struck and all difficulties had been put to rest. Work began in June 1910, but not until late 1911 did regular service move over the tracks.[15]

The railroad company announced that there would be four stations built along the extension from Fruitville; Palmer, Osprey, Laurel, and Venice were the preliminary names announced. Other stations would be added as needed. Even at this early stage, only months after their February visit to Sarasota, Bertha and her family had advanced their development plans significantly. They saw the rail extension as a development corridor, and each station was meant to be a profitable center of Palmer enterprise. Yet Bertha would soon find that some of her new neighbors did not entirely agree with her methods or her ambitions.[16]

The newspaper reports in June 1910 gave some hints about what the Palmers were intending to do with their huge land holdings. For example, it was reported that Bertha was planning to build a large Italian-style villa on her personal estate. Indeed, she later did commission not one but two architectural plans for such a structure, though neither was erected. It was also noted that Bertha owned 12 miles of bayfront property and intended to organize most of it into one-acre parcels that she would sell to well-to-do individuals looking for a winter retreat. The cost she estimated would be $100 per acre. Around her personal estate, later named Osprey Point, Bertha was said to expect many of her Chicago friends to buy land to be near her, just as they had when the Castle was built. According to the paper, Bertha had so far invested $300,000 in land purchases. Little appeared in the paper about her intentions for the great majority of the acreage she owned that was located inland.[17]

By June of 1910 Bertha and her family had made important decisions about how to manage her properties. She arranged through her lawyers for the state of Florida to incorporate the Sarasota-Venice Company, with her brother Adrian C. Honoré as president, J. H. Lord as vice-president, Honoré Palmer as secretary, and Potter Palmer Jr. as treasurer. Lord also served as general manager and oversaw land sales. The company was responsible for much but by no means all of the Palmer lands. As the name implied, the company was primarily responsible for the land originally bought from Lord south and southeast of Sarasota. It appears that this land differed from other Palmer properties in that it was purchased from trust funds created in Potter Palmer's will for his two sons, with Bertha and Adrian Honoré as trustees. A second Florida corporation, the Palmer Florida Company, was formed later, with Adrian Honoré as president and Honoré Palmer as vice-president. This entity managed Palmer properties in and around the town of Sarasota and on nearby keys. It was also responsible for land purchases Bertha made in the Tampa area. The funding for this corporation is not entirely clear, but it may have been from profits generated by Potter Palmer Sr.'s properties in Chicago and elsewhere. Bertha managed her personal estate, Osprey Point, and several other properties directly, with no corporate structure. She used the huge inheritance left her by her husband to purchase and manage them. Although important, the corporate structures did not keep Bertha from making decisions about all Palmer properties, regardless of where they stood in the organizational chart.[18]

After a summer in Paris at 6 Rue Fabert, Bertha made her way to Sarasota by mid-October of 1910, arriving with a large entourage aboard a private rail car. She brought along her new automobile, a French Cadillac purchased in Paris. There was, of course, nothing like it in Sarasota. Although most of the streets and roads were poorly built, the car, together with Bertha and her chauffeur, were soon familiar sights throughout the area. Soon after arriving she undoubtedly met with Joseph Lord, who had now given up his office in Chicago to assume his duties with the Sarasota-Venice Company and to manage his own extensive real estate holdings. He immediately moved his operations to the Gillespie Building, where the Sarasota-Venice Company paid half of his office expenses. The *Sarasota Times*, now published by the widow Rose Wilson, reported that Lord would be planting groves and draining lands for truck farms, a strong hint that Bertha and her family advisors now had sharpened their thinking about how to develop their properties for sale.

Sarasota in the fall of 1910 was a changed town. Since Bertha had arrived in February, the all-too-evident lassitude had evaporated, and the little settlement now exuded new energy. Bertha's land purchases alone had plowed hundreds of thousands of dollars into the local economy. People could reasonably anticipate that her estate and improvements on her holdings would create jobs, bring in tourists and investors, and generally create an age of growth and prosperity. The new railroad extension was visible proof that Sarasota had entered a new era. In rapid order Sarasota's government moved to establish better sewage, electric, and telephone service, and to pave local streets. Bertha was not alone in snatching up desirable city lots, thus driving up real estate prices. She also built a garage, the first of several buildings she would construct in the town. Dr. Jack Halton had assumed management of the old Belle Haven Inn, whose new owners had renovated the structure and added a wing, which Bertha and her family and servants occupied in October. Within a year a seawall would be erected to protect the bayfront thanks to the arrival of another Chicagoan, Owen Burns. Burns was a dynamic, creative individual who continued to serve his adopted town for many decades.[19]

In the middle of November, Bertha and a party of ten, including her father and two of her brothers, left the Belle Haven and boarded a train for Jacksonville. She had concluded the time had come to see the east coast of Florida, presumably to study what Henry Flagler had accomplished. The group spent weeks on the road, with stops in St. Augustine, Palm Beach, and Miami. There are few details known about this trip. One paper commented that among her party were men who could help her run her estate, which suggests she may have been looking at the layout of gardens and mansions for ideas. Presumably, she stayed at some of Flagler's sumptuous hotels and observed the rich men and women who lived in luxurious suites and enjoyed a wide range of leisure activities. In a few years Bertha would consider building a hotel at Venice to attract the rich to the Sarasota area, but that never happened.[20]

By December Bertha was back in Sarasota and buying more land. On December 8 a Jacksonville paper revealed that she had invested in lands rich in phosphate along the Peace River of central Florida. Phosphate was a principal export of the state. But the biggest news came in mid-December when Bertha purchased thousands of acres of ranch lands along the Myakka River, due

Left to right: Mrs. Potter Palmer with her daughter-in-law Mrs. Honoré Palmer, and her sister, Mrs. Frederick Grant. *Courtesy of Gulf Coast Heritage, Inc.*

east of her planned estate at Osprey. She bought the ranch of Garrett "Dink" Murphy, together with several thousand head of cattle. Later she would acquire other ranches in the area, eventually totaling 15,000 acres, and name the whole thing Meadowsweet Pastures. She spent her personal funds on this project and managed it directly, as she did her estate. Why she undertook this venture is unknown. She had no more knowledge of cattle than she did of truck farming or citrus growing. Unlike her other purchases, there was no apparent plan. Indeed, it would be awhile before she figured out what she wanted to do with this mega-ranch. Bertha spent over $70,000 just for Dink Murphy's property, but then she could easily afford it. By now she owned well over 100,000 acres, 25 miles of shoreline property, and about 50 lots in Sarasota.[21]

During the fall of 1910, Bertha had many visitors at the Belle Haven Inn. Her two sons and their wives and children spent time in Sarasota, as did her niece Princess Cantacuzene, the prince, and their children. She also spent time with her architect and garden designers, who were preparing plans for her estate at Osprey, 12 miles or so south of Sarasota. This was to be her very own home, and she meant to control every detail. If she had no real experience in agriculture, she did know a lot about gardens and estates from her experiences in Chicago and Europe, as well as from the fabulous Columbian Exposition grounds laid out by Frederick Law Olmsted. The Castle had gardens, of course, as well as a large hothouse. Her London home and the estate on the Isle of Wight had gardens she had worked in when she happened to be in residence. She had even bred a rose that bore her name.[22]

As 1911 began, Bertha and her family continued to acquire new properties. In Tampa, Bertha bought a 19,000-acre ranch northeast of the city as well as acreage inside the city limits that she meant to develop as a subdivision. Around her estate, Osprey Point, she bought out local settlers until her original 13-acre purchase had expanded to nearly 350 acres. In Sarasota she built a hotel, and just outside the town limits to the north she gained control of a large tract near the bayshore that she would subdivide and call the Boulevard Addition. All in all, it was a breathtaking performance—and it had all taken place in one year.[23]

Bertha had never been shy about personal publicity. Her world's fair experience, if nothing else, had made her adept at manipulating the public's large appetite to know about her plans and activities. The novelty of such a famous woman redirecting much of her energy to developing the frontier of Florida attracted great attention from newspapers and magazines. Bertha chose her moments to grant an interview carefully and always knew exactly what points she wanted to make. In the early months of 1911 she was eager to advertise her development plans as a way to attract tourists to Sarasota who might eventually become purchasers of land and builders of homes. To succeed in her business aspirations, she had to recognize and take advantage of the simple fact that she was one of the most effective boosters of Florida. Thus, on February 23, 1911, the *Sarasota Times* reprinted a lengthy story from the *Chicago Examiner*, which had sent a reporter to Sarasota to interview the great lady.[24]

Bertha told the reporter that she had traveled widely in the United States seeking out the perfect location for her winter home. She wanted to "beautify a great landed estate to be handed down to posterity." And at Sarasota Bay she had come upon an area as beautiful as her favorite place, the Bay of Naples. The reporter praised Bertha for carefully examining the vast lands before she purchased them, and hiring experts to evaluate the quality and economic potential of the acreage. She described Bertha as shrewd and said "she was behind it all." The reporter correctly identified the Seaboard Air Line Railroad extension to Venice as a critical element in making the new Palmer lands valuable by linking them to Northern markets.[25]

What is most interesting about this article is Bertha's description of further plans. She talked about attracting more Chicagoans to buy her land near her Osprey Point estate. She listed nearly a dozen well-to-do Chicagoans who already owned citrus groves and were intending to become permanent residents. She stated that it was her plan eventually to live most of the year in Sarasota. Bertha went on to say that she thought the west coast of Florida, like the east coast, would become "a rich man's paradise." These wealthy individuals would be attracted to wonderful weather and scenery. They would seek places to stay where they could hunt, fish, sail, swim, and golf. And many of them would build winter homes amid truck farms and groves. She was quick to point out that these groves and farms would be great investments, noting the rapid rise of property values since she arrived. Bertha went on to say that her architect and garden designers were currently with her, laying out the grounds of Osprey Point. She also noted that other members of her family would soon be erecting houses in the area. In this interview, interestingly, there was no mention of Bertha's father, her brother Adrian, or her two sons, Honoré and Potter, all of whom were very involved in developing the Palmer Empire. But of course there was little public interest in them. She understood that it was her glamorous aura that would attract the wealthy elite.[26]

During 1911 there were six major projects involving the Palmers moving forward: the railroad extension; work at Bertha's Osprey Point estate; the marketing of the Boulevard Addition; the building of Immokalee, Honoré and Potter Palmer Jr.'s winter estate; planning for the Acacias, where Bertha's aunt and uncle would live; and preparations for the development of Bee Ridge, the first of the Palmer agricultural mega-projects. Gangs of workers, mostly black but with some immigrants among them, were hired—mainly from out of state—to do the required work. Bertha had little confidence in the work ethic of Florida blacks or native white "crackers." On occasion she would employ up to 300 workers in building her estate or digging drainage ditches at Bee Ridge. She provided dormitories at Osprey Point for some of these men. She also paid the highest wages in the area and was soon the largest employer in all of Manatee County. Other employers were not happy with her methods, and many of her neighbors resented the influx of outside labor. The situation was bound to cause trouble eventually. In the short run it was hard to stay mad at a woman who was pumping an enormous amount of money into the local economy, with the promise of much more to come.[27]

The railroad was not, strictly speaking, a Palmer project, but much depended on its completion. The road building took longer than anticipated, due to the number of waterways that needed bridging. Originally, the Seaboard announced that it would begin regular service on the extension in June of 1911. However, not until November did the company conduct test runs along the track and let contracts for the construction of the four stations and minor support structures. In December scheduled service finally commenced. But as early as October the question of the name of one of the stations emerged as an issue. The third station, originally called Laurel, had been renamed Dundee, while the fourth station located at the end of the line was to be known as Venice. But no one had consulted those living around the proposed Dundee location in what is now called Nokomis. In fact, Jesse Knight, a cattleman who had founded the little community, had named it Venice after the U.S. Postal Service deemed his original name, Horse and Chaise, too long. So in 1911 the local post office carried the name Venice, as did the local school and church. Yet all of these structures were a full mile distant from the terminus of the railroad, which the Seaboard Air Line Railroad had dubbed Venice at Bertha's insistence. Rivalries between families in the two locales, particularly between the Knights and their relatives and the Higel family, complicated matters. The growing controversy over the true location of Venice set the stage for a years-long test of wills. The truly important facts were that the railroad extension was finished and the Palmer plans could proceed.[28]

No project was closer to Bertha's heart than the design and building of her great estate at Osprey Point. She appears to have had several objectives in mind. First and foremost, it was to be her principal home in the final years of her life. Second, she intended to indulge fully her passion for gardening. Third, she saw Osprey Point as a kind of giant billboard, advertising what could be made out of the Florida wilderness. Wealthy men and women could see how they, too, could establish order and beauty out of a jungle. They would then, she hoped, buy Palmer land. Finally, Bertha intended to show that this great estate could be made self-sustaining. Much of the estate property to the east of the manicured lawns and fancy gardens comprised what she called the Home Farm. Here Bertha directed the planting of groves and fields of vegetables. As soon as the railroad reached the area, she began shipping much of what she grew to Northern cities. The Home Farm also had facilities to handle farm animals as well as turkeys and chickens. If Bertha made money selling agricultural products to offset the ongoing costs of her estate, she also saved money by using products from the Home Farm for her own table as well as to feed the gangs of workers she employed.[29]

The site of Osprey Point boasted panoramic views of the water and nearby Casey and Siesta Keys, of which she owned parts. At the south end of the estate, a small peninsula jutted out into the bay. Here stood several structures previously owned by the Guptil and Webb families from whom Bertha had purchased the land, and which she now adapted to new uses. Along the south shore of this peninsula stretched a ridge nearly a mile long. In fact, the ridge was artificial, a vast dumping ground of shells, called a midden, that had been created by Native Americans over a thousand years ago or so. There were other middens at Osprey

Point, as well as a burial mound, testifying to the enormous span of years human beings had occupied the site. The region around Sarasota was once filled with similar middens and mounds, many of which were carelessly destroyed by land developers. Fortunately, Bertha and her family displayed greater sensitivity as stewards of these cultural assets.[30]

The work of creating Osprey Point and her mansion, which she named The Oaks, occupied much of Bertha's attention. The basic design work was completed in 1911. Although there had been talk of a grand Italian villa, Bertha felt that her permanent house should be architecturally consistent with the large system of gardens she was planning. Until those gardens actually existed, she felt design work on the mansion would be premature. Yet she needed at least a temporary structure to live in for a few years. She made the decision to renovate and expand the original lodge built by the previous owner. To design the temporary home Bertha hired Thomas Reed Martin, a Chicago architect from the firm of Holabird & Roche, who came up with a plan to add a sec-

The lodge Bertha purchased in 1910. Later it was expanded and named The Oaks. H. H. Honoré in foreground. *Courtesy of Gulf Coast Heritage, Inc.*

ond story and build broad verandas around the structure. Further additions and remodeling went on for years, but Bertha never got around to building the grand villa.

Osprey Point rapidly evolved into an entire village, housing workers, managers, domestic staff, farm operations, and storage facilities. Every week seemed to bring new breathless reports in the *Sarasota Times* about progress. Local citizens expressed astonishment when Bertha installed a complete electric power system for the estate at a time when Sarasota's electric lights worked only a few hours each day. They were also likely amazed at the sewage system installed at The Oaks, as well as the fresh water system that relied on deep artesian wells. A water tower provided enormous storage capacity. If a fire broke out, the tower's electric pumps could deliver more water than was available to most small towns. By the fall of 1911 Bertha inhabited at least part of The Oaks, although she continued to spend some of her time at the Belle Haven Inn.[31]

The Boulevard Addition was Bertha Palmer's first effort to plat a subdivision, develop infrastructure, and then resell the lots at a profit. The Palmer Florida Company financed and managed the project, located on the site of the Whitaker homestead, where the first cabin in the Sarasota area had been built in the 1840s. Born in 1821 in Savannah, Georgia, William Whitaker ran away at age 14 and worked as a seaman and fisherman for a few years before moving in with his half-brother Hamlin Snell, an attorney in Tallahassee. He soon left to join the army and spent four years as a soldier in the Seminole Wars. Taking advantage of a government offer of 160 acres to able-bodied men willing to settle in south Florida, Whitaker, along with his half-brother, sailed along the Manatee County coastline until they spotted some yellow cliffs. In December 1842 the two men landed to find an excellent locale for homesteading. They immediately set about building a cabin. Snell left before long to take up his legal career, but left his name on Snell Bayou. Whitaker married, had a large family, and was important in launching Sarasota's fish, cattle, and citrus industries. It was this historic land that Bertha had bought and developed as the Boulevard Addition, an area now completely changed around the modern intersection of 10th Street and North Tamiami Trail.[32]

By the end of 1911 the Palmer Florida Company created a plan and began work on the Boulevard Addition. Every lot faced a street, and every street right-of-way had been cleared and graded. The company sank a deep artesian well, thus ensuring fresh water for the inhabitants. The Boulevard Addition stretched west almost to the bay and east across the Bradentown Road, now paved and referred to as the "hard road." Those who purchased lots had to hire builders to erect houses. In 1911 the Boulevard Addition offered every amenity that the citizens of Sarasota enjoyed, but with the benefit of no city taxes. The location overlooking Sarasota Bay and Longboat Key was another attraction, as was easy access to the Bradentown Road. The Palmers offered generous terms for lot purchases. Buyers had to come up with a down payment, but then had several years to pay off the debt at a reasonable interest rate. The Boulevard Addition was one of the earliest subdivisions of its type in Sarasota. Many more would soon follow. As the year closed, however, Bertha could not be certain that enough people would buy lots to bring a profit. [33]

Very near the Boulevard Addition, at Yellow Bluffs, another Palmer project took shape. Bertha's aunt and uncle, Laura and Benjamin Honoré, built on Palmer land one of Sarasota's first grand mansions, the Acacias. In 1911 this couple had made the decision to relocate permanently to Sarasota. They commissioned an architect and agreed to pay $70,000, a very large sum at the time, to build a home with 7,000 square feet of living space, plus extensive balconies and porches. J. S. Mans of Sarasota agreed to handle construction.[34]

Besides The Oaks and the Acacias, the Palmers were prepared to lay the foundation for yet a third mansion in November of 1911. Potter Palmer Jr., or Min, as the family called him, and his wife Pauline had not made their way to Florida until the fall of 1910, but soon fell in love with the Sarasota area, as had other members of the family. By the fall of 1911 they realized that they would be spending at least part of every winter in Sarasota, if for no other reason than to help manage Palmer business affairs. The young couple began looking at possible locations for what they thought originally would be a small house. They chose a site south of Sarasota on Sarasota Bay close to the mouth of Philippi Creek and began preparations to build. However, things changed when Min and his older brother Cappy, as Honoré Palmer was called in the family, agreed to build a much bigger house named Immokalee, and to share it. When finished, Immokalee was ideally situated for boating and swimming and remarkable for the large number of very old, picturesque live oaks and other types of trees that graced the grounds.[35]

The Palmers remained very active in the Bee Ridge area. This was the first Palmer agricultural project linked to the new rail line extension to Venice, which was still under construction. Bee Ridge is an area located southeast of Sarasota and designated as the site of the first railroad station south of Fruitville. Originally, the Seaboard Air Line Railroad Company named that station Palmer, but Bertha later agreed that it should be called Bee Ridge, the name used by a small community already located there. In 1912 Bee Ridge, as a legal entity, referred to a town platted by the Sarasota-Venice Company. The plat showed a proposed rail station at the center of the town, whose streets bore names of American presidents. Lots were immediately placed on sale by the company. Around this emerging new town, the company planted and managed some groves and opened several experimental farms. No public announcements were made, but observers could tell that the Palmers intended to do something very big. Otherwise, how to explain the large groups of black workers digging irrigation canals in what was largely a jungle?[36]

As she reviewed the nearly two years since she first came to Sarasota, Bertha had to be pleased with her achievements. She had assembled a huge land empire, organized it, established plans for it, and begun the task of developing it. She was operating on a scale that made her one of the largest real estate investors in Florida. She had almost single-handedly lifted Sarasota out of a recession and stimulated a prolonged period of prosperity with

Immokalee in 1920, viewed from Sarasota Bay. *By permission of Sarasota County Historical Resources.*

her investments and her ability to attract other wealthy people to visit and settle in the area. She had mobilized her now extensive family to be part of her great enterprise. Her imprint was deep on tourism, civic improvements in Sarasota, and the local agricultural economy. Had she found in Florida the personal satisfaction and a purpose to life that she seemed to seek a few years earlier? The answer appeared to be emphatically positive, for nothing kept her coming back to Sarasota other than her desire to succeed in meeting the challenges she had set for herself.[37]

Self-interest now firmly linked Bertha and the Sarasota region. She had invested heavily in both the community and the surrounding backcountry, which provided the town with a growing agricultural economy essential to its success. The town she had first visited in 1910 was largely disappearing as improved public services, a growing population, an expanding commercial sector, and an influx of rich people transformed the formerly sleepy burg. New leaders like Owen Burns and very soon John and Charles Ringling would take Sarasota to higher levels of prosperity. However, it was Bertha who started it all, and her family kept Sarasota moving in positive directions for decades after she passed away.

Notes for Chapter 2

1. Jeff LaHurd, *Sarasota: A History* (Charleston and London: The History Press, 2006), 24, 146–147; Ross, *Silhouette in Diamonds*, 224; Karl H. Grismer, *The Story of Sarasota: The History of the City and County of Sarasota, Florida* (Sarasota: M. H. Russell, 1946), 143–146, 155–156.

2. *Sarasota Times*, Feb. 24, 1910.

3. Thomas Graham, "The First Developers," in Michael Gannon (ed.), *The History of Florida* (Gainesville: University Press of Florida, 1996), 276–282; Daniel Leon Chandler, *Henry Flagler: The Astonishing Life and Times of the Visionary Robber Baron Who Founded Florida* (New York: Macmillan Publishing Co., 1986), 95–225; *Sarasota Times*, Feb. 24, 1910; LaHurd, *Sarasota*, 146–149.

4. Arthur Britton Edwards Papers, Manuscript Division Sarasota County Historical Resources.

5. LaHurd, *Sarasota*, 24–26.

6. Arthur Britton Edwards Papers, Manuscripts Division, Sarasota County Historical Resources; Grismer, *Story of Sarasota*, 300–302.

7. Grismer, *Story of Sarasota*, 15–19.

8. Jeff LaHurd, *Sarasota*, 21–23; Grismer, *Story of Sarasota*, 101–154.

9. *Sarasota Times*, Feb. 24, 1810; Ross, *Silhouette in Diamonds*, 224–226.

10. Ross, *Silhouette in Diamonds*, 226–228; Black, "Mounted on a Pedestal," 88.

11. Black, "Mounted on a Pedestal," 89; *Sarasota Times*, March 10, 1910; *Tampa Tribune*, March 10, 1910.

12. *Sarasota Times*, April 21, 1910.

13. Ibid., May 12, 1910; *General Index to Deeds*, Manatee Historical Records Library, 1910.

14. Janet Snyder Matthews, *Venice Journey From Horse and Chase: A History of Venice* (Sarasota: Pine Level Press, 1989), 179–183; Ross, *Silhouette in Diamonds*, 226–227.

15. *Tampa Tribune*, June 24, 1910.

16. *Sarasota Times*, June 30, 1910.

17. Ibid., June 30, July 6, and Sept. 8, 1910.

18. Matthews, *Venice*, 184–190; Grismer, *Story of Sarasota*, 159.

19. *Sarasota Times*, Oct. 13 and 20, 1910; Grismer, *Story of Sarasota*, 159–166.

20. *Sarasota Times*, Nov. 10, 1910; *Jacksonville Metropolis*, Nov. 10, 1910.

21. *Jacksonville Metropolis*, Dec. 8, 1910; Ross, *Silhouette in Diamonds*, 182; Pete Eithus, *A History of Agriculture of Sarasota County Florida* (Sarasota: Sarasota County Agricultural Fair Association and the Sarasota County Historical Commission, 1976), 9–14.

22. *Sarasota Times*, Dec. 1 and Dec. 15, 1910.

23. Lana Burroughs, *et al.*, *Temple Terrace* (Charleston, SC: Arcadia Publishing, 2010), 15; *Sarasota Times*, Feb. 23, 1911; Matthews, *Venice*, 183–184.

24. *Chicago Examiner*, Feb. 23, 1911; Mathews and Mansperger, *Mrs. Potter Palmer*, 12; Ross, *Silhouette in Diamonds*, 230.

25. *Chicago Examiner*, Feb. 25, 1911.

26. Ibid.

27. *Sarasota Times*, March 16, 1911; Matthews, *Venice*, 133.

28. Matthews, *Venice*, 188–189; *Sarasota Times*, March 16, Oct. 5, Nov. 2, and Nov. 16, 1911; Ross, *Silhouette in Diamonds*, 227.

29. *Chicago American*, May 18, 1911; *Sarasota Times*, May 25 and Oct. 11, 1911; Ross, *Silhouette in Diamonds*, 228.

30. *Sarasota Times*, Dec. 21, 1911; Grismer, *Story of Sarasota*, 116–117.

31. *Sarasota Times*, April 27, and Oct. 19, 1911.

32. Ibid., Dec. 21, 1911.

33. Ibid., Feb. 19, 1912.

34. Ibid., Aug. 15, 1911.

35. Ibid., Dec. 21, 1911; Pauline Palmer to Mrs. Herman Kohlsaat, Nov. 16, 1911, in Eleanor Dwight (ed.), *The Letters of Pauline Palmer: A Great Lady of Chicago's First Family* (MTT Scala Books, 2006), 79.

36. *Sarasota Times*, Dec. 21, 1911, April 11 and 18, May 2, July 11, and July 25, 1912.

37. Ibid., Nov. 24 and Dec. 21, 1911.

CHAPTER THREE

The Flowering of Empire
1912–1915

In October of 1911 Bertha added a personal dimension to her relations with the leaders of Sarasota. She gave a reception for the members of the Board of Trade and their wives at the Belle Haven Inn. The Queen of Chicago Society stood in the parlor of the hotel and welcomed each couple personally. After refreshments in the dining room came the speeches. Owen Burns gave a toast to Mrs. Palmer, who then asked Mayor Harry Higel to respond on her behalf. C. B. Fish and Dr. Joe Halton spoke representing the Board of Trade and praised Bertha for her great impact on the community. The vice-chair of the board, W. A. Sumner, also spoke. Since he worked for Bertha as an official of the Sarasota-Venice Company, his remarks were most certainly also laudatory. The *Sarasota Times* reported that the guests were well pleased with the event and found Bertha charming. Such events do not appear to have been common during Bertha's time in Sarasota, but she certainly showed once more how her superb social skills could promote close political and business ties.[1]

The reception for the Board of Trade showed that Bertha and the Sarasota business community had forged a firm alliance of self-interest. They shared a common belief that their potential for profits relied on the development of infrastructure that facilitated movement of people and products. The rail extension to Venice served as an excellent example, as did the paving of Sarasota streets and the "hard road" from Sarasota to Bradentown, the county seat. Yet these improvements were not sufficient for the Sarasota area to realize its full potential. Through the Sarasota-Venice Company and the Palmer Florida Company, as well as her personal contacts, Bertha worked with Sarasota's leaders to build and pave more roads. She also expressed interest in improving transportation by water from the Venice area to Sarasota. When government engineers arrived from Washington to investigate Sarasota's needs, they enjoyed dinner with the Board of Trade at the new Automobile and Boating Club by the bay, a club to which Bertha belonged. The next morning at a breakfast, local leaders argued the need for federal support in carrying out a dredging project. Mayor Harry Higel argued for deepening the channel to accommodate bigger boats transporting citrus crops from the southern part of Manatee County to the railroad station at Sarasota. W. A. Sumner, the vice-chair of the Board of Trade, who also was an employee of the Sarasota-Venice Company, agreed. The production of citrus and vegetables intended for Northern markets had exploded, he said. The huge size of the crops spurred by the rapid development of agricultural areas had nearly surpassed the capacity of the railroad extension to Venice. An improved water route was critical to keep production growing. It took time, but the channel project received federal funding. The U.S. Army Corps of Engineers handled the planning and management of the project.[2]

Bertha understood that she would have great trouble selling her lands without good transportation systems as well as other amenities that would attract reasonably well-to-do investors. In April of 1912, at the offices of the Palmer Florida Company in downtown Sarasota, a meeting of local leaders heard from Honoré Palmer and W. A. Sumner about a plan to create the Sarasota Golf and Country Club. The idea assumed that rich men and their families were more likely to stay in hotels and resorts around Sarasota if they had access to golf, tennis, and the refined social environment of a country club. Palmer and Sumner proposed raising $10,000 to build the facility. They also suggested setting initiation fees at $25 for residents and $15 for nonresidents. This idea proved only moderately popular, although Bertha and her family continued to promote it for years, as they did a similar institution in Venice.[3]

Bertha also supported Sarasota's development by erecting more buildings in addition to the garage and hotel she commissioned in 1911. In May of 1912 she announced through the Sarasota-Venice Company that a new two-story office building for the exclusive use of the two Palmer companies would soon be completed. A month later both companies had moved all their operations to their new headquarters on Pineapple Avenue. In early 1914 the Palmers revealed plans to build two other business buildings in Sarasota.

Perhaps Bertha's most useful building efforts in Sarasota in the 1912 to 1914 period related to the need for a modern post office. The growth in numbers of people and businesses since

Bertha's arrival in early 1910 had been truly remarkable. Sarasota had completely changed, and its aspirations were enormous. Town leaders now believed that Sarasota required a proper post office, not one housed in a general store, if the town was to grow and prosper.

In May of 1912 the U. S. government authorized the construction of a new post office building, and the Palmer Florida Company took on the role of general contractor. By July construction was well advanced. Plans called for a two-story building on Main Street. The post office would be located on the first floor, while a rental apartment would occupy the top floor. The Palmers hired architect Lester Avery to design the 25′x 40′ structure. It featured handsome red and buff brick on the outside front wall, plaster and oak for the interior. The new post office, claimed the *Sarasota Times*, possessed the most modern equipment, including two writing desks in the lobby and a bulletin board mounted in a glass case for notices. Most importantly it had 40 large, 40 medium, and 190 small call boxes made of bronze and glass, each accessible by key. There were also windows for money orders and general delivery. It did, indeed, appear that Sarasota had entered a new era of efficiency and modernity. The Palmers received praise for erecting a post office that strictly adhered to government contract requirements but also pleased the public's aesthetic sense.[4]

The era of good feelings did not last long. By January of 1914 the *Times* declared the post office building inadequate because the government badly underestimated the current and future needs of the community. Postmistress Carrie Abbe reported great public demand for additional call boxes. Because all existing call boxes were leased, long lines formed at the general delivery window. A waiting list for box assignments exceeded fifty individuals. As Bertha had been responsible for constructing the building, town leaders contacted her and found her "anxious that the city should have a post office calculated to meet future demands and that would be a credit in its appearance." Since the government would not pay for yet another new post office, Bertha offered to build it herself. The Board of Trade enthusiastically supported the plan and thanked their benefactor for her generosity. Bertha not only funded the structure, but threw in extra dollars to pay for fancy brickwork on the front of the building. It served Sarasota until 1923.[5]

During these years Bertha wrote checks supporting many institutions in Sarasota, but perhaps none of them was closer to her heart than the Sarasota Women's Club. The town's women had worked as a group for some years to improve Sarasota. In 1913 they organized the Sarasota Women's Club, which incorporated a year later. Bertha, who knew a great deal about women's clubs and their good works from her time as president of the Board of Lady Managers, was among the first to take out a membership, and then contributed generously to the building fund for the group's clubhouse on Palm Avenue and Park. She even brought in an art lecturer from Chicago to make a presentation before the club. Later she donated land on Main Street to support a Women's Club park project. Thus, in both small and very large ways, Bertha sought to help Sarasota grow into a pleasant, civilized community that would attract visitors and settlers.[6]

Florida communities in this era understood that in the race for new residents, wealthy tourists, and Northern markets for local agricultural products, advertising was a vital element. Thanks to Bertha and her corporations, professional public relations men arrived from Chicago to design and write advertising booklets. Ostensibly, these public relations materials were prepared and sent out by the Sarasota Board of Trade, but in fact the Sarasota-Venice Company and the Palmer Florida Company financed most of the costs and arranged for distribution. In this effort they asked for everyone in Sarasota to participate to boost the town nationally. The Board of Trade requested all Sarasota residents to mail out at least one and as many as six copies of the brochure to friends and relatives in other states. Many Sarasotans cooperated in this campaign.[7]

Such commercial advertising was important, but no more so than the drumbeat of positive publicity about Bertha's activities and her huge vision for her holdings in Florida. Newspapers continued to cover her movements to and from Chicago and Europe and around Florida. When she joined the Florida Citrus Exchange, the Strawberry Cooperative, or other such organizations, it was reported. The Board of Trade and the local paper endlessly repeated her comment that Sarasota Bay rivaled the Bay of Naples in its beauty. Her words became, in effect, a Sarasota Board of Trade slogan.[8]

Besides incidental publicity, Bertha and Sarasota appeared in lengthier pieces. In February of 1912, R. W. Grinton published an article on her in the Joliet *Evening News*, which he had once edited. Bertha, he said, had visited the world's great beauty spots and was, therefore, an expert on such places. She had discovered Sarasota and put it "on the map in brilliant colors." So many Chicagoans had followed her lead that "Sarasota and vicinity are sort of suburbs for Illinois." A few months later Richard Edmonds, editor of *Manufacturers Record*, a Baltimore publication specializing in analysis of the Southern economy, praised Bertha and her family. He said she was a suitable successor to Henry Plant and Henry Flagler in her vision to transform the entire west coast of Florida. Edmonds talked of her estate and its global collection of plants. He noted that the Palmers had platted two or three towns and were building great mansions for themselves. "To only a few wealthy and ambitious individuals such as Bertha Palmer is a chance given to create and develop an entire principality," he wrote, concluding that the Palmers' "plans are broad, their wealth great, and their enthusiasm in keeping with both."[9]

In January 1913 the *Sarasota Times* reprinted an article from the *Tampa Times* that quoted an unnamed man from Oregon now living in Sarasota. The anonymous commentator said that the article in the *Manufacturers Record* had been very influential in attracting attention to Sarasota Bay, and that even more progress had occurred since its publication. He described the Palmer's Bee Ridge project as "the ideal suburban community," where prosperous men might purchase 10- or 20- acre lots to grow vegetables and citrus. A large labor force, he noted, was building roads and a drainage system in the Bee Ridge area. For those who preferred to live close to the water, the Palmers offered for sale sites along the miles of shoreline they controlled. The writer went on to praise the other members of the Palmer and Honoré families for living in the community and contributing to its improvement.[10]

In the next few years newspapers and magazines published many such stories, all positive and all portraying Bertha as a dynamic and visionary leader who used her great wealth to build, populate, and improve the Sarasota area. In fact, Bertha and Sarasota became so intertwined in the public mind that one of her real estate competitors brazenly used her presence in Sara-

The Seaboard Air Line Railroad Company was crucial in the development of Bertha
Palmer's properties. *By permission of Sarasota County Historical Resources.*

sota to market his own subdivision. The company sold property
in Indian Beach near Bertha's Boulevard Addition subdivision.
The company's message was that buying in their Indian Beach
development would put investors in the same community as
Bertha and her fabulous Osprey Point estate with its spectacular
gardens. Even this episode underlined how important Bertha
and her family were to Sarasota. It was her cachet as a transat-
lantic social figure, the novelty of the Queen of Chicago Society
devoting herself to civilizing the Florida frontier, and the amaze-
ment at what she was achieving as a woman that kept her, and
therefore Sarasota, at the center of public and press attention.[11]

While Bertha occupied a unique spot among those Sarasota
leaders who recognized her powerful effect on the town's development, not all her neighbors were as generous in their judg-
ments. In fact, some of them harbored so much hostility towards
her that she faced years-long legal and political battles, as well as
violence against her workers at Osprey Point. Interestingly, the

Venice Freight Depot, built by Bertha Palmer.
Courtesy of Gulf Coast Heritage, Inc.

press never really linked her to the issues causing these problems, further testimony to her mastery of publicity even when it meant masking unpleasant facts from the public.

The question of the location of the Venice post office had arisen soon after Bertha had arrived in Florida. Through her financial clout she had persuaded the Seaboard Air Line Railroad to build a rail extension to a terminus that she named Venice. In fact, there was already a community named Venice a mile or so north of the "new" Venice. The original Venice had a church and a school with "Venice" in their titles, as well as a post office to serve the forty or so residents. The new Venice, which Bertha had plans to develop, was only lightly settled at the time. From the beginning of the controversy in 1910, the original Venice residents were angry over the apparent hijacking of their community's name. The key family was headed by Jesse Knight, who had named the area Venice. But Knight had never platted the settlement and there were disagreements about the boundaries.

Some argued that the new Venice was always considered a part of the original.[12]

Although the residents of "old" Venice, led by Charles Curry, postmaster and son-in-law of Jesse Knight, protested to the railroad about the name issue, Seaboard officials largely ignored their concerns. That left several questions. First, what would the railroad station at old Venice now be called by the railroad, since that would *de facto* become the new name of the community? Second, would the post office in old Venice still be called the Venice Post Office, or would an entirely new building be erected at new Venice and claim the Venice name? If all this seems confusing, well, it is as confusing now as it was in the second decade of the twentieth century. Bertha certainly felt that she had something at stake in the naming controversy. She wanted the Venice name because it conveyed the image of Europe, wealth, and a playground for the rich. It would not do to have letters and packages addressed to the Venice post office delivered over a mile away from the new Venice train station. Her opponents also thought they had major interests at stake, including their brief history as a place called Venice. Perhaps more importantly, they simply resented the rich lady from Chicago sweeping in and taking the name they considered their own.[13]

In January 1912 the Seaboard Air Line Railroad further angered the residents of old Venice by rejecting the name Dundee for the new station to be built in old Venice. Local residents proposed that name when they learned the Venice name had been given to the terminus station, but the railroad noted that another community already claimed Dundee. Instead, the railroad company said the new station would be called Potter, a decision sure to inflame the residents who were already angry at Bertha.

Now they believed that she had not only taken their community's name, but had substituted her husband's name for it. At almost the same moment the U.S. Post Office Department dictated that as of January 21 the current post office named Venice would be moved one mile southeast to the terminus of the railroad. Bertha appeared to have won the fight, and she prepared to erect a building next to the new Venice railroad station to house the post office.[14]

Vehement protests by the residents of old Venice to the Post Office Department and Congress quickly changed things. Rather than move the existing Venice postal operation a mile southeast to new Venice, the Post Office Department accepted a plan to move it a mile and a quarter northwest and allow it to keep the name Venice. Thus, the Venice post office was no longer near the Potter rail station, which soon had another post office named Potter. New Venice residents were now over two miles away from the post office with their community's name. Bertha had the Venice name on the railroad station, but not on the post office next to the station. Things became so heated that the *Sarasota Times* refused to print a letter that appears to have attacked Bertha directly. All was confusion, the communities in the area were badly split, and competing petitions to the U.S. Post Office Department were pushed in the faces of all area residents. The *Sarasota Times* became a principal battleground, as "Nemo," the regular correspondent from the Venice area whose real name was George Higel, sparred with supporters of the Knight family. Higel and his family were mostly residents of the new Venice. Increasingly, he allied himself with the Palmers.[15]

At no point did Bertha Palmer reach out to her adversaries or seek some compromise. Her reaction to this challenge mirrored her response to the threat to her authority posed years before by Phoebe Couzins, the secretary of the Board of Lady Managers. Bertha took it personally and would accept nothing but total victory, no matter how long the struggle went on.

As in many of her business activities, Bertha relied heavily on her brother, Adrian Honoré, who was president of both of the Palmer corporations operating in Florida and her co-trustee of the Potter Palmer estate. By November of 1912 the two of them realized that they had a major fight on their hands. They hired a Washington, D.C., law firm, Britton and Gray, to represent their interests before the United States Post Office Department. With their attorneys beside them, Bertha and Adrian went to the H Street office of P. V. DeGraw, Fourth Assistant Postmaster General and the man responsible for straightening out the mess. It appeared they were close to obtaining a transfer of the post office now named Venice to the new Venice rail station, but further protests and petitions from residents halted the effort. The lawyers advised Bertha to build a structure for the post office and to put residential lots around the rail station on the market as soon as possible. By December 5, George Higel, writing as Nemo, reported the Palmers would plat the town of Venice shortly. But things were, in fact, at a standstill, although lumber arrived at the new Venice to finish the interior of the building meant to house a store and the post office. A year later, in January and February of 1914, the battle resumed when the Post Office Department once again contemplated moving the Venice post office to new Venice. As before, petitions were circulated and letters of protest dispatched to congressmen. No action was taken.[16]

In 1915 the controversy did reach a conclusion when Bertha again persuaded federal authorities to move the Venice name to the post office building she had built several years earlier in new Venice. This led to an interesting exchange of letters between Charles Curry, the leader of the opposition, and Bertha. On July 10, 1915, Curry invited Bertha to attend a convention at his home to select a new name for the Potter railroad station and post office. "While we have fought zealously and untiringly for Venice," he wrote, "yet when we realize that our defeat is certain, we wish to surrender on terms of amity." He asked her for any suggestions she might have and said he rather liked, surprisingly, the name Palmer. Since Curry sent the letter on the day of the meeting, this was not a serious invitation. Bertha's response sent five days later lacked graciousness, as she pointedly referred to his "defeat." There were no words of solace. Indeed, Bertha's attitude sent Curry off on another wave of oratorical hyperbole. "If democracy prevails," he wrote the First Assistant Post Master General, "the p.o. will remain where it now stands and still bear the name of Venice. If plutocracy prevails the office will be removed." If anyone was unclear as to the plutocrat he had in mind, his final sentence spelled it out: "Is a community to be stabbed to the very heart to satisfy the selfish whims of Mrs. Potter Palmer?" The answer, apparently, was yes. In the end, the former town of Potter became Nokomis. Bertha had won, as she usually did, but was the prize worth the hard feelings left among some of her neighbors?[17]

Even as she struggled with Charles Curry over the naming of Venice, Bertha engaged in another and far more serious local dispute. This time she was challenged not only by some of her neighbors, but by a few of the top leaders in her own organization. Bertha's letters in 1914 revealed that bands of night riders on several occasions over the past few years had attacked her

Osprey Point estate, shot up the quarters occupied by her black laborers, and chased them away. This was always done while she was absent from Osprey Point, so there was never a question of her personal safety. In the past she had not notified the county sheriff or done anything else that would bring this violence to the attention of the press, figuring that news of such lawlessness would drive away potential investors and settlers, the very people she was counting on to purchase her land.[18]

News that night riders had once again raided Osprey Point reached her aboard the S.S. *Danfers* carrying her to France in April of 1914. She speculated to William F. Prentice, her overseer at Osprey Point, about which of the local "crackers" were responsible for the outrage, and fixed on a fellow named Johnson, who was himself employed by her. The Georgia blacks she had brought in by train as laborers, she thought, might be a cause of the disturbance. Bertha ordered Prentice to fire Johnson as well as "any other crackers about" if there was another raid. A few days later, she wrote someone called U. B., perhaps one of her attorneys, to discuss the recent raid. She now said a dispute between Prentice and one of the men reporting to him led to the raid as an act of revenge. She expressed shock that such a minor event could lead to such violence towards her property and employees and "depreciate every value in the vicinity, for what prospective buyer could invest there after learning how I was treated who has spent a large amount of money to show what the soil and climate can do and to create values." As she wrote, she became increasingly excited: "No community can prosper and grow with such a gang of desperados (that is perhaps too flattering a term—I should say sneaks and cowards) allowed to go at large." She instructed

U. B. to collect evidence concerning the perpetrators, which she vowed to act on when she returned to Sarasota.[19]

Bertha obviously knew that Prentice was not a popular figure at Osprey Point. He lacked tact and tended to treat his subordinates in an arrogant manner. She made it clear to U. B. that whatever others thought of him, she considered him indispensable. As she put it, "I'll never let him leave me." She spent a page or more telling U. B. all of the duties Prentice handled. She said he had responsibility for everything at Osprey Point other than The Oaks. He had charge over all the men and machines, the boats, the pump house, cutting and hauling firewood, the gardens, the animals, the Home Farm, and the stables. Moreover, he bought everything needed by Thomas Reed Martin, Bertha's architect, who was remodeling her mansion. Above all, Prentice kept her fully informed by weekly written reports. Other managers might come and go and be easily replaced. That was not the case with Prentice. Bertha expressed sympathy for her overseer, noting that although he was British, British male servants in The Oaks disliked him because he gave up his British citizenship to become an American.[20]

In May of 1914, Bertha, now settled in her home in Paris, heard a great deal more not only about local community hostility to Prentice, including threats to his safety, but also about the attitudes of other Palmer managers, who thought things might go more smoothly without Prentice. She wrote Albert Blackburn, overseer of the Palmer groves in Venice, who had told her that Prentice had refused to pay a man for work he had done and had threatened to kick the employee off the estate for even asking to be paid. Bertha fired back that she did not believe the story and accused Blackburn of "harboring a deep prejudice against Prentice." She also began checking into H. C. Gibbons, general manager of both Palmer companies, whom she also suspected of "disloyalty" to Prentice. She was pleased to hear he was saying only positive things about her estate superintendent.[21]

Bertha reserved her greatest wrath for Thomas Reed Martin, believing him to be the central plotter against Prentice. Martin worked for Bertha for years and transformed The Oaks from a modest home into an impressive country mansion. On May 12 Bertha wrote him from Paris. Her opening words were ominous: "The more I hear from Osprey the more surprised I am at the disloyal role you have played to me and my interests." She then terminated his employment, noting she had paid him a great deal of money for his professional services.[22]

Martin proved to be one of Bertha's great gifts to Sarasota. He did not return to Chicago and the firm of Holabird & Roche,

Thomas Reed Martin, the architect hired by Bertha Palmer to oversee the design of The Oaks. She later fired Martin for being "disloyal." *By permission of Sarasota County Historical Resources.*

choosing instead to set up his own firm in his adopted town. He emerged as one of Sarasota's most important and prolific early architects, designing more than 500 structures over the years, including the Civic Auditorium and the Chidsey Building, the city's first library building, both of which still stand near each other on the bayfront. At least one of his sons worked in his firm, and another, ironically, obtained a job with the Palmers in the 1920s.[23]

Having put down the uprising in her organization, Bertha turned her full attention to permanently ending the raids on her estate. Learning that a group of men planned another raid at Osprey Point and a physical assault on Prentice, Bertha ordered her overseer and his wife to seek safety elsewhere. She turned to Gibbons and instructed him, should a raid take place, to go to Osprey Point afterwards and gather evidence. She even told him whom he should talk to in order to get the names of participants. Walter Blackburn, presumably contrite, appeared on her list as willing to supply information. Bertha also insisted that Gibbons consult with the law firm of Sparkman & Carter: "I want no mistakes, but to act with great speed. Get evidence at once. Have criminals and abettors indicted and convicted. Spare no reasonable expense for getting evidence." These were tough words from a tough lady who felt herself pushed to the wall.[24]

While she defended Prentice, she hoped some friendly employer advice would help him avoid future confrontations. She had to begin that advice by suggesting a good lawyer Prentice could hire to fend off a lawsuit brought by the man he had supposedly insulted. She then told him to go back to Osprey "and be perfectly civil and pleasant with everyone. *You owe* it to me and to yourself to straighten all of this out and go on quietly and peacefully." She added that it was "not necessary to have words with anyone or any bad feeling." She urged him to be "civil to good employees and positive about what they must do & how they do it." She even advised on how to criticize a worker without a confrontation. Above all, she told him not to talk to the local citizens unless a conversation could not be avoided.[25]

As her final action in this drama, Bertha wrote a letter to J. A. Saunders who ran the only store in the Osprey community. Everybody living in the vicinity visited and exchanged information at his establishment. In her letter Bertha talked about the recurrent raids on her property aimed at her black workers. But more recently, she said, Prentice had been the object of these criminals. She said she sent Prentice away to prevent his being whipped and beaten, but now she had ordered him to return. She continued: "I send notice to these lawbreakers that there will never be but one more riot at my place. I have put it in the hands of two of the best lawyers in Tampa who are instructed to take appropriate action in case of any lawlessness." She pledged to pursue any raiders to the full extent of the law and to bring civil suits against them. She asked Saunders to pass this information on to his customers and "tell them to keep off my property (where they have no right to be)." No part of this story reached the general public, although many knew some of the details. Sitting thousands of miles away in Paris, Bertha had shown an iron will and a mental toughness she had first displayed earlier in her life as president of the Board of Lady Managers. There would be no more raids on Osprey Point, and Prentice remained superintendent of the estate.[26]

Despite these serious disputes with some of her neighbors, evidence suggests that the local community generally liked

Bertha. She often went out of her way to promote good community relations around Osprey Point. For example, in January of 1913 she hosted a dance with refreshments at the estate for her neighbors. The *Sarasota Times* reported that everyone had a good time and the dancing went on until a late hour. For music, Bertha hired the Sarasota Band. In 1914 she held a Christmas party for local children and another party for young adults. She ordered Japanese lanterns hung from the limbs of many of her trees, which created quite a view from the bay. During March she organized yet another party at Osprey Point for young people and then took them on her yacht *Raven* to Sarasota to see a movie. When they arrived very late and missed the last showing of the day, she arranged to pay the projectionist for a private screening. Bertha sometimes visited her neighbors at their homes, and was in turn visited by them. She also invited local women to The Oaks to discuss art and other subjects. Decades later, elderly residents living near Osprey who had enjoyed her hospitality remembered her fondly and recalled many small kindnesses she had extended to them.[27]

There were, of course, many other things happening in the 1912 to 1914 period besides Bertha's involvements with the community. Her estate took shape, and her mansion, The Oaks, was rebuilt and came to be seen, together with its gardens, as one of the great residences on the Florida west coast. At the same time, Bertha's family completed work on two other grand homes, Honoré and Potter Palmer's Immokalee and her aunt and uncle's much-praised mansion called the Acacias. Sarasota would soon boast far more impressive residences, such as John Ringling's Cà d'Zan, but in this earlier period the three Palmer-Honoré homes, together with New Edzell Castle on Bird Key in Sarasota Bay, offered evidence to Northern visitors and investors that the city had already attracted influential and wealthy individuals.[28]

Although Bertha had many personal and business interests that claimed her attention, she did not allow herself to be distracted from building her estate or her mansion. Spread over 350 acres, Osprey Point included The Oaks, the gardens, a village for her employees, and a working agricultural operation known as the Home Farm. By 1912 most visitors to Sarasota of any social stature made their way to Osprey to see what Bertha had wrought out of the wilderness. They were joined by newspaper and magazine journalists, many of whom obtained interviews with Bertha as well as personal tours. All praised Osprey Point as an oasis of beauty and order that somehow managed to unite formal garden planning with the use of local plants and trees and the preservation of ancient mounds and middens left by earlier Native American civilizations.[29]

While Bertha made the decisions about how her estate would look, she freely sought the advice and design services of professional architects. She also received information on botanical matters from the U.S. Department of Agriculture as well as various universities and their extension services. As in almost everything she did in her Florida venture, Bertha highly valued scientific and technical expertise in building Osprey Point.[30]

A visit to Historic Spanish Point today offers insight into what Osprey Point looked like at its peak between 1912 and 1918. There are a few of Bertha Palmer's gardens still in existence, including the Pergola, the Duchene Garden, and the sunken garden. But Spanish Point today takes in only 30 of the 350 acres where Bertha's estate was located. The Oaks itself has long since been torn down, as have the many other structures she built

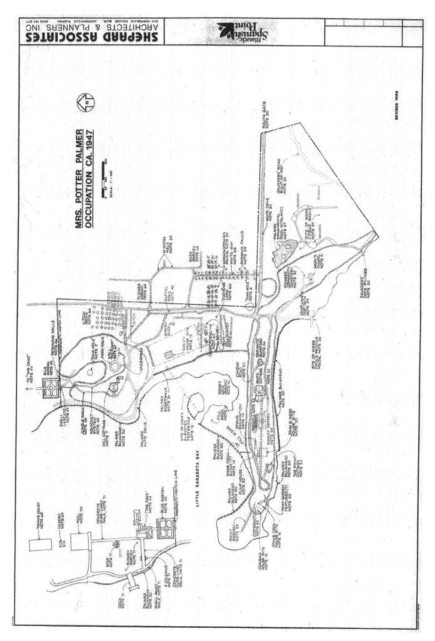

Map of Bertha Palmer's estate, Osprey Point.

Courtesy of Gulf Coast Heritage, Inc.

to house staff and provide water, electricity, and other services to the estate. A look at a map of Osprey Point during Bertha's lifetime reveals the complexity of her vision. The Osprey Point estate at the height of Bertha's power and influence included a tennis court, swimming pool, beach, and a pier with a boathouse for her two speedboats.

Osprey Point featured nine major gardens, including the Jungle Walk through native flora, the Blue Garden, Mirror Lake, Duchene Garden, the Great Lawn Garden, the Pergola and Sunken Garden, and the Rose Garden. Between the gardens were great swaths of live oak trees and palms. Gazebos and other garden structures appeared throughout the grounds. Formal and informal walkways as well as larger roads with names like Acacia Trail and Orchid Walk connected all the parts of the garden. Around the gardens flourished plants and trees from many parts of the world that Bertha had imported. All of this reflected Bertha's experience with English gardening design. Certainly her association with King Edward VII and his social circle allowed her to visit many great country houses throughout England. Edwardian-era gardens demonstrated nearly all the features Bertha later incorporated into her plan for the gardens at Osprey Point. Of course, her estate was located in a semi-tropical setting, requiring plantings very different from those found in Great Britain. Still, any educated and wealthy English visitor would have felt quite at home in the naturalistic setting Bertha created with water features, rock gardens, picturesque paths, and charming vistas.

Bertha refurbished several old houses built by early settlers for her own purposes. The head gardener had his own home, as did the superintendent, W. H. Prentice, and his wife, who not only cooked for the workers but also took care of the large flocks

Gardens and pergola at Osprey Point.
By permission of Sarasota County Historical Resources.

of chickens and turkeys. There was housing for staff and for laborers as well as a dining hall. At the nearby Home Farm could be
found barns, animal pens, and storehouses. One building housed
the electric power plant, and a huge water tower provided water
for domestic purposes and, if needed, to fight fires.[31]

At the northern end of the Osprey Point stood Bertha's mansion, The Oaks. Before his disgrace and dismissal, Thomas Reed
Martin had spent years in Bertha's employ designing The Oaks
and overseeing construction. The Oaks began as a relatively simple structure that had served as a winter home for Lawrence Jones
of Louisville, Kentucky, the man from whom Bertha had bought
the first 13 acres of her estate. By the time Martin had finished,
The Oaks had expanded into a two-story mansion surrounded by
pillared porches and set amongst lush plantings, including lines
of huge palms flanking a broad walkway leading to the front door.
The home itself had 31 rooms, 5 porches, 9 bathrooms, a huge

The Oaks, after years of expansion and remodeling.
By permission of the Sarasota County Historical Resources.

kitchen, a living room that was 40 feet long and 35 feet wide, and a dining room where Bertha kept her 16 sets of china. On one of the verandas perched a large cockatoo with white wings lined with bright yellow. Although an impressive edifice, The Oaks retained a general air of informality and lacked the quality of grandeur. Bertha repeatedly told reporters that she could not build the grand mansion she wanted until the gardens had been developed. Her permanent home, she said, had to grow naturally out of the gardens that would surround it, a cardinal principle of Edwardian garden design. Before her death in 1918, she had approached two architectural firms that had suggested concepts for the proposed mansion, which was never built.[32]

The Home Farm in 1914 included 1,040 orange and grapefruit trees as well as litchi trees. Some cattle and hogs were kept at the farm. Estate records show the cultivation of many types of crops: 40 acres of corn, 15 acres of velvet beans, eight acres of sorghum and cowpeas, 15 acres of hay, ten acres of sugar cane, one acre of Irish potatoes, and five acres of sweet potatoes. After harvesting these crops, workers replaced them with turnips, carrots, and other vegetables "suitable to the season." Some food raised on the Home Farm fed workers or farm animals on the estate. Bertha shipped the remainder by rail to Northern markets at a profit.[33]

The Home Farm also experimented with growing different crops not normally cultivated in Florida, such as avocados and alfalfa. Bertha, as always, relied on the U.S. Department of Agriculture and university extension services as major sources of advice and seeds. On one memorable day, Bertha used the Home Farm to test a new method of creating drainage canals. Representatives of the DuPont Company persuaded her to let them plant explosives and detonate them in order to establish a drainage ditch. This method, they said, would be far cheaper that using laborers for the job. The *Sarasota Times* reported on the experiment, but the results apparently did not impress Bertha, as she never adopted the technique[34]

The Osprey Point estate employed a large work force, although the number of laborers fluctuated with the growing seasons, building projects, and whether or not Bertha was in residence. The Oaks staff was quite separate from any other workers on the estate. The butler, maids, her personal secretary, the chauffeur, footmen, and cooks were with Bertha wherever she went for the most part. Carpenters, gardeners, the apiarist, those men harvesting shellfish in the bay at a site leased from the state, and cattle and hog herders were all local residents who were considered quite lucky by their neighbors because Bertha paid high wages. Blacks mainly from Georgia made up the workforce that picked citrus and vegetables, as Bertha continued to see Florida blacks and "crackers" as largely unskilled and unreliable.[35]

Bertha's letters show that she closely observed every aspect of Osprey Point estate operations. She insisted on annual projections of production, kept detailed lists of every machine, tool, and object used by her workers, and personally examined the credentials of every man seeking employment as a gardener. She ordered books and pamphlets on plants, animal husbandry, and many other subjects to educate herself on agriculture generally and horticulture in particular. She considered herself an expert on gardening, based not only on reading but also on her experience with gardens at her homes in Chicago and Europe. She felt perfectly comfortable issuing orders on what to plant, when to mow and water lawns, and how frequently to weed and apply fertilizer. When living at The Oaks she often walked the grounds with her subordinates, giving instructions. When away in Chicago or Europe, she demanded frequent reports on how her gardens were faring, and wrote detailed orders for her force of gardeners. The society queen had already shown she could cope with the rough-and-tumble frontier society of west Florida. Now she demonstrated that she could master the challenges of managing a large estate workforce.[36]

While Bertha oversaw the building of The Oaks, her sons and their spouses were busy erecting their own winter home, Immokalee, on the bayshore a few miles north of Osprey Point at the mouth of Philippi Creek. Potter Jr. and Pauline had identified this site in 1911 for a home near Sarasota. Later Honoré and Grace decided to join them and build a larger house for both families. The two brothers named W. E. Walker of Chicago, who had designed the Palmer House Hotel, to be the architect of Immokalee, an Indian word thought to mean "my house." The building contractor was C. A. Hallat & Son. By the middle of May 1912, the mansion was under construction and estimated to cost $35,000 to $45,000. In early August Immokalee was completed and Honoré and his family moved in around Christmas.[37]

The mansion extended 110 feet along the shore of Sarasota Bay. Built of wood, it had large airy rooms and extensive screened porches on both floors. Immokalee occupied a beautiful 140-acre lot, boasting both wonderful views and many impressive trees. The estate included a pier and boathouse as well as a fancy beach cabana. Honoré and Potter Jr. occupied Immokalee until 1918 when Bertha died. Potter then sold his half interest in Immokalee to his brother and moved into The Oaks as his winter home. In 1921 Immokalee burned to the ground at an estimated loss of $60,000. Honoré expanded an existing home on the grounds, gave it the same name, and lived there until his death in 1964.[38]

The third of the three great mansions associated with the Palmer era was the Acacias, built north of Sarasota at what is now the intersection of the Tamiami Trail and 12th Street. In 1912 Benjamin and Laura Honoré, uncle and aunt to Bertha and her sister Ida, bought seven acres that had once been part of the Whitaker homestead, Sarasota's first residence. Indeed, workers found foundations of the old house from the early 1850s when they started work on the Acacias. The lot had 600 feet of frontage on Sarasota Bay and extended east for 400 feet. It was filled with beautiful trees including, of course, acacias with their yellow flowers. The lot also had an Indian mound that the Honorés left untouched. At the front of the house was a striking arch as well as several freestanding pillars. The arch and some of the pillars now rise by a fishpond behind the Sarasota Bay Club, the structure on the site once occupied by the Acacias. The steps where Honorés walked down to the water and their pier also remain.[39]

Built of concrete, the mansion had five bedrooms. Broad verandas surrounded the main area of the house and Spanish tile covered the roof. The interior walls were white plaster with white woodwork. Visitors entered rooms with large fireplaces and magnificent views of the grounds, the bay, and the nearby keys. A number of other buildings on the estate housed staff, the gar-

Acacias, home of Bertha Palmer's aunt and uncle, located on Sarasota Bay just north of the town of Sarasota.

By permission of Sarasota County Historical Resources.

dener, a laundry, a garage, and a tool house. The *Sarasota Times* called it "one of the most beautiful structures on the west coast of Florida."[40]

Benjamin Honoré died in 1913 soon after moving into the Acacias. Bertha's sister, Ida Honoré Grant, made the Acacias her winter home after her husband died. In 1918 Prince and Princess Cantacuzene and their children also moved in, following their escape from Russia and almost certain death at the hands of Bolshevik revolutionaries. Thus Laura Honoré, Benjamin's wife, who lived until 1922, never endured loneliness in her final years. The Acacias remained in the Honoré family until after World War II. In 1994, long abandoned and neglected, it was torn down. In its earliest years, however, the Acacias was much admired by local citizens and visitors. Many boats filled with tourists cruised past to catch sight of the mansion.[41]

The Oaks, Immokalee, and the Acacias helped establish Sarasota very early as a haven for the wealthy. The elegant houses served to advertise the city as one possessing a cultured and refined elite that had heavily invested in its future. Not everyone drawn to Sarasota was wealthy, of course. A growing and prosperous American middle class generated by industrialization also wanted to enjoy the perquisites of living in sunny Florida, at least during the dreary winters in the north. These families had both some leisure and some excess income, and they became prime targets for the Palmers and many others who had real estate to sell. Bertha certainly wanted to sell land to the super-rich like herself, and frequently succeeded; however, many of the 140,000 acres she owned were not suitable for this market. Some of her parcels were located near Sarasota Bay, but proved unattractive to investors interested in erecting large mansions. Most of the remaining Palmer property was located inland and needed considerable preparatory work to make it salable at all. Far away from the beach areas, filled with mosquitoes, alligators, and rattlesnakes, these areas also did not attract the wealthy. Thus, out of necessity, Bertha and her family conceived strategies for development and marketing that appealed to a much larger group of prosperous professional men, corporate managers, and other members of America's blossoming middle class. The Boulevard Addition just to the north of Sarasota near the shore of Sarasota Bay was among the first efforts of Bertha and her family to appeal to this group.

As the years went by Bertha spent more of her time at Osprey Point and less in Chicago and London. She did insist on her annual summer pilgrimage to Paris and her residence at 6 Rue Fabert, which sometimes included a motoring trip around parts of Italy. There were other changes in her personal life. In April of 1913, her sister Ida's husband, General Frederick Dent Grant, suddenly died in New York at Governor's Island, his headquarters as commander of the Eastern Division of the United States Army. Only a few months earlier he and Ida vacationed at Osprey Point. Grant's death was a staggering blow for Ida and her children, Princess Cantacuzene and Ulysses S. Grant III, as well as to all the Palmers and Honorés. Fred had a long and distinguished diplomatic and military career, but he was not a rich man, and it now fell upon the rest of the family to be sure Ida was properly supported. Bertha immediately postponed her 1913 visit to France and returned to Sarasota and The Oaks, where Ida intended to spend the summer. Julia Cantacuzene left Russia and joined her mother. As noted earlier, in November 1913, Benjamin L. Honoré, builder of the Acacias and uncle to Bertha and Ida, died at age 90. He never had much of a chance to enjoy his mansion, but his wife, Laura, remained there for the rest of her life, surrounded by many visiting Honorés.[42]

Bertha's sons continued to prosper. Their professional lives were entirely devoted to managing the huge family real estate and business empire started by their father and now further expanded by their mother. Honoré and Grace had two sons, Potter D'Orsay and Honoré II. Potter II (Potter Jr.) and Pauline raised four children: Potter III, Bertha, Gordon, and Pauline. Most of the grandchildren spent considerable time at The Oaks, often without their parents. Bertha lavished attention on them, and in future years would try to shape their values as she had those of her sons. One thing was clear—an aging Bertha Palmer, always committed to her family, now gathered the members about her as closely as she could.[43]

When the great World War broke out in August 1914, Bertha fled France, even abandoning one of her cars at the dock in her haste to board an ocean liner bound for America. She had to rely on friends to store her belongings, worth over $350,000. She eventually turned over her Paris residence to the Red Cross. Bertha would never again see Europe. The war affected many aspects of her social, business, and personal life. Not long after the war began, Princess Cantacuzene shipped her children, Prince Cantacuzene II and Princesses Bertha and Zenaida, to Osprey Point for safety—to the delight of their Aunt Bertha. Princess Cantacuzene remained in St. Petersburg, Russia, where her husband, now appointed major general, served on the military staff of the Grand Duke Nicholas. After Michael suffered serious wounds leading a cavalry charge in the Ukraine against German forces, his wife managed to move him from Russia to The Oaks while he recovered. But as soon as possible the couple returned to Russia, only to flee the country in 1918 to escape the Bolsheviks.

While Bertha doted on her family, she also paid close attention to her real estate interests. Her first significant initiative, the Boulevard Addition, reflected her interest in selling land to middle-class Northerners who wanted both the Florida climate and the amenities they enjoyed in their Northern homes. The Great Florida Land Boom that began a few years after Bertha's death in 1918 usually featured the platting and sale of subdivisions near the coasts. Bertha, as she did in so many ways, pioneered this form of development in Sarasota. Relatively small town lots dotted the subdivision, and the developer attracted buyers through infrastructure improvements and advertising. The Palmers and Honorés would have been very familiar with this kind of growth from their Chicago experiences. Subdivision development had only a limited history in Sarasota in this period, although the Scots colony certainly was an early example. Still, Bertha's Boulevard Addition subdivision near the Acacias was among the first projects of its kind in Sarasota. However, competitors soon grasped what the Palmer's were doing and quickly jumped into the market.[44]

In 1912 the Palmer Florida Company platted the Boulevard Addition, constructed roads, and dug wells. The company then hired the Bowman Realty Company to handle sales. That organization opened offices on Main Street in Sarasota and launched an advertising campaign directed at current residents of the area and visitors interested in owning property near the city. The company emphasized the subdivision's location along the road to Bradentown, the county seat, and touted the relatively large lots, at least some of which had views of the bay. Ads stressed that the lots were good investments. They described Sarasota as a city on the move, where real estate values would continue to increase. Repeatedly the Bowman Company asserted that you could live in the Boulevard Addition, enjoy many urban amenities, and pay no city taxes. Moreover, the company promised liberal payment terms. While some lots sold, apparently the pace of sales disappointed the Palmers. The Bowman Company then organized a public auction for all the unsold lots on March 14, 1912. "No shrewd businessman will fail to invest in Sarasota property," said one advertisement, adding, "prizes will be given."[45]

The auction idea seems to have fallen flat. However, by middle April and into May, reports surfaced of increased sales with twelve lots sold in a single week. In July the local paper asserted the Bowman Company had made additional sales. Other stories appeared about new home building, such as a doctor erecting a home for $2,000 on the corner of Paradise and Florida Avenues in the Boulevard Addition. Some buyers purchased multiple lots, either for investment or in order to build larger houses. A number of builders announced plans to construct cottages in the Boulevard Addition in the fall, making the area "one of the best residence parts of the town." There are no records to show how successful the Palmer Florida Company was in marketing its Boulevard Addition, but given the immediate entry of other developers into this type of development, it can be inferred it made a reasonable profit. The area around 10th Street and the Tamiami Trail in Sarasota has been completely remade over the years, and nothing remains of the houses or streets of the Boulevard Addition.[46]

By 1914 it seemed obvious that Bertha had exercised tremendous influence over Sarasota's development through her extensive building program, the opening of the Boulevard Addition, support for roads and navigational improvements, the huge amounts of money she had pumped into the economy, the increase in population, the rise of property values, the opening of the railroad line to Venice, and her incomparable ability to generate national publicity for herself and the city. However, the bulk of her economic activities would not be in the city of Sarasota itself. To maximize their real estate profits, she and her family had to figure out how to persuade middle-class citizens in the North to migrate to Florida, purchase Palmer lands to the south and east of Sarasota, and become farmers. Since most members of the middle class were not farmers, but worked and lived in cities and towns, the family's task was not an easy one. Yet they did ultimately succeed in turning near-worthless land into prime farmland, using their great wealth, technology, and modern management techniques. They attracted thousands of people to Sarasota County from all over the North to settle on Palmer lands and live in planned agricultural communities, a concept that the Palmers may have invented.

Notes to Chapter Three

1. *Sarasota Times*, Oct. 26,1911.

2. *Sarasota Times*, April 17, 1913.

3. Ibid., April 8, 1912.

4. Ibid., May 2, 1912.

5. Ibid., Jan. 15, 1914; Grismer, *Story of Sarasota*, 268.

6. *Sarasota Times*, April 10 and July 13, 1913.

7. Ibid., April 25, 1912, Feb. 20, 1913.

8. Ibid., Feb. 20, 1913

9. Ibid., Feb. 8, 1912, April 2 and June 11, 1914.

10. Ibid., Jan. 7, 1913.

11. Ibid., February 8, 1912, and April 20, 1916; Ad Brochure for Indian Beach, 1913, Sarasota County Historical Resources Archives.

12. *Sarasota Times*, Aug. 15, 1912.

13. Joan Berry Dickenman, "The Homesteaders: Early Settlers of Nokomis and Laurel," typed manuscript, 38–41, Sarasota County Historical Resources, 1987.

14. *Sarasota Times*, Jan. 11, Jan. 18, and April 4, 1912; Adrian C. Honoré to Bertha Honoré Palmer, Jan. 1912, Bertha H. Palmer Papers, Vol. 5, Sarasota County Historical Resources.

15. *Sarasota Times*, Aug. 15, 1912.

16. P. V. DeGraw to Britton & Gray, Nov. 30, 1912, and Britton & Gray to Adrian C. Honoré, Dec. 2, 1912, Bertha H. Palmer Papers, Vol. IV, Sarasota County Historical Resources; *Sarasota Times*, Feb. 13, 1913, and Jan. 29, 1914.

17. Charles Curry to Bertha Honoré Palmer, July 10, 1915;Bertha Honoré Palmer to Charles Curry, July 15, 1915; and Curry to First Assistant Postmaster General Dickerman, Aug. 3, 1915. In Bertha H. Palmer Papers, Vol. III, Sarasota County Historical Resources.

18. Ross, *Silhouette in Diamonds*, 236–239.

19. Bertha Honoré Palmer to William F. Prentice, April 23, 1914; Palmer to Walter Blackburn, April 28, 1914.

20. Bertha Honoré Palmer to Mr. U.B., April 28, 1914.

21. Bertha Honoré Palmer to Walter Blackburn, May 5, 1914.

22. Bertha Honoré Palmer to Thomas Reed Martin, May 12, 1914; Grismer, *Story of Sarasota*, 316–317.

23. Grismer, *Story of Sarasota*, 316–317.

24. Bertha Honoré Palmer to J.A. Saunders, June 19, 1914; Palmer to H. C. Gibbons, May 21, 1914, Bertha H. Palmer Papers, Vol. V., Sarasota County Historical Resources; Ross, *Silhouette in Diamonds*, 236–238.

25. Bertha Honoré Palmer to William F. Prentice, June 19, 1914.

26. Bertha Honoré Palmer to J.A Saunders, June 19, 1914.

27. *Sarasota Times*, Jan 7 and Jan. 21, Feb. 26, and March 19, 1914: Dickenman, "The Homesteaders," op. cit., 134.

28. *Sarasota Times*, June 20, 1912.

29. Ibid., Feb. 8, April 25, and June 20, 1912; April 20, 1916.

30. *Sarasota Times*, April 22, 1915.

31. Master Plan for Spanish Point at the Oaks (Shepard Associates, Architects and Planners, Inc., 1982), Historic Spanish Point Archives; David Ottewill, *The Edwardian Garden* (New Haven: Yale University Press, 1989), 1, 2, 51. Ottewill says the Edwardian Garden is best thought of as a "succession of outdoor rooms," which describes the garden Bertha Palmer created at Osprey Point quite well.

32. Matthews, *Venice*, 181–182; Virginia Robie, "Home Beautiful," (Jan. 1920), 34–59; *Sarasota Times*, Feb. 19, 1914.

33. Estimated Cost of Fertilizing, Spraying, and Cultivating Grove, 1914; Home Farm Estimates, 1914, Bertha H. Palmer Papers, Vol. V, Sarasota County Historical Resources.

34. P. H. Rolfs, Director, University of Florida Agricultural Experiment Station, Gainesville, to Bertha Honoré Palmer, Jan. 29, 1912; Samuel Hood, Scientific Assistant, United States Department of Agriculture, Bureau of Plant Industry, March 13, 1912 to Palmer; C. V. Piper, Bureau of Plant Industry of the USDA to Palmer, December 2, 1912; and Home Farm Estimates, 1914, Bertha H. Palmer Papers, Vol. V, Sarasota County Historical Resources; Sarasota Times, April 18, 1812.

35. Bertha Honoré Palmer to William F. Prentice, April 23, 1914, Bertha H. Palmer Papers, Vol. V, Sarasota County Historical Resources.

36. Bertha Honoré Palmer to William F. Prentice, July 6, 1914, Ibid.; Sarasota Times, July 6, 1914.

37. Sarasota Times, April 18 and 25, May 9, July 25, and Dec. 19, 1912; Matthews, Venice, 183.

38. Sarasota Herald Tribune, Feb. 28, 1921; Chicago Tribune, April 16, 1944.

39. Sarasota Times, Dec. 26, 1912.

40. Ibid.

41. Ibid.

42. Sarasota Times, Jan. 11, April 18 and 25, 1912, and Nov. 13, 1913.

43. New York Times, Sept. 18, 1914.

44. William W. Rogers, "Fortune and Misfortune: The Paradoxical 1920s" in Michael Gannon (ed.), The History of Florida, (Gainesville: University Press of Florida, 2013), 296–298.

45. Sarasota Times, Feb. 29, 1912.

46. Ibid, March 7, April 18, and July 25, 1912.

CHAPTER FOUR

The Empire Experiments 1912–1918

Much of the story of Bertha Palmer in Florida between 1912 and her death in 1918 revolves around three great initiatives: the development of two path-breaking planned agricultural communities called Bee Ridge Farms and Osprey Farms, and Bertha's decision to enter the local cattle industry and transform it technically and economically. Bee Ridge Farms and Osprey Farms had everything to do with selling 78 square miles of her land to small farmers at a profit. Meadowsweet Pastures, on the other hand, had little to do with the real estate business, but Bertha intended to make money from raising cattle and hogs.

Bee Ridge Farms

The town of Bee Ridge, located at the modern intersection of Proctor and McIntosh Roads, had been platted by the Sarasota-Venice Company in 1911 as the new railroad extension to Venice neared completion. The plat showed twelve blocks each containing around 23 lots for houses. The north-south streets were named First, Second, Third, and Fourth. The east-west streets were Randolph, Washington, Madison, Adams, Jackson, Harrison, and Polk—a roster that mirrored the street names in Chicago's Loop. The railroad ran through the town in a northeast to southwest direction. The original small railroad station occupied a location bounded by Adams, Madison, First, and Second Streets.

In the spring of 1911 the Sarasota-Venice Company commenced selling lots in the town. But there was much more at stake here than creating a new town, although that alone was a considerable undertaking. The town existed to support the development and sale of 8,000 acres of Palmer land stretching from Philippi Creek to Cow Pen Slough between two modern avenues named Bee Ridge Road and Clark Road. The Palmers called the project Bee Ridge Farms. To support the growth of the village of Bee Ridge and Bee Ridge Farms, the company established a sawmill at the north end of the town, which also served local settlers. The demand for the mill's products was so great that in April of 1912 it had a 60-day backlog of orders.

As 1912 advanced, the pace of development in the Bee Ridge area quickened. Large groups of workers arrived and began clearing land and digging canals. As at Osprey Point, the bulk of these men were black and came from outside the Sarasota area. To house these workers the Sarasota-Venice Company ordered construction of a "row of tenements" in the town of Bee Ridge. In July the Sarasota-Venice Company announced it would begin building a massive drainage system to service the entire 8,000 acres of Bee Ridge Farms. Soon train cars full of tools began arriving at the Bee Ridge Station. The company also revealed that work crews had almost completed preliminary work for an 80-acre citrus grove, while another group of workers prepared seedbeds for fall crops of celery and tomatoes at one of the experimental farms. Meanwhile, five more cottages had gone up in the town of Bee Ridge. In late July news stories related that the Sarasota-Venice Company had hired the H-K Construction Company to build a large store and hotel on a lot 150´ x 25´ in Bee Ridge. On the yet-uncleared land that the Palmers intended to sell for farming, another company drilled artesian wells to irrigate the property.[2]

As the huge scope of the Palmer plan for Bee Ridge emerged, public curiosity grew. Automobiles owned by the Sarasota-Venice Company daily drove potential buyers to see the company town rising up in what had been a jungle not long before. They witnessed the first steps taken to establish an innovative agricultural community. The place blazed with intense activity, as buildings and houses seemed to appear almost magically, while large crews prepared the land to grow citrus and vegetables. Even though the expansive Palmer advertising campaign for Bee Ridge Farms property was yet in the future, some locals, such as A. B. Edwards, who had helped sell Bertha the land originally, now bought some of it back, sensing big profits to come. By middle September the company store opened in the town and conducted a brisk business. Close by, the temporary Bee Ridge railroad station handled increasing numbers of passengers. A local Bee Ridge resident now writing occasional columns in the *Sarasota Times* stated in October that the town of Bee Ridge was still "booming" and had among its residents eight clerks and four merchants. The article also boasted of its two stores, two hotels, and a post office. Several boarding houses serviced the community and the growing number of travelers arriving by rail.[3]

The importance of the Sarasota-Venice Company experimental farms at Bee Ridge became clearer in November when the *Sarasota Times* published a lengthy story on the company's intentions. Two experimental farms were part of the 8,000 acres encompassed by Bee Ridge Farms. One experimental farm of approximately 100 acres soon produced celery and tomatoes in large enough quantities to send north by rail for sale. The flourishing crops showed potential buyers how well vegetables grew at Bee Ridge and how the railroad made shipment to market relatively easy and—above all—speedy. The second experimental farm covered but two acres surrounded by a pine and palmetto forest. This small area was drained and irrigated, just as the entire 8,000 acres would be before long. The company used this farm to test and demonstrate which vegetables grew best in the type of sandy soil that covered much of Bee Ridge Farms. In addition, the company operated the 80-acre citrus grove, which also tested ideas on the best methods of growing oranges and grapefruit. Like the other experimental farms, the grove helped persuade possible buyers that the land could produce marketable crops. W. A. Sumner, general manager of the Sarasota-Venice Company, personally oversaw the test farms, an indication of how important the company viewed this aspect of the Bee Ridge project. Bertha and her family continued to believe in the value of science, technology, and expertise in developing their Florida empire and improving the corporate bottom line. This last quality, expertise, undoubtedly inspired the company to hire George F. Miles to manage the company's experimental farms and grove at Bee Ridge. Miles formerly worked for the United

States Department of Agriculture as an expert in truck farming and diseases of vegetables. To help him manage the celery crops, which required considerable experience and special knowledge, the company hired a Mr. Frank of Sanford, Florida, the state's leading area for celery farming.[4]

Through 1913 and 1914 Bee Ridge hummed with activity as the hard work of digging miles of drainage ditches continued. An important new development was a technological one. A major problem in preparing Bee Ridge Farms for occupation and farming related to the types of trees and shrubs that grew everywhere and whose tough roots spread widely but not deeply. It took perhaps a day for a farmer to clear a single acre using fire and simple hand tools. Since the Palmers intended to sell their land to well-to-do buyers, many of them having little knowledge of farming, they thought it essential to make the land as attractive as possible. They believed that pulling up the roots and clearing out the thick growth would increase land sales. But to commit their labor gangs to such work made no economic sense in financial or labor-efficiency terms.

The company, therefore, sought out machines such as the Hercules stump puller, which company workers tested at Bee Ridge in September 1914. It performed so successfully that the company ordered a second one. Each Hercules required a crew of four men and was drawn by a pair of mules. Pulling out the stumps and roots entirely not only made planting easier, but also eliminated the possibility of wood lice and other pests infesting newly planted citrus trees The Palmers also obtained the Chattanooga disc plow, which prepared the land for planting after the Hercules did its work. Together these machines made seemingly worthless land quite valuable. The company immediately assigned the new machines to clear 10- and 20-acre farms already purchased so that visitors thinking of buying land could see what their parcels would look like. The machines allowed the Palmers to launch their major national advertising campaign for Bee Ridge Farms property immediately.[5]

The Palmers hoped to sell land at Bee Ridge to several different groups, including Northern farmers seeking better weather and a longer growing season. However, they counted most on attracting Northern middle-class buyers, as they at done at the Boulevard Addition. But marketing a town lot near Sarasota Bay and the city of Sarasota presented a very different challenge from persuading nonfarmers to purchase ten or twenty acres inland where they could grow citrus and vegetables. The Palmers targeted Northern town and city dwellers unhappy with urban life and seeking a physical and metaphysical return to the simple virtues of country life—specifically self-sufficiency and independence. This latter group, of course, lacked farming experience and would need quite a bit of help. These individuals represented a widespread belief in America at the time that life would be better on farms than in cities.

The back-to-the-land movement in America arose in the late nineteenth century and was at its peak in the 1910s and 1920s. The movement represented a reaction to the massive relocation of Americans from rural areas to industrial cities. One of the chief exponents of the movement was William Ellsworth Smythe, a southern Californian who saw urbanites reclaiming their lost independence by establishing small farms. In 1908 he organized the Little Lands Colony in San Ysidro, south of San Diego, California, which offered moderately priced land, a public irrigation system, and cooperative mechanisms to market agricultural products. By 1915 he had founded three more such colonies in California. Three years later the California state government opened its own agricultural colony in Dunham in the Central Valley. Like Smythe's Little Lands Colonies, the State Demonstration Colony offered cheap land on easy terms, a strong community life to avoid the usual isolation of farm communities, and cooperative transportation, sales, and purchasing arrangements. But the back-to-the-land movement extended far beyond California. In 1914 the United States Department of Agriculture conducted research on the subject, concluding that a significant back-to-the-land movement existed in many parts of the country. Other research identified the stress and dreariness of city life as the chief motives driving the white-collar middle class—encompassing such groups as teachers, librarians, journalists, middle managers, and some doctors and lawyers, as well as a few clerks and salesmen—to seek peace in a rural setting. Many of them found the allure of the back-to-the-land movement most compelling. It was precisely these individuals that the Palmers sought out as customers.[6]

Yet the innovative agricultural community the Palmers built at Bee Ridge differed in several important respects from other similar projects. For one thing, the California experiments relied on government initiatives or on the leadership of visionary reformers such as Smythe. Bee Ridge Farms and subsequent Palmer planned agricultural communities were entirely capitalistic in their organization and intent. The California communities, both public and private, sought family self-sufficiency and assumed participants would live on and work the land on a full-time basis and subsist on what they could grow. The predominately gentlemen farmers at Bee Ridge, on the other hand, sought freedom and independence, but they also intended to make a profit from their investment. Subsistence farming was not their goal, nor were they all committed to living year-round at Bee Ridge. A goodly number spent part of the year in the North. For these reasons the Palmer planned agricultural communities appear to be unusual for the times, if not unique.

The era of the Bee Ridge Farms project also coincided with a significant movement of Northern farmers westward into the upper plains states of Minnesota, the Dakotas, Montana, and Wyoming. Cheap land, easy payment terms, and the blandishments of railroad companies, real estate developers, and chambers of commerce persuaded thousands to pack up and migrate. New types of farm machinery and theories of dry farming seemed to promise farmers a great era of expanded production and prosperity. Like the back-to-the-land enthusiasts, the new plains farmers benefitted from high food prices caused by World War I. Sadly, the whole thing proved to be a fragile bubble that burst with prolong drought, grasshoppers, and collapsing agricultural prices after the war ended. In the aftermath, many farmers abandoned their land and returned to the East, but the Palmers could reasonably expect that at least some of them could be enticed to purchase farms at Bee Ridge and, in fact, at least a few did just that.[7]

The Bee Ridge Farms advertising campaign kicked off in October of 1914, but not with an appeal to the back-to-the-land group or displaced plains farmers. Rather, Lamar Rankin, the chief salesman for the Sarasota-Venice Company, went after the local market in and around Sarasota. His initial ad made some interesting points. He urged local people to buy now, because the company was "rapidly selling" the best of its combination citrus fruit and vegetable land at Bee Ridge. The company, he said, would sell only to actual settlers and not to real estate investors in order to drive up the value of the land, which now went for $60 per acre. Bee Ridge, he noted, was but six miles from Sarasota, and the company lands "comprise the largest body of uniformly good land near Sarasota." Rankin listed a number of men who had bought farms of ten or twenty acres and were having them cleared. He claimed 700 acres had already been sold at Bee Ridge Farms.[8]

Bee Ridge, named for the large number of hives in the area, was itself a beehive of activity as houses were built, roads constructed every half mile, and miles of drainage ditches excavated. Trains brought construction materials and potential buyers to the town of Bee Ridge, and Sarasota-Venice Company workers carefully tended company fields filled with celery, tomatoes, cucumbers, and orange and grapefruit trees. On the new farms the Hercules stump puller and the Chattanooga disc plow methodically cleared vast stretches of land, while Sarasota-Venice Company autos continued conveying families thinking about an investment around the enormous site. They did not see isolated farms, but rather a tightly organized agriculture community, with a town, stores, businesses, good roads and rail transportation, examples of successful crops, and experimental farms demonstrating other possible crops. They also saw a comprehensive system of irrigation and drainage canals.[9]

One of the founders of Sarasota, Colonel John Hamilton Gillespie, also purchased a farm. He made the arrangements from Scotland, where he had rejoined his regiment to support the British war effort. Many land purchasers came from Chicago or other Midwestern cities and had visited Sarasota before.

Even at this early stage, however, Bee Ridge attracted people who had never seen Sarasota yet wanted to be part of the great Palmer enterprise. For example, in October 1914 four farmers from Kalamazoo, Michigan, described as being Dutch, suddenly appeared and bought tracts of adjoining land from the Sarasota-Venice Company. They lived in tents as they prepared to plant vegetable crops and citrus groves. They also drained ponds to open up muck land for celery crops. Their plan was to build three houses and bring their families to join them. In fact, they did build houses in "picturesque Holland style" that caused many in Sarasota to drive the six miles or so to Bee Ridge to view the unusual architecture. The Dutch farmers said that many of their Dutch friends would eventually join them.[10]

By the end of October 1914, Lamar Rankin and the Sarasota-Venice Company went national with their advertising campaign. He put together a booklet to mail to those who sent in a coupon from one of the company's newspaper advertisements. The booklet served mainly as a booster piece for Bee Ridge as well as other Palmer lands in the Sarasota area. Rankin wrote for a literate audience, but not one particularly knowledgeable about agriculture, generally or Florida specifically. Prospective settlers learned about the kind of crops that could be cultivated, the costs of planting, reaping, and transportation, as well as the profits that investors might reasonably expect based on current prices. Generally, Rankin presented the information in a straightforward and reassuring manner.

The booklet maintained that Florida was an excellent place for farming because of its pleasant and healthful climate and its good soil. Farmers could be assured of making a living and accumulating wealth if they put in the necessary effort. The ultimate aim for farmer-investors, it said, was to own a productive citrus grove, but it took as long as five years for citrus trees to mature. Until then Bee Ridge farmers could make a living by growing and shipping vegetables. At Bee Ridge Farms they would have artesian wells, good drainage, and no winter fuel costs. Investing in Bee Ridge Farms offered a way to retire early. It was an "opportunity for the man in moderate circumstances who is willing to work to earn his living from the soil for a few years until his grove comes into being." Potential buyers learned from the booklet that the Sarasota-Venice Company had researched the land scientifically using government reports on soil production and expert analysis of both topsoil and subsoils. Before beginning any work, the company had acquired detailed maps of topographical features, reports on drainage requirements, charts of underground water reservoirs, and climatological analyses of annual temperatures and rainfall. This information, the booklet asserted, would cost individual farmers a great deal to obtain, but the Sarasota-Venice Company would make it freely available to Bee Ridge investors. The piece went on to say that the land at Bee Ridge could be purchased now because thirty-year timber and turpentine leases had only recently ended. Moreover, the railroad had reached the area but a few years earlier, thus connecting it with the national market. Professor P. H. Rolfe, Director of the University of Florida Agricultural Station, told readers that most of the land at Bee Ridge Farms could support citrus groves. The professor also stated that same soil could yield two to three crops of vegetables each year.

A major appeal of the Sarasota-Venice Company related to the promise of profits. One section of the booklet was titled "The Citrus Grove—Your Endowment Policy." The company claimed a citrus farmer at Bee Ridge could count on a profit of $200 to $500 per acre growing grapefruit, while for oranges the figures were $200 to $350 per acre per year. Once mature, citrus trees produced fruit for 35 to 40 years. The booklet went into great detail on fertilizer applications and other aspects of cultivating citrus trees, as well as the financial arrangements to purchase a 10- or 20-acre farm. Other sections covered living conditions and the many amenities and activities available in the Sarasota area. The company emphasized the many new hard-topped roads that made automobile travel quite convenient, a matter of some importance to Americans caught up in the early stages of their love affair with the car. The booklet described the town of Bee Ridge with its hotels, stores, churches, a school, and a women's club as the social and commercial center of the Bee Ridge Farms district. This interesting bit of national advertising shows that the company aimed its marketing appeal at educated and prosperous Northerners who desired both greater personal freedom and economic security by owning their own Florida citrus grove. The Palmers promised potential investors a heady combination of independence, profits, and the attractions of Florida's location and climate.[11]

As 1914 drew to a close, the momentum of development at Bee Ridge Farms seemed to accelerate. Over 8,000 acres, men and machines prepared the land for large-scale farming. The people of the Sarasota region had never before seen anything that compared with the magnitude of the Palmers' operation at Bee Ridge or the audacity of their ambition. As settlers arrived, they immediately began planting crops and sending out carloads of produce. So rapid and impressive was the progress that the

Seaboard Air Line Railroad sent top managers to Bee Ridge in December to tour the site and talk with Sarasota-Venice Company executives. They came away astounded at the scope of the enterprise and the large number of 10- and 20-acre farms already sold. They particularly liked the company's policy of charging investors a modest down payment per acre and then giving them a number of years to pay off the rest at a reasonable interest rate. This encouraged new owners to invest immediately in their lands and count on future profits to pay the Sarasota-Venice Company what they still owed. Vice President C. R. Capps of the railroad said he and his colleagues had found Bee Ridge "in a well advanced state the making of a great agricultural community."[12]

The railroad men also commented favorably on the massive drainage channels under construction and the draining of ponds to create muck land for celery growing. They expressed admiration for the expansive road system that unified the community by ensuring that a road ran in front of each tract of land. They described Bee Ridge Farms as a "farm village" with houses close enough for "neighborly interchange." Capps then proclaimed that the railroad planned to expand service to Bee Ridge and along the entire Venice extension. He also announced that the Seaboard would build a rail station suitable for a town of 5,000 near the new Sarasota-Venice Company hotel. At that moment, only a few hundred individuals lived in and around the town of Bee Ridge. Erecting such a large depot reflected the railroad's faith in Bertha Palmer and her family, and its confidence that Bee Ridge Farms would be a great success. The Palmers soon pledged that they would contribute funds so that the station could be made of brick and tile rather than wood. The well-publicized visit of the railroad delegation increased public interest in the Sarasota-Venice Company and its Bee Ridge Farms project.[13]

Reports of land purchases at Bee Ridge became staples of the weekly news reported by the *Sarasota Times*. Most transactions involved town and city people from the Midwest, citizens who appeared to fit the model of back-to-the-land advocates. Such, however, was not the case with Mr. and Mrs. R. M. David of Colorado, who learned of Bee Ridge Farms from a Sarasota-Venice Company ad and made a sight-unseen purchase of land very near the town of Bee Ridge. Their current home, they wrote to Lamar Rankin, was the Valley View Ranch in Colorado. They could not leave for Florida until November 20, 1914, in order to get their crops in. This would not have been a problem except that they decided for financial reasons not to travel by train. Instead, they intended to come by wagon. In fact, they had packed their family and belongings into two covered wagons, each pulled by two horses. They carried camping equipment, so they did not have to pay for accommodations along the way. Their route took them through mountainous country ranging from 8,400 to 10,400 feet high.[14]

It being winter, the David family faced harsh conditions. Reaching New Mexico, the family confronted a blinding snowstorm. They had no choice but to halt and wait for better traveling conditions. Texas weather provided little respite for the Davids, as they endured temperatures below 20 degrees Fahrenheit, blowing snow, and a powerful east wind. Writing December 24, the David family reported to Rankin that they had covered 550 miles. On Christmas Eve the family camped not far from Wichita Falls, Texas. They could not predict when they would reach

Sarasota. Not until middle September of 1915 did the David's eastward trek end when their two prairie schooners reached Bee Ridge, some ten months and 2,800 miles after their adventure started. It turned out that after leaving Texas the David family encountered terrible roads and then ran out of money. Mr. David took a position as a sharecropper in Louisiana for two months. Ever energetic, Mr. David had now found employment in Bee Ridge while the Sarasota-Venice Company cleared his land and prepared it for cultivation. The David family trek was a remarkable story of courage, resilience, and perhaps foolhardiness. Their adventures surely rivaled those of earlier pioneers who crossed the continent to seek a better future on America's Western frontier.[15]

Spurred by publicity and special low rail rates from cities like Washington and Chicago, public interest in Bee Ridge Farms continued to grow in 1915. By now, Lamar Rankin had assembled a large sales force that operated out of offices in downtown Sarasota. This group handled the hundreds of inquiries about Bee Ridge that poured in from people all over the United States. The staff responded with booklets and other materials that provided detailed information on Bee Ridge Farms. In a story printed January 21, 1915, the *Sarasota Times* specifically mentioned the back-to-the-land movement and its appeal. The paper portrayed Bee Ridge Farms as a place where Northern city and town dwellers could enjoy economic security, independence, and freedom from winter storms. The article asserted that on just ten or 20 acres an investor could grow both vegetables and citrus for market. The bounty of the nearby Gulf of Mexico assured easy fishing and vast numbers of shellfish. The paper argued that this economic diversity helped protect Bee Ridge residents against unpredictable markets that might collapse for one kind of product but not likely all of them at the same time. For example, 1914 had not been a good year for citrus prices, but vegetables did well. The newspaper cited claims by the Sarasota-Venice Company that it had sold 1,000 acres at Bee Ridge Farms before the big advertising campaign began. As had become common in its stories on Bee Ridge, the *Sarasota Times* ended its article with a list of new purchasers, this time from places like Chicago; Cuyahoga Falls, Ohio; and Minneapolis, Minnesota. Sometimes the paper listed the occupations of buyers, such as E. C. Bode, head of the advertising department for William Randolph Hearst's *San Francisco Examiner*; Professor George A. Clark of Yankton, South Dakota; Clyde A. Nelson, who supervised railroad building in Panama; and George Hull, a lawyer from Bristol, Connecticut.[16]

As 1915 progressed, the Sarasota-Venice Company stepped up its advertising and stated it now spent $1,000 a month to spread the word about Bee Ridge Farms. In the town of Bee Ridge, work crews laid the foundations for the new railroad station as well as a 20-room hotel. Both structures served the purposes of Lamar Rankin's national advertising campaign. People interested in Bee Ridge land purchased discounted rail tickets to the Bee Ridge station from the Sarasota-Venice Company and then stayed in the hotel while they surveyed possible locations. These marketing techniques accelerated land sales. In March the company announced total sales of more than 2,000 acres. Moreover, it reported that produce from the company's experimental farms and from newly established farms at Bee Ridge filled over 100 rail cars with citrus, celery, and other vegetables. In late April Lamar Rankin revealed that 2,800 acres had been sold, and his ads began to warn potential buyers that time was running out because the best Bee Ridge Farms lands would soon be taken. They needed to act quickly. And, indeed, in August the Sarasota-Venice Company's new general manager, H. W. Mackintosh, stated that nearly all the prime 10- or 20-acre farm sites had been sold.[17]

In the spirit of the back-to-the-land movement as well as to attract investors, the Palmers continued to develop methods of supporting Bee Ridge Farms residents who lacked agricultural experience. The company's grove and experimental farms already provided models for neophytes to follow, and the experts who ran them offered advice. But more was needed to help these amateurs succeed. By late summer of 1915, the Palmers assisted in forming a farmers' cooperative association at Bee Ridge. At a meeting on August 12 at the Sarasota-Venice Company hotel, the farmer-owners gathered at the invitation of G. C. Vowell, a company employee and agricultural specialist, for a preliminary discussion on forming an association. Farmers' cooperatives had been around for some years and shown themselves effective in helping members purchase seed and farm machines more cheaply and assisting farmers to market their crops. Some viewed the collective nature of these groups as a danger to farmers' independence and even un-American. The Bee Ridge farmers, however, had no such qualms. A week later they reassembled at the hotel and enthusiastically elected R. J. Sawyer, an early settler at Bee Ridge Farms, as their temporary chair. They agreed that the cooperative should build a cannery, packinghouse, and fertilizer mixing plant. Of these three, the members believed the cannery of most immediate utility. Farmers growing tomatoes lost a significant part of every crop because of delays in harvesting or transportation. They simply discarded over-ripe tomatoes. Canning offered a way to turn this waste into a marketable product and thus enhance farmers' incomes.[18]

G. C. Vowell spoke eloquently at this second meeting about other benefits of farmers' cooperative. Buyers in Northern markets would continue to purchase Bee Ridge produce if the cooperative uniformly graded each crop for quality and properly packed it. Transportation costs for individual farmers would drop, he said, because the cooperative could lease entire rail cars for its members' products. Otherwise, individual farmers would have to pay more to use only a part of a car. Vowell also pointed out that a cooperative could purchase in bulk for its members and thereby obtain lower prices for seed and the ingredients of fertilizer that would be mixed together in the proposed fertilizer factory. The still inexperienced gentlemen farmers of Bee Ridge Farms obviously found the idea of professional help in these areas most attractive. The headline in the *Sarasota Times* of September 2

New hotel at Bee Ridge, built by the Sarasota-Venice Company.
By permission of Sarasota County Historical Resources.

summed it up: "Will Market Together; Cooperation to be Given a Trial among Settlers on Bee Ridge."[19]

The new farmers' cooperative, now officially called the Bee Ridge Growers Association, established a Farmers' Institute as one of its first actions. Run in partnership with the Cooperative Extension Work in Agriculture and Home Economics at the University of Florida at Gainesville and the U.S. Department of Agriculture, the institute sessions took place in the Bee Ridge Hotel. The first institute, on February 10, 1916, featured two professors lecturing on staple crops and livestock. Other farm topics were discussed in later meetings. The Farmers' Institute again underlined the extensive web of support services put in place at Bee Ridge by the Sarasota-Venice Company. It also once again demonstrated Bertha Palmer's belief in the importance of science and expertise in running any enterprise.[20]

The growth of Bee Ridge continued at a remarkable rate. Investors had purchased much of the original 8,000 acres offered by the Sarasota-Venice Company. These new farmers had planted many thousands of acres with a wide variety of crops by the middle of 1916. Hundreds of rail cars rolled north every growing season, stuffed with the produce of a land that had been jungle only a short time earlier. The population of the new community soared, as immigrants from 30 states as well as Canada, Panama, and South Africa poured into the area. Illinois led the way with 40 purchasers. The elements of a true community began to form as early as December 1914 when 65 newcomers held a community party on a yacht in Sarasota Bay. Soon new businesses, such as a lumber company, took root. The community expanded the local school and hired additional teachers to educate the growing number of children. Religious groups built churches, at least one with Bertha Palmer's financial support, and community-minded women formed a women's club, which they originally called the Get Together Society.[21]

In an ad published in January of 1916, the Sarasota-Venice Company commented on social life at Bee Ridge Farms. It noted the important role of the Get Together Society, the Bee Ridge Growers Association, and the new library located in the Bee Ridge Hotel. In this ad the company asserted that the development of a vibrant community was very much part of the master plan for Bee Ridge. By keeping farms small, close together, and linked by good roads, it had aimed to nurture community spirit and provide opportunities for social exchanges similar to those that took place in cities. As a result, it said, Bee Ridge Farms attracts city and town dwellers accustomed to an active social life rather than the physical isolation common in most farm areas.[22]

It was not uncommon for people to migrate to Bee Ridge Farms in groups called colonies. Usually these individuals came

Bee Ridge Women's Club.
By permission of Sarasota County Historical Resources.

from a particular state or area, like the Dutch farmers, or had a religious connection. In 1915, for example, as many as 20 people from Portland, Maine, arrived by train to inspect Bee Ridge as guests of the Sarasota-Venice Company. Some of them had put down money on farms even before they arrived. The Maine colony took up adjacent properties along Philippi Creek, and other Down-easters soon joined them. Reflecting a common interest, the Maine colonists formed the Old New England Yacht Club, which became the social center of their sub-community. The club's membership elected Lamar Rankin—the Sarasota-Venice Company executive who helped persuade the New Englanders to relocate to Bee Ridge Farms—to the honorary post of vice-commodore.[23]

The *Tampa Tribune* extensively covered the amazing story of Bee Ridge's sudden appearance and rapid development as an agricultural community. The reporter correctly perceived the role of Bertha and her family working through the mechanism of the Sarasota-Venice Company. The company earned praise for not only platting and clearing such a huge area, but also building the infrastructure of roads and irrigation and drainage canals. Noting the lack of preparedness of these new farmers, the reporter emphasized the importance of the experimental farms and the other support service the Palmers provided. The article pointed out that some of the land purchasers at Bee Ridge lived there year-round, while others came for part of the year. Many settlers built houses at Bee Ridge, although a few chose to live in Sarasota and drive six miles to tend to their property.[24]

In this same article, the *Tampa Tribune* addressed the transformation of Sarasota since the Palmers and Honorés had arrived in town. From a small fishing village, Sarasota had grown to a population of 2,500 with 12 miles of paved streets and 30 miles of sidewalks. It boasted many urban conveniences, such as electricity, telephone service, railroad and boat connections, and entertainment options. The downtown area had 13 two-story buildings, four hotels, five churches and numerous businesses. The bayfront had been beautified and a seawall erected. Evidence of prosperity appeared everywhere, the paper added, and even the Negro section of town had its own stores. Bee Ridge, of course, was an important reason for that prosperity, as all the newcomers brought with them new money and a need for goods and services. The Sarasota-Venice Company was the largest economic entity in all of Manatee County, just as Bertha remained the single largest employer.[25]

Osprey Farms

Bee Ridge had been a great and profitable success for Bertha and her family. Now, with most of the land sold, they moved on to the next phase of their business plan. The new project, named Osprey Farms, called for opening up 5,000 acres of Sarasota-Venice Company land south and west of the original Bee Ridge Farms project. The prime tracts were along the lower Philippi Creek and south along the coastline to Osprey, near Bertha's estate. The Sarasota-Venice Company's plan repeated much of what it had done at Bee Ridge Farms. The company intended to build roads every half-mile and install irrigation and drainage systems. Once more, the railroad extension to Venice would be crucial to the development plan. The station just to the south of Bee Ridge was Osprey, and the company meant to make it another major shipping point for vegetable and citrus production. Bee Ridge Farms relied heavily on the Sarasota-Venice Company town of

Bee Ridge for hotels, businesses, and community social life. The equivalent company town at Osprey Farms was to be Bayonne, located on the shore of Little Sarasota Bay. The Palmers platted the town, emphasizing the wonderful views of the bay. Bayonne sat on rising land east of the shoreline. The slightly curved streets gave every lot a water view. As was their usual procedure, the Palmers graded the town, dug artesian wells, and built roads lined with shade trees.[26]

The plan for Osprey Farms foresaw Bayonne and the Osprey rail station two-and-one-half miles away as complementary. Bayonne could serve as an alternative way to move agricultural products to market. Farmers could ship by boat from Bayonne or by rail from Osprey, depending on cost. Osprey would have stores to serve the farmers. The Sarasota-Venice Company also saw Bayonne as an attractive housing site for farmers. They could have all the benefits of living next to the bay and then drive a short distance east to tend their fields. As they had done before at Bee Ridge, the Palmers opened a nationwide advertising campaign in 1915, including subsidized trips to Florida for interested buyers. The *Sarasota Times* described the campaign as immense, involving all the major newspapers and magazines in the United States and Canada and reaching into nearly every household "where English is spoken." Hundreds of inquiries poured in daily, and sales of tracts made sight unseen by the purchasers rose rapidly. By the end of March 1916, investors had snapped up all the land between the Osprey station and Bayonne.[27]

The Sarasota-Venice Company ads once more appealed to the urban and town middle classes. They extolled the beauties of Bayonne together with its amenities and proximity to Sarasota. The company promised that a new hard road near Bayonne, later named the Tamiami Trail, would soon allow access to the Northern cities and to the rest of Florida by automobile. Osprey Farms offered sociability to people used to living in close proximity to their neighbors. As at Bee Ridge Farms, many of those purchasing lots and farms at Osprey Farms came, said the *Sarasota Times*, "because of the attraction of the back to the land movement." But was that enough to keep them in Florida? The Sarasota Venice-Company realized their new settlers might easily return home unless they found a rewarding life filled with outside pleasures and neighborliness. The company seemed confident that the weather, beaches, fishing, and a thriving community environment would persuade newcomers not to abandon their investment in Osprey Farms or, for that matter, in Bee Ridge Farms. This was to be farming Sarasota-style: part-time, assisted by professionals and cooperative enterprises to relieve the individual farmer of many burdens and uncertainties, and offering urban amenities, lots of social interaction, and a ready-built infrastructure of roads, drainage, and irrigation. Like Bee Ridge Farms, Osprey Farms was to be a planned agricultural community.[28]

The terms and conditions laid out for purchasing land on Osprey Farms mirrored those at Bee Ridge Farms. Buyers had to provide a small down payment per acre and were given considerable time to pay off the remaining amount at a modest borrowing rate. Buyers had to occupy their land to prevent speculation, and the land had to be cleared, fenced, and under cultivation. The only major difference from Bee Ridge Farms was that the base price of an acre went up from $60 to $70. As Bertha bought this acreage for a song in 1911, the profits were huge even with the costs of development. Of course, she had steadily made money from the Sarasota-Venice Company farms and groves at Bee Ridge for years.[29]

It is difficult to evaluate the success of Osprey Farms. While farmland sold well, the Bayonne lots drew only modest interest from buyers. Bayonne does not even appear in the 1920 census, while the town of Bee Ridge boasted a healthy 508 residents and Sarasota had a population of about 2,500. The reason that the town of Bee Ridge did well while Bayonne did not could have been the result of changing circumstances. While the Sarasota-Venice Company remained the largest real estate developer on the west coast of Florida, it now had competition in both the Sarasota and Venice districts. For example, in 1913, two sisters, Katherine and Daisietta McClellan, platted McClellan Park on the south side of the newly designated City of Sarasota. The sisters sought the same well-to-do buyers courted by the Palmers. Just as the Palmers had broken new design and marketing ground with the Boulevard Addition, the McClellan sisters figured out ways to make their subdivision attractive to those with money. By altering the street layout to moderate the boring look created by grid systems and adding in tennis courts, a yacht club, and other amenities, they presented an attractive upscale neighborhood that impressed many buyers. Meanwhile, the Southern Development Company opened up a large development project on Manasota Key, just south of the Palmer lands at Venice. This offered another option for affluent people thinking of building a winter home who might otherwise have purchased land at Venice. These new developments likely undercut the Bayonne project. They also heralded a far larger tidal wave of real estate speculation that would soon envelop all of the Florida: the great Florida land boom. In 1924 the Palmers sold all or at least a large part of Bayonne to the founders of the community of Vamo, itself a product of the mid-1920s land bubble. When the bubble burst in late 1926 and early 1927, the ambitions of the Vamo developers were dashed.[30]

Bertha Palmer often visited all parts of her Florida empire. It is interesting to speculate how she felt seeing the progress of Bee Ridge Farms and Osprey Farms in late 1916 and early 1917. Nearly 13,000 acres had been sold, cleared, and planted. Hundreds of people, perhaps a few thousand, had migrated to her lands in Florida. Although not all of them were year-round residents, these newcomers built houses and created communities. At the town of Bee Ridge, the new $7,000 train station handled ever-expanding incoming and outgoing cargoes. The new cannery, incorporated by the State of Florida, now produced carloads of canned tomatoes and other vegetables. The road system was complete. Everywhere wood planks from the Palmer sawmill went into residences, shops, and businesses. New towns such as Bee Ridge, Venice, and Bayonne had sprouted, thanks to the Sarasota-Venice Company. Bertha and her family and the employees of the Sarasota-Venice Company had shown that brains, planning, organization, and lots of capital could bring a profit. More importantly for the future of the Sarasota area, they had transformed nearly 80 square miles of jungle and pine forests into productive planned communities.[31]

Meadowsweet Pastures

After Bertha had purchased Garrett "Dink" Murphy's 15,000-acre ranch and 2,000 head of cattle for $93,000 in December of 1910, she continued to buy property in the Myakka River area until she controlled an estimated 30,000 acres. Unlike most of her other Florida enterprises, there did not appear to be a plan guiding the development of what she named Meadowsweet Pastures. Neither she nor any members of her family had even the slightest experience with or knowledge of the cattle industry. She did not intend to develop and sell off the land as at Bee Ridge or the Boulevard Addition. From the beginning, she saw Meadowsweet Pastures as part of her personal domain, which, like Osprey Point, she managed directly. She seemed drawn to the natural beauty of the area around the Myakka River, with its vistas of water, jungle, and prairie; and she often went by buggy and later by car to enjoy the peaceful spectacle with friends and family.[32]

It does not appear that Bertha thought much about what to do with Meadowsweet Pastures until 1914 or 1915. She had hired a few men to look after the cattle, installed fencing to keep out wild hogs, and sold and shipped at least one substantial trainload of cattle to buyers in Texas. There are references after 1915 to Bertha hosting shooting parties to hunt local birds at Meadowsweet Pastures. Bertha was a good shot, and this kind of sporting activity may have taken place there earlier. By May of 1914 her correspondence showed an increasing interest in the business of cattle raising. She observed to her brother Adrian that she believed it better to sell cattle on the hoof rather than already slaughtered because slaughtering allowed butchers effectively to control prices and therefore profits. Around the same time, the foreman of the ranch demanded a substantial pay increase, and she found that she was losing cattle to predators. In Paris at the time, she could not realistically dismiss the foreman and, for the moment, capitulated to his demand. She also instructed Adrian to place all her cattle in fenced pastures.[33]

Finally, in May of 1915, Bertha made the decision to fully engage in the cattle raising business and to approach it with the same vigor and professionalism she had displayed in her real estate dealings. She began by dismissing the foreman and seeking a new leader for Meadowsweet Pastures. She selected Albert Blackburn, a local man with considerable experience in the cattle industry. A copy of the contract shows that Bertha was now paying very close attention to details. Blackburn's duties were carefully listed, along with what he would be paid. He could buy a horse and employ three or more men for "calf marking" at two dollars a day plus food. Bertha reserved to herself the right to terminate the agreement "at any time without notice."[34]

To support Blackburn's operations and provide housing for his family, Bertha ordered the building of a two-story ranch house whose second floor was surrounded by a screened-in porch. Screening, except for Palmer residences, was a rarity at this time. Eventually Bertha added a barn, cabins for ranch hands, a corral, an artesian well, three silos, a large water tower, and other structures necessary to a large cattle ranch operation. But feed for cattle was a problem that Bertha never satisfactorily solved. In late 1915 she built a feeding shed at the Home Farm, some 18 miles away. Calves being raised for market and the prized Brahman bulls she brought in from Texas were kept for long periods at Osprey Point. This, however, did not solve the main problem. Later she would explore selling her cattle at a younger age to reduce the costs of feeding them. Another answer was to grow more silage on Meadowsweet Pastures, but much of the richest soil was near the Myakka River and flooded regularly. Moreover, the silos she built did not adequately protect their contents from rotting as a result of the pervasive dampness in the river bottom area. She brought in experts who proposed a plan for canals to open new drainage to Philippi Creek while expanding existing drainage to the Myakka River and down to Charlotte Harbor. She mounted a long but ultimately unsuccessful effort to persuade the U. S. government to undertake the drainage project. Even after fencing and planting her fields located outside the Myakka River flood zone, she never quite satisfactorily addressed the problem and often found that buying needed food for her cattle significantly cut into her profits.[35]

Despite this disappointment, Bertha pushed on, hoping to realize her developing vision of Meadowsweet Pastures as a model cattle ranch utilizing the latest scientific information on cattle raising and cattle breeding. She intended to take the hardy but runty native cattle of Florida and mix them with some of the finest cattle breeds in the world. Their offspring would be worth far more on the market, and some could be sold as breeding stock to other ranchers. As she had for other aspects of her agricultural

Bertha with some of her purebred hogs at Meadowsweet Pastures at Myakka.
By permission of Sarasota County Historical Resources.

activities, Bertha turned again to the U.S. Department of Agriculture and university extension services in Florida and throughout the nation. She began breeding top quality Duroc Berkshire hogs as well as cattle and entered them for judging at the Florida State Fair, even winning a few prizes.[36]

Bertha was so committed to cattle raising that she joined the Florida Stock Association. She had earlier joined the Citrus Exchange and other agricultural associations. But for the first and only time, she actually accepted an office as first vice president of the livestock group. She did not, however, attend even

Cattle-dipping vat at Meadowsweet Pastures. One of Bertha's most important contributions to cattle raising in southwest Florida was cattle dipping to eradicate the scourge of the Texas tick.

By permission of Sarasota County Historical Resources.

one of the group's meetings, much to the disappointment of the group's president.[37]

Bertha Palmer may not have attended cattlemen's conventions, but she did take a key role in modernizing the Florida cattle industry, particularly in the western part of the state. A problem common throughout the lower South was the Texas tick, which infected untold numbers of cattle. The U.S. and state agricultural agencies were well aware of the problem, and all promoted tick eradication through a cattle-dipping process. By 1915 many Southern states had made progress against the pest, but Florida lagged behind. One problem was the abysmal ignorance of many cattle ranchers, who harbored odd ideas about cattle dipping: Some believed it would kill the cattle if ticks were washed off them.[38]

When Bertha had fenced in her pastures, cattle ranges, and fields of silage, she had drawn much criticism and some malicious damage from fellow cattlemen for violating the unwritten rule of the open range. In 1916 she stirred up new controversy when she announced that dipping vats would be built at Meadowsweet Pastures. Her men constructed the first vat about two-and-one-half miles east of the ranch home. A year later Bertha ordered the building of a second dipping vat some 16 miles away from the first one. The design of dipping vats forced cattle to proceed into and out of them in a single file. Each animal had to swim through a coal tar–based emulsion. The cowhands repeated the process every two weeks. Once freed of ticks, cattle were moved into fields where no cattle with ticks had ever grazed. The process worked well; cattle lived longer and weighed more when sold. Within two decades, cattle dipping would be required by law in Florida and the tick problem permanently solved.[39]

At its peak, Meadowsweet Pastures reflected some of the same qualities as Bee Ridge Farms. It was certainly a huge enterprise, and it utilized science, technology, and planning to the fullest extent possible. Just as Bee Ridge Farms ranked among the most advanced planned agricultural communities in the nation, Meadowsweet Pastures made most other cattle and hog ranches look primitive. Only a few days before Bertha died in May of 1918, the *Sarasota Times* published a detailed report on what a "party of ladies and gentlemen" found when they visited the "celebrated stock farm." They concluded that Bertha "had converted a wilderness into one of the most valuable stock farms in the South." They described a vast 120-square-mile area that had been fenced and cross-fenced, thus dividing much of the ranch into fields and pastures. In the fields they observed crops of corn, rice, sorghum, peas, and beans. To support the farm work and store the crops as feed for the livestock, Bertha built several huge barns and a series of silos, each one capable of holding 185 tons. The fenced-in pastures contained herds of the finest cattle and hogs in the entire region, the result of Bertha's introduction of superior breeds. They also saw horses and sheep. The cattle and hogs were graded by quality and age, and each group kept in a separate grazing area. The visitors praised the dipping vats and all the other innovations that Bertha introduced to make Meadowsweet Pastures a showcase for modern stock raising.[40]

In sum, Bertha transformed the cattle business in Manatee County through four innovations: cattle dipping, fencing the open range, improving the herd through the introduction of superior breeds, and growing at least a percentage of the food needed to fatten up her herds for sale. She also experimented with building silos to store feed. Finally, she demonstrated that federal and state governments could help cattle growers succeed through research conducted by the United States Department of Agriculture and state university agricultural extension services. She used many of those same tactics to build up her hog herd, which reached around 2,000 head. However, she did encounter problems beyond the hostility of some of her neighboring ranchers, which was often expressed in fence cutting and killing some of her cattle. She had, for example, frequent confrontations with nearly all of her ranch managers, which usually led to dismissals or resignations. She simply did not trust any of them to act in her best interests and always feared they were incompetent or perhaps lackadaisical. In her final years, perhaps distracted by her health problems, she became near-paranoid in her mistrust. She even ordered the accountants at the Palmer Florida Company's Sarasota headquarters not to honor any requisitions from Meadowsweet Pastures' managers unless she had first given her personal approval.[41]

Meadowsweet Pastures represented more than a business to Bertha. It was also her personal retreat. As her young grandchildren, nieces, and nephews began to grow up, she saw the ranch as a place where youngsters could have fun, learn to appreciate the beauty of the outdoors, and acquire camping skills. In 1916 Bertha had five grandchildren. Potter D'Orsay and Honoré Jr. were the sons of Honoré Palmer. Potter Palmer Jr.'s four children were Potter III, Bertha, Gordon, and Pauline. In addition, Prince and Princess Cantacuzene had three children, Michael, Bertha, and Ida. All of these children spent considerable time with Bertha Palmer, and she doted on them.[42]

In 1916 Bertha decided to create a family camping site on Upper Myakka Lake not far from the ranch house. She ordered concrete pillars sunk in the ground in a circle, with three feet of each one showing above the ground. On top of the pillars her workers built a platform made from cypress logs. She then had large tents raised on the cypress platform. A nearby wooden building housed a kitchen. Placing the camp area atop pillars made sense given the rattlesnakes, alligators, and wild hogs that abounded at Meadowsweet Pastures. Unlike many, if not most, Floridians, those who camped at Meadowsweet Pastures had the benefit of electric lights. Bertha ordered installation of a large Delco generator that powered lights around the camping area as well as colored lights strung up in the trees and Spanish moss. The generator also supplied power to the ranch house. Besides electricity, campers also benefitted from having the butler, the cook, and other staff members from The Oaks come along to take care of their needs. This was roughing it—Palmer style.[43]

W. H. "Big Bill" Ferguson (right) and Potter Palmer III on horseback at Meadowsweet Pastures at Myakka. *By permission of Sarasota County Historical Resources.*

Bertha very much desired that her grandchildren, nieces, and nephews cultivate a love for the outdoors. As she had insisted with her two sons, she wanted this new generation to learn to ride, shoot, fish, and play competitive sports. During a stay at her son Potter's ranch in Colorado, Bertha met a relatively young cowboy named "Big Bill" Ferguson who impressed her. Ferguson stood an imposing 6´3˝, and possessed a certain charm as well as a reputation as a master of woodcraft and bronco busting. A native of Central Point, Oregon, Ferguson joined Bertha's staff as "woodcraft tutor" to the younger Palmers and Cantacuzenes. His other duties were not spelled out, although he apparently had some managerial responsibilities at Meadowsweet Pastures. Contemporaries described him as young, clean cut, wholesome, and good with a rifle as well as fishing gear. Ferguson also could tell a good tale about cowboys, soldiers, and Indians on the Western frontier. Once Ferguson was hired, Bertha purchased ponies for the children. Thanks to this Western cowboy, family visits to Meadowsweet Pastures were not only fun, but educational.[44]

Meadowsweet Pastures was one of Bertha's last projects before her death. Given the short period of time, four years at most, that she devoted to developing her Myakka River property, she accomplished a great deal. When she died in 1918, she passed the ranch on to her brother Adrian who had so faithfully served her for many years. But Adrian died in 1926, leaving no children. He in turn willed all his possessions to his sister, Ida Grant. In 1934 the state of Florida purchased Meadowsweet Pastures from Adrian's estate to be part of the planned Myakka River State Park. A.B. Edwards, the man who first showed the Myakka area to Bertha in 1910, then persuaded Honoré and Potter Palmer Jr. to donate an adjacent parcel of 9,300 acres to the park in tribute to their mother. Anyone visiting Myakka River State Park today will appreciate the magnificent natural asset that it is to Sarasota and all of Florida.[45]

Notes to Chapter Four

1. *Sarasota Times*, April 18 and May 2, 1912.

2. Ibid., May 2 and July 11, 1912.

3. Ibid., Aug. 8, Sept. 12, and Oct. 17, 1912.

4. Ibid., Nov. 14, 1912, and June 12, 1913.

5. Ibid., Sept. 10, 1914.

6. Dona Brown, *Back To The Land: The Enduring Dream of Self-Sufficiency in Modern America* (Madison WI: the University of Wisconsin Press, 2011), 1–6, 81–84, 106–124.

7. Jonathan Raban, *Bad Land: An American Romance* (New York: Pantheon Books, 1996), 180–183.

8. *Sarasota Times*, Oct. 22 and Nov. 5, 1914.

9. Ibid. July 11, 1912.

10. Ibid., Jan. 7, 1915.

11. Ibid., Oct. 29, 1914; the Sarasota-Venice Company booklet from 1915 is located in the Vertical File, Sarasota County Historical Resources.

12. *Sarasota Times*, Feb. 11, March 4, Nov. 5 and 26, and Dec. 10, 1914.

13. Ibid., Dec 10 1914.

14. Ibid., Jan. 14, April 1, April 15, May 20, May 27, July 15, Aug. 26, and Sept. 16, 1915; Manatee County General Index to Deeds, 1910–1920, Manatee Historical Center, Bradenton, Florida. Shows a large number of deeds granted by Sarasota-Venice Company in Bee Ridge and Bayonne areas.

15. *Sarasota Times*, Dec. 24, 1914, and Sept. 16, 1915.

16. Ibid., Jan. 21, 28, March 4, and Sept. 21, 1915.

17. Ibid., March 4 and April 29, 1915.

18. Ibid., Aug. 12 and 19, 1915.

19. Ibid., Aug. 9, 1915.

20. Ibid., Jan. 3, 1916.

21. Ibid., Dec. 3, 1914, June 17, July 22, Oct.7, and Nov. 4, 1915.

22. Ibid., Ibid, Jan. 6, 1916.

23. Ibid., Sept. 16, Nov. 25, and Dec. 7, 1915; *Sarasota Herald Tribune*, Feb. 6, 1950, report on Maine Club picnic at Philippi Crest clubhouse in the Maine Colony of Sarasota.

24. Ibid., Dec. 14, 1915, reprinted from *Tampa Tribune*.

25. Ibid.

26. Ibid., Dec. 16, 1915, March 16, 1916.

27. Ibid., Dec. 16, 1915, Feb. 17 and March 30, 1916,

28. Ibid., March 30, 1916.

29. Ibid.

30. Ibid., March 16, 1916; Census, State of Florida, Department of Agriculture, 1920, 151; William Frazer and John L. Guthrie, Jr., *The Florida Land Boom: Speculation, Money, and the Banks* (Westport, CT: Quorum Books, 1995), 1–8; *Sarasota Herald*, Jan. 17, 1926, and April 14. 1928; *Sarasota Herald-Tribune*, March 1, 1997 and Nov. 23, 2012.

31. *Sarasota Times*, June 1, 1916, Jan. 22, 1917.

32. Ibid., Dec. 15, 1910; Matthews, *Venice*, 182; Ross, *Silhouette in Diamonds*, 232–236; Esthus, *History of Agriculture*, 8–9; Dickenman, "The Homesteaders," 102–110; Manatee Historical Records, Plat Book, 22, 23. Refers to 14 parcels of land bought from Garret Murphy and others between June 27, 1910, and Dec. 13, 1910.

33. *Sarasota Times*, May 18, 1911; Bertha Honoré Palmer to Adrian C. Honoré, May 14 and 15, 1914, Bertha H. Palmer Papers, Vol. IV, Sarasota County Historical Resources.

34. Albert Blackburn Contract, May 1, 1915, Bertha H. Palmer Papers, Vol. IV, Sarasota County Historical Resources.

35. Bertha Honoré Palmer to Sarasota Furniture Co., Nov. 15, 1916, and W. H. Prentice to Palmer, Dec. 14, 1915, Vol. V ibid.

36. Esthus, *A History of Agriculture*, 8; Press Bulletin 181, July 28, 1916, University of Florida Agricultural Experiment Station, sent to Bertha Palmer; Dept. of Animal Husbandry at Iowa State College, Agricultural Experiment Station, report dated May 2, 1916, sent to Palmer, Bertha H. Palmer Papers, Vol. IV, Sarasota County Historical Resources.

37. *Sarasota Times*, Feb. 22, 1917.

38. Ibid., Sept. 14, 1916; Esthus, *History of Agriculture*, 8.

39. *Sarasota Times*, June 22, 1916, Esthus, *History of Agriculture*, 8.

40. *Sarasota Times*, May 2, 1918.

41. Ibid., Feb. 22, 1917, and March 21, 1918; Joe G. Warner, *Biscuits and 'Taters: A History of Cattle Ranching in Manatee County*, (St. Petersburg, FL: Great Outdoors Publishing, 1980), 65–68.

42. Ibid., Dec. 3, 1916; Ross *Silhouette in Diamonds*, 245–247.

43. P. J. Benshoff, *Mayaka* (Sarasota: , Pineapple Press, 2002), 124.

44. *Sarasota Times*, Dec. 3 and 17, 1916.

45. Ibid., Dec. 17, 1916; Grismer, *Story of Sarasota*, 207.

CHAPTER FIVE

The Fringe of Empire: Tampa and Venice

By 1915 the Palmer empire in Florida had become complex and very active. Thousands of acres had been cleared, graded, irrigated, and drained. Roads had been constructed and new towns formed at Bee Ridge and Bayonne. Palmer corporate agricultural operations at Bee Ridge and at Bertha's Osprey Point estate filled hundreds of railroad cars headed to Northern markets. Her Meadowsweet Pastures ranch yielded profits and served as a model of modern cattle ranching. Wherever the citizens of southern Manatee County looked they saw the results of what Bertha and her family had achieved in only a few years. New hard-topped roads, the Venice rail extension, buildings in downtown Sarasota, the three impressive Palmer and Honoré mansions, rising property values, and a growing population testified to the sweeping impact of Bertha's ideas and investments on what had been only a sleepy village before her arrival.

Bertha remained the largest employer in the area. Her payroll, the purchases made to support her many economic initiatives, and her direct investments in land and machinery channeled large amounts of money into the local economy and contributed to rising prosperity. Her real estate operations attracted hundreds of prosperous, ambitious people to the Sarasota area, and they in turn contributed to the growing wealth of the community. The official ad campaigns of the Sarasota-Venice Company as well as the constant newspaper focus on Bertha kept Sarasota in the public eye.

Yet the now 66-year-old Bertha Palmer gave no sign of slowing down in any way. Indeed, she pushed ahead with existing and new projects from 1915 until her death in May of 1918. For example, in 1915 and 1916 she directed a major expansion of The Oaks and moved forward vigorously in designing and enhancing her gardens. Gardening, along with collecting oriental porcelains, continued to be Bertha's great passions. In August 1915 the *Chicago Herald* interviewed her about her life in Florida. She told the reporter: "I have found my one talent if I have any at Sarasota Bay. It is to watch beautiful things grow and see blossoms bloom as I plant them." She went on to explain that she considered Sarasota practically her permanent home, and that while she loved Chicago society's "vast and merry whirl," she craved more from life. As she had since her arrival in Florida, Bertha continued to experiment with plants like the mango that could prove profitable commercially. Her papers contain numerous letters to and from state and federal agricultural officials on a wide variety of topics. She also communicated with horticulturalists around the nation.[1]

Besides the many moneymaking operations at Osprey Point, such as poultry, eggs, citrus, cattle, hogs, and vegetables, Bertha added two others in 1915. She took out state licenses to farm oyster beds in Sarasota Bay, hiring local men with knowledge of the business to manage operations. She also employed an apiarist named Thomas McLaine to run a bee farm and collect honey. Bertha learned a great deal from McLaine, as she did from other bee experts with whom she corresponded. With McLaine's patience and expertise, bee operations at Osprey Point grew to 10 hives producing a total of 200 quarts of honey, some of which she sold to the Palmer House Hotel in Chicago.[2]

Bertha in these years continued to be very involved in the affairs of the town of Sarasota, as did the chief officials of the Sarasota-Venice Company and the Palmer Florida Company. She supported new road building as she had in the past, becoming an advocate for the emerging "Good Roads Movement" in Florida. Indeed, one of her employees, the energetic Lamar Rankin, headed the Sarasota Good Roads Committee. Good roads, of course, served her economic interests, as they made it easier for tourists to reach Sarasota and visit the land she was selling. Good roads also meant that trucks could carry a larger percentage of her citrus and vegetable crops to out-of-state markets. Therefore, she would be less dependent on the railroads, which often set exorbitant rates in the absence of competition.[3]

In 1915 Bertha and her brother Adrian as well as J. H. Lord, who still drew a salary from the Sarasota-Venice Company, sought public support for a bond issue to build a bridge across Sarasota Bay and a road from Sarasota to Venice, which eventually became part of the Tamiami Trail running from Tampa to Miami. The road would connect Bertha's land holdings along the coastline. Despite some political problems and disagreements over the quality of the proposed road, the bond issue won approval. Bertha took an active interest in the Sarasota-Venice road's construction, even providing housing for some of the workers. In early 1916 the Sarasota-Venice Company placed ads in papers talking about the commercial possibilities of the new road, which would bring thousands of tourists to the Sarasota area by automobile. The company urged investors to buy Palmer land along the route and put up hotels and restaurants to serve the anticipated influx of people. Bertha also supported improved surfaces for Fruitville Road, which ended at her undeveloped property known as Camp Sawgrass; Old Bee Ridge Road, now called Proctor Road; and a paved road from the town of Bee Ridge to the Myakka River. The first road would give the Palmers a truck route to Florida's east coast, once the cross-state road was completed, while the latter two linked their Bee Ridge operations more closely to Meadowsweet Pastures and Sarasota, thus increasing the value of her lands throughout the area.[4]

Besides roads, Bertha contributed to Sarasota in other ways. She had already built two post offices, a hotel, and a garage, as well as donating a park for children on Main Street and helping fund the Women's Club clubhouse. She now put money into J. H. Lord's renewed efforts to establish the Sarasota Golf and Country Club, an amenity she still considered essential to attracting wealthy tourists and investors to the town.[5]

The Sarasota Board of Trade, long dominated by Sarasota-Venice Company executives, had been a close ally of Bertha's in mounting advertising campaigns to attract potential land purchasers to the city. In boosting the Bee Ridge Farms development nationally, the Sarasota-Venice Company had arranged for professional public relations experts to write a Board of Trade brochure on Bee Ridge, funded the costs of publication, and paid for most of the mailings. The relations between the Palmers and the Board of Trade had grown so close that few were surprised in late 1916 when Bertha offered the first floor of her corporate headquarters on West Pineapple in downtown Sarasota as the new meeting place for the Board. She charged them no rent.[6]

On at least one occasion, the generally unapproachable Mrs. Potter Palmer surprised everyone by turning up personally at a meeting of the Sarasota Women's Club. The purpose of the meeting was not to discuss roads, railroads, city beautification, or political reform. Rather, J. H. Lord, Vice President of the Sarasota-Venice Company, acting in his capacity as president of the Board of Trade, proposed establishment of a farmers' market in Sarasota, where farmers could sell their food products directly to town dwellers. Lord asked Bertha if she wanted to say anything. She replied that she had listened with great interest: "Like many others here I am eager to learn what it is you are going to do and where so we can send anything we have to spare from home." One can only imagine the impact on her neighbors of a world-famous millionairess owning over 140,000 acres of land attending a meeting to see if she could sell some ears of corn or a few oranges. The once-a-week market opened for business at 8 A.M. on December 16, 1916. There is no record as to whether Bertha participated.[7]

In these final years of her life, Bertha turned her attention to large tracts of land she had purchased in and around Tampa and to the southernmost reaches of her empire in Venice. She began acquiring the Tampa properties soon after arriving in Florida in 1910. Just outside the city limits, to the northeast and along the northern shore of the Hillsborough River, she obtained a 19,000-acre tract she called Riverhills Ranch, which her brother Adrian administered in his capacity as president of the Palmer Florida Company. Bertha said little in her letters as to why she purchased this property or what she intended to do with it. She occasionally ran some cattle and hogs on the ranch, but there are no references in her papers to any plan of development. The few letters she wrote on the subject speak of establishing a hunting preserve. In 1914 she discussed erecting a fancy hunting lodge for rich sportsmen, but backed off when her son Honoré expressed reservations. He felt that such an investment should be delayed until he could determine how much game actually inhabited the ranch. He also voiced concerns about security, saying that he lacked confidence the existing fencing could keep interlopers off the property. She instructed the staff to construct several lesser buildings, including a more modest hunting lodge and several bungalows, according to plans Honoré provided. This appears to be the extent of major improvements at Riverhills Ranch.[8]

Family members, including Bertha, hunted at Riverhills Ranch and sometimes slept in tents. Local historians in the area believe that just before she died in 1918, Bertha conceived a grander scheme for the ranch. This scheme, they say, included a planned golf community, one of the first in Florida. But if so, she never had a chance to implement such an idea. Her will treated Riverhills Ranch as part of her personal estate. She passed it on to Adrian Honoré as she had Meadowsweet Pastures. Adrian in turn sold the 19,000 acres to real estate speculators who formed two companies, one to create the community of Temple Terrace and the other to develop a huge orange grove. Adrian's death in 1926 ended the relationship between the Palmers and Honorés and the former Riverhills Ranch.[9]

Bertha exerted considerably more energy developing her holdings inside the Tampa city limits. Her major investment, a subdivision called Virginia Park in the south Tampa area, stretched along Bay to Bay Drive for a mile between Palma Ceia Park on the east and Sunset Park on the west. By the summer of 1915 the Virginia Park subdivision had been laid out, although no development work would begin for months. Even so the Palmer Florida Development Company hired sales agent L. P. Bottenfield, who commenced selling lots. Indeed, he soon reported to Bertha that he had already sold 46 lots and exhausted his initial list of prospects.[10]

It was not until December 1915 that Bertha received a financial plan and marketing concept for Virginia Park. This plan projected that the subdivision would have a total of 144 lots on 12 blocks. The entire area required grading, sidewalks, curbs, sewers, storm drains, street paving, and land clearing and grubbing. Bertha learned from her experts that she needed immediately to extend Tampa Boulevard through Virginia Park and to complete construction of the street grid within the development. The report estimated that the costs of developing Virginia Park would come to $158,463.67, a remarkably precise figure. If all the lots sold, Bertha would receive $978,855, leaving her a profit of $565,627.43. No mention was made of marketing costs or potential legal expenses if buyers did not keep up with their payments on the property.[11]

The report offered several other pieces of information about Bertha's plans for Virginia Park. The plat showed ten streets in the development. Five of them the Palmer Florida Company designated as locations for larger, more expensive homes where lot prices would be higher. These streets were Palmira, Barcelona, Granada, Empedrado, and Bay to Bay Boulevard. The other five streets would feature more modest housing, set on cheaper lots. The names of those streets were Santiago, San Juan, San Pedro, Obispo, and Tacon. As at the Boulevard Addition, the Palmer Florida Company offered easy financial terms. Corner lots cost an average of $725 while inside lots sold for an average price of $600. The company required buyers to pay 4 percent down and pay the rest in equal monthly installments of not less than 2 percent. The company charged 6 percent interest per annum on the unpaid amount.[12]

While some work on sewers and roads took place in 1915, the major development effort did not begin until August of 1916 when the Palmer Florida Company installed concrete curbs. Street paving followed, as did the laying of six-foot-wide sidewalks. Plans also called for the installation of electric lights. To implement the idea that about half of Virginia Park would be a more elite neighborhood, the Palmer Florida Company insisted that sales documents for the affected lots include a provision that the buyer spend a minimum of $3,500 on the construction of the house. To set a standard the company financed the building of two houses, each costing about $5,000. The Palmers expected that at least two high-end purchasers would welcome the chance to buy not only a prestigious lot, but an architect-designed home as well. Other investors would be encouraged to build houses similar in size and aesthetic appeal. In addition, Bertha financed construction of the Palma Ceia Golf and Country Club as a further inducement to potential wealthy investors.[13]

In order to add to the snob appeal of Virginia Park, Bertha announced in August 1916, as part of the publicity surrounding the start of work on the subdivision, that she herself would build a home there and occupy it part of the year. She pointed out that she had substantial land holdings around Tampa and frequently stayed at Henry Plant's Tampa Bay Hotel while conducting business. It would be convenient for her to have a home in Tampa, as it would be for her father, H. H. Honoré, who also had business interests in the town. This proposed mansion would stand at the corner of Bay to Bay and Tampa Boulevard, the most prominent location in the subdivision.[14]

In making this announcement, Bertha repeated a marketing ploy used by her husband when he built the Castle in part to boost sales of Gold Coast properties. He estimated correctly that many wealthy couples in Chicago would have economic and social reasons for moving in near one of the city's richest men and his highly visible and glamorous spouse. Bertha herself had done the same thing when she encouraged members of the social elite to buy her lands around Osprey Point to associate themselves with such a famous and wealthy lady. There was nothing spontaneous in her public statement about residing in Virginia Park. In fact, sales agent Bottenfield referred to the idea more than a year earlier and urged her in July 1915 to start work on the home immediately as a way to "stimulate sales." It is not known if anyone actually bought a lot in Virginia Park because Mrs. Potter Palmer said she was going to build a home there. If some did, they were sadly disappointed, for Bertha never carried through on her announced intention.[15]

Virginia Park was not one of Bertha's success stories. Despite huge infrastructure investments and the employment of a sales force entirely dedicated to selling lots in the subdivision, the project floundered. Bertha did not give up easily. She thought that people's reluctance to buy lots in Virginia Park related to the current empty and barren look of the property. She financed one builder to erect additional houses in order to give a more settled and attractive look to the subdivision. That initiative not only failed to attract more buyers, but also led her to conclude the builder had committed fraud by putting up inferior structures. She brought in outside financial experts who told her that while her books showed many of the lots were under contract, a number of investors had not kept up their payments or erected homes. Bertha also continued to finance development of a golf club that her new sales agent, W. L. Nevins, assured her would boost business. "Conditions were never brighter for Virginia Park," according to Nevins. But in June of 1917 one of Nevins' associates, Mae Thomas, told Bertha that the public was skeptical about the future of Virginia Park. She advised, "We must do the necessary things to make Virginia Park the *one* and *only* high class subdivision in Tampa." Bertha fired sales agents and hired others, only to find they were no more successful. Finally, she sacked the entire sales staff in February 1918 and hired an outside firm to do the job—and it all made little difference. Bertha soon sold all the property she controlled in Virginia Park to another developer in 1918 shortly before her death.[16]

While Bertha struggled to make her Tampa properties profitable, she, along with her brother Adrian and her two sons, turned their attention once more to Venice. She had won the battle over the name of the town, developed groves, dredged the nearby coasts to allow deeper draft vessels to reach shore, and sold some property to rich individuals. She had erected buildings near the terminus of the Seaboard Air Line Railroad. But she and her family, acting through the Sarasota-Venice Company, had not promoted major development activity. The reason for this likely related to legal problems similar to those she faced at Bee Ridge. Pine forests grew over much of the Venice area, and corporations had negotiated rights to harvest the sap of the pines to make turpentine, pitch, and tar, products long associated with the maintenance of sailing ships. Bertha may have owned the land, but not the trees. Until these leases expired she could do little to improve much of her Venice holdings.[17]

Bertha always viewed Venice as a rich man's paradise. If the hotel-golf-tennis-fishing-hunting-swimming-boating model pioneered by Henry Flagler on the east coast would work anywhere on the west coast, Venice was that place, she felt. She aimed to attract the wealthy to enjoy all these pleasures, but her real objective was to persuade them to buy land from her and build winter estates as she had at Osprey.

Not until 1915 when the pine forest was mostly gone and the corporate leases had run out did Bertha and her family feel they could begin a major development effort at Venice. Other positive signs included the new hard road connecting Venice to Sarasota and the renaming of the post office. The Sarasota-Venice Company had already created the core of a town around the rail station, including a freight station, a store that also housed the post office, and workers' quarters. The population remained quite small, but the residents now raised a surplus of vegetables. The Sarasota-Venice Company operated two large groves in the area that produced significant amounts of citrus for export to Northern cities. Based on these circumstances the company took the legal step of platting a downtown area. The development plan seemed modest, showing a district of only six streets and four square blocks, located adjacent to the train station. A mere 64 lots that could be sold appeared on the plat. Purchasers of these lots would reside far from the Gulf of Mexico, because Bertha had other ideas about developing the beachfront area.[18]

Bertha had met an architect named Charles Wellford Leavitt during one of her trips to New York. Leavitt was something of a multitalented genius who designed gardens, parks, hotels, homes, and entire towns. He had worked on projects for many wealthy clients, including Walter P. Chrysler, William C. Whitney, Charles C. Schwab, and John D. Rockefeller. He also designed racetracks and Forbes Field, home of the Pittsburgh Pirates. Bertha may have been drawn to him because he was a major figure in the City Beautiful movement, one of the many important outcomes of the Columbian Exposition. Bertha joined him in visiting Garden City, New Jersey, where Leavitt had done design work. She apparently liked what she saw and invited him to Florida to look at her properties in Venice. He agreed to come saying, "I think I can give you some useful suggestions."[19]

Leavitt continued to correspond with Bertha during the following weeks, and it is clear they exchanged ideas. Interestingly, one of Bertha's letters discussed building a racetrack at Venice "if it is legal." Given his experience designing racetracks, this may have been an idea he proposed to her. Sometime in late June or early July, Leavitt reached The Oaks and began his investigation of the Venice district.[20]

During his stay at Osprey Point Leavitt had many opportunities to talk with Bertha and the officers of the Sarasota-Venice Company about what they wanted to do in Venice. She told him that she was interested in erecting an "attractive resort and sporting center" where rich men and their families could spend a few months in the winter and enjoy a variety of outdoor activities. Leavitt quickly came up with ideas that he verbally discussed with his hostess. He talked about a beachfront hotel with every room enjoying direct access to the water. He suggested there be an "adjoining colonnade quadrangle for reading [and] serving tea and coffee." Guests, he said, would have access to facilities for tennis, fishing, boating, shooting, golf, and motoring. Finally, he proposed that a path should lead from the hotel to a nearby orange and grapefruit grove where the guests could sit in a pavilion and drink citrus juice squeezed from fruit picked from the trees right before their eyes. Bertha and her family expressed interest in this vision and asked Leavitt to prepare a more detailed plan for their review.[21]

By late July Leavitt returned to New York and began working on a proposal. He reported good progress to his patroness, and said he soon expected to receive data from several experts that would help his efforts. "As the days go on," he told her, "I grow more and more enthusiastic about Venice and I am very much pleased with the way things are shaping themselves."[22]

On August 9, 1915, Leavitt wrote Bertha once more and described what his plan for Venice would contain. He said he had come up with specific ideas for the resort and golf club. However, he revealed that his plans for Venice went far beyond a beachfront resort. He told her his plan included a railroad station, civic squares, a town hall, a market, a church, a school, stores, a yacht club, docks, a commercial hotel, a residence district, and a farm. There was provision for an "orange parkway," presumably the path to the citrus juice pavilion he had talked about with Bertha. Leavitt added that he would also provide designs for canals, roads, streets, and parks. His formal report, he said, would show "how, when, and in what order these improvements should be made." He said he would attach cost estimates to the report. Leavitt, in other words, conceived his task to be nothing less than planning an entire city.[23]

The next letter Leavitt received came from Adrian Honoré, President of the Sarasota-Venice Company. He told Leavitt that the company had reviewed his plan and decided to reject it because "it has grown far more complex and costly than when you proposed it to us." The company's board, he continued, did not wish to go forward with such an "extensive, expensive, and hazardous plan of development." Honoré noted that the company felt his plan failed to grasp that its lands in Venice were of two types. The area near the Gulf and Venice Bay was suitable for a luxury, winter-tourist resort, but the bulk of the land was inland and had to be developed for agricultural pursuits. Leavitt's plan, Adrian continued, would cost much to implement and "leave a small profit per acre and not add materially to the value of the rest of the lands." The Sarasota-Venice Company believed that when the agricultural lands were settled, "the mere existence of this population will add value to the Venice Bay lands to make them salable at such a price as to return to us a larger profit than outlined in your plan." He added that this would occur with little expense or risk on the company's part.[24]

Adrian Honoré's polite and reasoned letter should have been enough to convince Leavitt that he had misread or misunderstood what Bertha wanted from him. Instead, he wrote her directly asking that she personally explain to him the rejection of his plan. On February 16, 1916, he got his wish. Bertha wrote back, reminding him of their previous discussions and pointing out that his plan contained many things that neither she nor her brother had ever authorized him to include. Above all, his plan would cost far more than she wished to pay. She told him bluntly that what he had proposed did not serve her purposes.[25]

Bertha then proceeded to give Leavitt a basic education in real estate transactions. "This, as we explained to you is a practical business," she wrote, "with the aim of furnishing such necessary improvements and attractions as would sufficiently develop our property to enable us to sell it at a profit." She made it clear that neither she nor the Sarasota-Venice Company wanted to assume any additional effort or cost not absolutely essential to that goal. Bertha derided that part of Leavitt's plan calling for four civic centers: "What functions do they handle? What civic life and activities will go on? Social service or civic projects, she said, would not add to the value of the land, but the cost of construction would certainly reduce profits from land sales. She claimed the costs of his plan would be more than Henry Flagler spent developing Palm Beach.[26]

Bertha concluded her critique of Leavitt's plan by pointing out that she paid $75 per acre for her Venice property, and that it was currently marketable even in its undeveloped state at $875 per acre, earning a profit of $800. If Leavitt's planned community were actually built, his own estimated costs of funding the development would reduce her profit to only $500 per acre. Bertha's analysis demonstrated why she rejected the Leavitt plan. But it also seems to represent her views on all the lands she was trying to sell, including the agricultural areas located in the interior.[27]

Bertha never hired another architect to produce a plan for Venice. She did not build a resort hotel nor a pavilion in a citrus grove for the wealthy to drink freshly squeezed juice. However,

Bertha did come up with an alternative strategy to attract wealthy winter vacationers to Venice. In her travels she had met a transplanted Englishman named M. T. C. "Mike" Evans. Evans operated two resorts, one in Wyoming and the other in Virginia. He demonstrated a gift for attracting and entertaining rich people, and had developed a loyal following of repeat customers. Bertha persuaded him to visit Venice and showed him a 24-acre site that sat astride the new hard-surfaced road under construction between Sarasota and Venice. Covered with tall pine trees, the area jutted out into Roberts Bay. In their discussions, Bertha returned to some of the same ideas she had hoped Leavitt would embrace. She wanted to attract moneyed individuals and families to spend the winter in Florida in fairly simple accommodations, engaging in a variety of healthful physical activities while enjoying Florida's spectacular climate. She talked again of the back-to-the-land movement and an allied concept, back to nature. The railroad extension and especially the new road would bring many people to Venice. Evans could relate to this vision, for it was very close to what he was already offering people in Wyoming.[28]

A deal was struck, as Evans agreed to lease the newly named Eagle Point Camp. The Sarasota-Venice Company did some dredging to allow small boats to dock at the boathouse that would soon be built. Over the next two years the company also constructed ten one-story cabins, some as big as 1,400 square feet, and all facing west. A two-story clubhouse contained the dining area and bachelor's quarters upstairs. Tennis courts were soon added. On January 11, 1917, Evans welcomed his first guests to what the *Sarasota Times* called the "most up-to-date and modern equipped resort on the west coast."[29]

Among the first guests were Honoré and Grace Palmer and Mr. and Mrs. H. W. Mackintosh. Mackintosh served as general manager of the Sarasota-Venice Company. Most of the other guests were wealthy East Coast types who had stayed at one or both of Mike Evans' other resorts. During the day the guests swam, boated, hunted, golfed, fished, or played tennis. At night, thanks to the electrical generator installed by the Sarasota-Venice Company, they engaged in different kinds of games organized by Evans, such as bridge tournaments. At the end of the second season Evans purchased Eagle Point Camp from the Sarasota-Venice Company. The resort continued to operate for decades, and in 1991 the area was declared a National Historic District. Today it is a gated private community known as Eagle Point Club. Behind the fences and walls still stand most of the cabins, the clubhouse, the water tower, and even the dinner bell. There is also a section of the original Tamiami Trail on the property.[30]

A cabin at Eagle Point Camp, Bertha Palmer's major effort to attract the wealthy to Venice as a vacation site. *By permission of Sarasota County Historical Resources.*

Bertha did try to build on the success of Eagle Point Camp in the final months of her life. She and her family launched an effort to organize a golf and country club in Venice. For the post of secretary and chief organizer of the club, Bertha and Adrian decided to bring in one of the Sarasota-Venice Company's most effective employees, Lamar Rankin, who had been sales manager for the very successful Bee Ridge Farms project. The officers of the new club included Honoré Palmer, Potter Palmer Jr., and Edson Keith, a Chicago businessman whose son married a sister of Grace Palmer. Keith built a historically significant mansion in Sarasota that still stands in Philippi Estate Park on the south bank of Philippi Creek. The club's officers instructed Rankin to sell enough $2,500 memberships and lots to finance the building of the club and golf course. Bertha urged Rankin not to use an out-of-state firm to do the construction, as it inflated costs. She talked about her experience at Virginia Park, and how she saved money by using a local contractor to build the Palma Ceia club.[31]

Bertha obviously thought of the Venice Golf and Country Club as a way finally to get her "sporting club" that Leavitt was supposed to design along the waterfront. But Bertha did not live long enough to achieve the kind of success she had hoped for in Venice. It would be left to others, particularly the Brotherhood of Locomotive Engineers and Trainmen and a talented urban planner named John Nolen to attempt what Bertha declined to undertake: the creation of a planned city. They built their city in the 1920s during the height of the Florida land boom, but the venture turned into a colossal financial failure during the subsequent hard times. Unlike Bertha, these entrepreneurs lacked clarity of purpose and prudence. The Brotherhood nearly bankrupted itself and left behind a virtual ghost town. It took years before Venice recovered. Fortunately, subsequent generations have been able to appreciate Nolen's masterpiece.[32]

World War I erupted in August 1914 and affected Bertha and her family in many ways. The war helped their business interests by spurring an increase in food prices, as European countries competed to buy more agricultural products from the United States. U-boats and widespread military operations kept most Americans away from Europe. The wealthy who usually spent "the season" in London or Paris or Rome now wintered in places like Florida. On the other hand, the war may have affected the availability of bank credit for home loans, a shortage that may partly explain why the Virginia Park project was not as successful as expected.[33]

The war also affected Bertha on a personal level. Some of her English servants now served in the British army. Many of her long-time friends among the nobility of Europe now stood in harm's way. She knew well the King and Queen of Belgium and was appalled, as many Americans were, by the suffering of the Belgian people as a result of the German occupation of that country. In December 1915 she wrote the king a personal note reminding him of their friendship at Newport when he was still a prince and came to her cottage for dinner. She enclosed a contribution for the Belgian relief fund. As war came closer to the United States, she became even more concerned. In January 1917 she responded to a request for funds from an American group trying to set up trade schools for maimed French soldiers. Two months later she learned that two Wedgewood pieces she ordered from England were lost when the ship carrying them was torpedoed. Finally, the United States officially entered the war in April 1917, after many U.S. ships had been sunk by German U-boats.[34]

In August of 1917 one of Bertha's friends in Sarasota, Dr. Jack Halton, who had welcomed her in 1910 at his sanitarium/ hotel, left for Oglethorpe, Georgia, to take up his duties as a captain in the Medical Officers' Reserve Corps. She later would send jars of honey from her Osprey Point hives to him and his friends. By January of 1918 she was writing her brother Adrian in Chicago that she was thinking of turning over the Castle to the Red Cross for use as a hospital. In that same month she experimented with growing castor beans in her orange groves because the army said the beans produced a substance that made airplane engines more efficient. The bean crop did not flourish, however, and she abandoned the effort. To help the American Expeditionary Force in France, Bertha gave the two cars, a Rolls Royce and a Renault, she had left behind in 1914 to Dr. George E. Brown, a consulting surgeon to the U.S. Army, for war purposes. It was a measure of her anxious concern about the war that she ordered a large-scale map of the Western Front from C.S. Hammond & Co. of New York so she could better understand the ebb and flow of battle. On May 1, 1918, only days before her death, the *Chicago Herald and Examiner* printed a letter from Bertha Palmer in response to one the paper had written her. Almost her last public words referred to the war and her duties as a citizen. "I am hoping to be able to return to Chicago soon," she said, "to take part in such war work as seems most important. I hope to plunge into this work immediately on my arrival."[35]

Bertha Palmer suffered from breast cancer. In 1917 she underwent a mastectomy at a New York clinic, but the cancer returned. She must have been in terrible pain through the late winter and early spring of 1918, but made no public acknowledgment of her condition. According to her biographer, Ishbel Ross, who was able to interview surviving family members around 1960, they did know of her illness but never said anything outside their circle. The only indication of something amiss was Bertha's testiness towards her employees and a tendency to mistrust their judgment. Her letters show that, almost to the end, she remained involved in all phases of her multifaceted empire, and she often spoke of plans for the future. She died on May 5. The death certificate cites pneumonia as the cause and that was the official reason given to the newspapers. Adrian Honoré told acquaintances that she fell ill only a week before her death. She had caught a cold, which turned into pneumonia. He said her "death was most unexpected."[36]

For a brief time, Bertha's body lay at The Oaks. Word of her passing spread quickly, and the mayor of Sarasota ordered the city flag to fly at half-mast in a sign of respect. Her coffin was returned to Chicago by private railcar, accompanied by Honoré and Grace, Potter Jr. and Pauline, Ida Grant, Adrian Honoré, and the Prince and Princess Cantacuzene. Her body lay in state in the Castle while large crowds clustered around the famous old structure. Newspapers in Chicago, New York, and elsewhere printed extensive obituaries summarizing her life, her achievements, and her significance. The *New York Times* estimated her worth at $15 million, including the Castle, the Palmer House, 150 other Chicago properties, and her personal possessions. That figure did not include the $6 million Potter Palmer had left in a trust for his two sons. The Florida properties were valued at only $1 million. When all sources of wealth are considered, Bertha may have come close to doubling the $12 million left by her husband in his will, a tribute to her business skills and those of her family. The New York paper went on to note her support of women's causes, her contributions to the Columbian Exposition, her un-challenged leadership of Chicago society, and her patronage of the Chicago Art Institute and other Chicago institutions. The *Chicago Tribune* summarized Bertha Palmer's importance in this manner: "At the height of her fame she was the most renowned American woman of her time." By and large the obituaries said relatively little about her activities in Florida other than referring to her reputation as a sagacious businesswoman.[37]

The funeral was held at 3 P.M. on May 10 at the Castle. Flowers surrounded the casket, particularly 'Bertha Palmer' roses she had bred. Afterwards the casket passed along Chicago streets jammed with people jostling to see the spectacle. The procession entered Graceland Cemetery located on the city's north side, where her husband and parents were interred. Today as in 1918, the Palmer burial ground is the most impressive in the cemetery.

Palmer family burial site in Graceland Cemetery, Chicago. The structure was designed by the New York architectural firm of McKim, Mead, & White, which had also designed the Agriculture Building at the Columbian Exposition in 1893. *Photo courtesy of Frank A. Cassell.*

The form of the structure is oblong and outlined by Ionic columns suggesting a Greek or Roman temple. The columns surround a raised platform upon which rest two huge sarcophagi, one for Bertha and the other for her husband. In later years many other Palmer family members have been buried beneath the platform. The structure was designed by the New York architectural firm of McKim, Mead, & White, which had also designed the Agriculture Building at the Columbian Exposition in 1893.[38]

Not long after the funeral Honoré and Potter Palmer Jr. probated her final will. She left everything to them except a lengthy list of bequests to family members, servants, and various civic and cultural organizations in Chicago with which she had been affiliated. The will named her two sons as executors of her estate. She did not dismantle the trust created in her husband's will to manage half his estate on behalf of his sons, with Bertha and her brother Adrian as trustees. This had important tax implications and spared the Palmers a huge tax bill. That trust would now be in the hands of her sons and Adrian. Bertha provided in her will that the Riverhills Ranch outside Tampa would go to Adrian, as would Meadowsweet Pastures. The Osprey Point estate now belonged to her sons. Despite the large amount of land given to Adrian and the huge amount of acreage sold at Bee Ridge Farms and Osprey Farms, the Palmer family still controlled tens of thousands of acres east and south of Sarasota. The question Sarasotans asked in 1918 was, What would Honoré and Potter Jr. choose to do with all that property?[39]

It would not be too much to say that Bertha Palmer made Sarasota. In eight short years she transformed a small frontier community into a thriving resort town with a solid agricultural base. She had attracted other wealthy individuals who in turn invested in property and supported a growing array of cultural assets. Through her own investments and her position as the county's largest employer, she had pumped great amounts of money into the local economy. She was responsible for the vital railroad extension to Venice, and built or arranged to have built a large web of roads in the area that connected communities, encouraged commerce, and made it much easier for automobile tourists to reach Sarasota and its surrounding area. Thanks to her, Sarasota's population had doubled and real estate values had climbed dramatically. She created whole towns in Sarasota County including Bee Ridge, Venice, and Bayonne, introduced modern agricultural technology, and systematically experimented with growing new commercial crops. She also modernized cattle and hog production in the Sarasota area. As in agriculture, she employed science and technology to grow and sell bigger and better cattle and hogs for market. Fencing in pastures, growing silage crops, eliminating tick disease in her herds, and crossbreeding local cows with Brahman bulls were all very important innovations that broadened and improved the economic base of Sarasota.

Bee Ridge Farms alone constituted a major triumph for Bertha and her family. They cleared thousands of acres and sold them in 10- or 20-acre lots to hundreds of middle-class Americans, many of who were seeking escape from the emerging industrialized and urbanized American society. At Bee Ridge a vast infrastructure of roads, wells, and drainage ditches made it possible for untrained town and city people rapidly to launch themselves as farmers. Experimental farms demonstrated what crops would do well. Various cooperative organizations sponsored by the Palmers helped the new farmers grow, transport, and sell their crops most efficiently.

At the end of her life Bertha felt pride in what she had accomplished in Florida. She had come seeking a challenge, and she had certainly found more than a few in carrying out her projects. She had tested herself by doing a great many things that she had never done before in her life. She remade herself from a society leader into a businesswoman and a hands-on manager. And she had succeeded. The fact that she was a woman in a male-dominated society makes her achievements all the more remarkable. She benefitted from being wealthy, but few wealthy women of her era would have considered doing what she did in Florida. So, in the end, Bertha and Sarasota both prospered from this relatively brief association.

Bertha found much to love about Florida, including the climate and the natural beauty of the area. However, she never developed the same attachment to Sarasota that she had with Chicago. Her will, for example, left nothing to anyone or any institution in southern Manatee County, although she had often been generous in her contributions to this community during her life. But of course her true legacy to Sarasota was to be found nearly everywhere in the great works she left behind. Chicago, however, was the center of her life, where her closest friends lived, the place where her family life unfolded, and the scene of her greatest triumphs. Although no one in Sarasota could know it on May 5, 1918, Bertha actually had left a very specific inheritance to the people she had lived among since 1910—her family. Bertha may have been gone, but a very capable group, including her brother and her two sons, were about to take over full direction of family operations in Sarasota.

Notes to Chapter Five

1. *Chicago Herald*, Aug. 5, 1915.

2. Charles T. Curry to Bertha Honoré Palmer, Dec. 3, 1915; Thomas McLaine to Palmer, March 1, 1915, and May 24, 1916, Bertha H. Palmer Papers, Vol. IV; Palmer to William E. Riemers, Palmer House, March 19, 1918, Bertha H. Palmer Papers, Vol. V, Sarasota County Historical Resources.

3. *Sarasota Times*, Feb 24, 1916, Sarasota-Venice Company ad on land adjacent to the Tamiami Trail; May 10, 1917; R N. Rowlands to Bertha Honoré Palmer, Feb. 20, 1917, and W. W. Savage to Palmer, Jan. 18, 1918, Bertha H. Palmer Papers, Vol. IV, Sarasota County Historical Resources.

4. Unknown to Bertha Honoré Palmer, March 10, 1915, and undated broadside, likely April, 1915, signed by Lamar Rankin, Bertha H. Palmer Papers, Vol. III, Sarasota County Historical Resources; *Sarasota Times*, Feb. 24, 1916.

5. W. W. Savage to Bertha Honoré Palmer, Jan. 18, 1918, Bertha H. Palmer Papers, Vol. IV, Sarasota County Historical Resources.

6. *Sarasota Times*, Dec. 14, 1916.

7. Ibid., Dec. 7 and 14, 1916.

8. Matthews, *Venice*, 183; Lana Burroughs, Tim Lancaster, Grant Rimbey, *et al.*, *Temple Terrace*, (Charleston, SC: Arcadia Publishing, 2010), 7; Bertha Honoré Palmer to H. C. Gibbons, July 18, 1914, Bertha H. Palmer Papers, Vol. III, Sarasota County Historical Resources.

9. Burroughs, *Temple Terrace*, 7; Bertha Honoré Palmer to H. C. Gibbons, July 18, 1914, Bertha H. Palmer Papers, Vol. IV, Sarasota Historical Resources; Matthews, *Venice*, 183–184.

10. L. P. Bottenfield to Bertha Honoré Palmer, July 14, 1915, Bertha H. Palmer Papers, Vol. IV, Sarasota County Historical Resources.

11. Ibid., Statement of Costs to Develop Virginia Park, Dec. 31, 1915, Bertha H. Palmer Papers, Vol. III.

12. Ibid.

13. Ibid., H. C. Gibbons to Bertha Honoré Palmer, Jan. 27, 1917; *Sarasota Times*, Aug. 3, 1916.

14. *Sarasota Times*, Aug. 31, 1916.

15. L. P. Bottenfield to Bertha Honoré Palmer, July 14, 1915, Bertha H. Palmer Papers, Vol. IV, Sarasota County Historical Resources.; *Tampa Times*, Aug. 31, 1916.

16. W. L. McNevin, agent for Virginia Park, to Bertha Honoré Palmer, Jan. 28, 1917; D. C. Gillet to Palmer, Feb. 24, 1917; Mrs. Mae Thomas to Palmer, June 19, 1917; Maude Littlefield Braithard to Palmer, Jan. 17, 1918, Bertha H. Palmer Papers, Vol. III, Sarasota County Historical Resources.

17. *Sarasota Times*, July 7, 1910; Adrian Honoré to Bertha Honoré Palmer, March 6, 1915; J. H. Lord to Palmer, March 20, 1915; Bertha H. Palmer Papers, Vol. III, Sarasota County Historical Resources.

18. Matthews, *Venice*, 195.

19. Charles W. Leavitt to Bertha Honoré Palmer, May 28 and June 21, 1915; Bertha H. Palmer Papers, Vol. III, Sarasota County Historical Resources.

20. Ibid., Bertha Honoré Palmer to Charles W. Leavitt, June 23, 1915.

21. Ibid., Charles W. Leavitt to Bertha Honoré Palmer, July 24 and Aug. 9, 1915.

22. Ibid., Leavitt to Palmer, July 24, 1915.

23. Ibid., Leavitt to Palmer, Aug. 9, 1915.

24. Ibid., Adrian Honoré to Charles W. Leavitt, Dec. 29, 1915.

25. Ibid., Bertha Honoré Palmer to Charles W. Leavitt, Feb. 26, 1916.

26. Ibid.

27. Ibid.

28. *Sarasota Times*, March 23, 1916.

29. Ibid., Jan. 11, 1917; Ross, *Silhouette in Diamonds*, 248–249.

30. *Sarasota Times*, Jan. 28, 1917. Mackintosh is the usual spelling of this name in contemporary sources. I have stayed with Mackintosh except for references to McIntosh Road. The road was likely named for the Palmer company executive, but county officials chose this less common spelling.

31. Ibid., Jan. 21, 1918; Lamar Rankin to Adrian Honoré, March 14, 1918, Bertha H. Palmer Papers, Vol. III, Sarasota County Historical Resources.

32. Matthews, *Venice*, 219–259.

33. Ross, *Silhouette in Diamonds*, 243–245.

34. Bertha H. Palmer to King of Belgium, Dec. 16, 1915, Vol. IV; Mrs. Edward Baylies to Bertha Honoré Palmer, Jan. 30, 1917, Vol. I; Potter Palmer Jr. to Bertha Honoré Palmer, March 5, 1917, Vol. III; Bertha H. Palmer Papers, Sarasota County Historical Resources.

35. *Sarasota Times*, Aug. 2, 1917; Bertha Honoré Palmer to William H. Riemers, Palmer House, Jan 17, 1918, Vol. III; Palmer to D. R. McQuarrie at Bee Ridge, Jan. 23, 1918, Vol. IV; Palmer to Ernest Harvey in Paris, Feb. 5, 1918, Vol. II; Palmer to Dr. Brown in Paris, March 20, 1918, Vol. IV, Bertha H. Palmer Papers, Vol IV, Sarasota County Historical Resources; *Chicago Herald and Examiner*, May 1, 1918.

36. Ross, *Silhouette in Diamonds*, 250–254; *New York Times*, May 7, 1918.

37. *New York Times*, May 7, 1918; *Chicago Tribune*, May 7, 1918; *Chicago Daily News*, May 8, 1918, Coakley Rollins Collection Box I, Sarasota County Historical Resources.

38. *Chicago Tribune*, May 9, 10, and 11, 1918.

39. Bertha Honoré Palmer will, Bertha H. Palmer Papers, Sarasota County Historical Resources.

CHAPTER SIX

The Empire Continues: Hyde Park Grove and Palmer Farms

Bertha Palmer's death led to a pause in the family's business operations. She had been the driving force behind everything they had done since 1910. Moreover, it took time to straighten out the legal and tax questions surrounding her will. The Palmer business holdings were national in scope and very complicated, involving Chicago real estate, manufacturing, natural gas production, and much more. The family needed time not only to grieve, but also to figure out what organizational changes were needed and to plan for the future.

The pause came at an interesting point in Florida's history, as the state stood on the brink of the great Florida land boom, a short but intense few years of incredible growth as everyone, it seemed, sought land on one of America's last frontiers. The stories of excess, instant wealth, and widespread chicanery seem almost unbelievable; but more times than not they were true. Florida in the early and mid-1920s was a land of dreamers, of highly ambitious men, of loose banking practices, and of corrupt politicians. Rarely has a state advanced so far and so fast in terms of population and land development. By railroad and automobile, a vast tide of people swept into Florida seeking quick riches. As in most economic bubbles, those living through this one thought it would go on indefinitely. But like all such phenomena it soon collapsed, leaving many people destitute and cities and towns mired in debt. By late 1926 and early 1927, the edifice of dreams had come tumbling down.[1]

Sarasota was not immune to this era of excess. The city's population nearly quadrupled, to 8,398, between 1920 and 1930. The area witnessed an unprecedented boom in building, including Andrew McAnsh's Mira Mar Hotel and Apartments, the Hotel El Vernona, a new high school and a number of grammar school buildings, Sarasota Memorial Hospital, the Sarasota County Courthouse, the Sarasota Terrace Hotel, John Ringling's home (Cà d'Zan) and his art museum. In 1927 Ringling also brought his circus to Sarasota, making it its new winter quarters. In this period, John Nolen's Venice was built and the Tamiami Trail completed. Never before had the city or county witnessed such a burst of development. But it was all based on easy access to capital made available through obliging banks. Sarasota also had its share of dishonest or at least underhanded subdivision developers, who sold lots that either did not exist or which lacked basic amenities. By 1926 there were 46 real estate companies listed as operating in the city of Sarasota alone.[2]

The 1920s brought another major change to the Sarasota area. In 1921 the legislature approved dividing Manatee County and establishing Sarasota County, thus ending a long struggle. Bertha Palmer and other leaders of the south Manatee County area had long resented how the county allocated tax income, the great distance many had to travel to conduct business in Bradentown, and the lack of effective policing by the county sheriff. The new Sarasota County was free of these restrictions. The citizenry joyfully celebrated this event, but no one had thought far enough ahead to consider where this new government entity would be housed. In the short term, it was placed near the Sarasota city government in the Hover Arcade located on the bayfront. Interestingly, a Palmer employee was named to the new county commission while an old Palmer loyalist, J. H. Lord, won election as the county's first representative to the Florida House of Representatives, thus giving the family a stronger voice in state politics.[3]

Against this background, the next phase of Palmer operations in Sarasota commenced. Bertha's death deprived the family of its leader and left her survivors with a number of tasks to handle before they could turn their full attention to the future of the Palmer-Honoré holdings in and around the city of Sarasota. In the months following the funeral, Honoré and Potter II carried out her final wishes with regard to bequests to her family and staff as well as to the Chicago Art Institute and various charitable organizations she had supported during her lifetime. Together with their spouses, the brothers also divided her personal property, including artworks and jewels. The four of them then traveled to France after the Armistice ended the Great War and allocated the $350,000 worth of possessions that had been stored away there since Bertha hurriedly left for America in 1914. It was during this period that her sons determined that Potter would take over The Oaks as his winter home, as well as the Castle in Chicago. Honoré became the sole owner of Immokalee.[4]

Besides Honoré and Potter II, the Palmer business and real estate interests benefitted from the expertise of a cadre of corporate administrators and managers in Chicago, Florida, and Louisiana. The greatest force for organizational continuity after 1918 was Adrian C. Honoré, although his energies now had to be divided between the Palmer Empire in Florida and his need to manage Meadowsweet Pastures and the Riverhills Ranch, which he now owned. Still, Adrian was the family member most knowledgeable about all aspects of the Palmers' investments. He had been close to Bertha as her brother, as her co-trustee of the Potter Palmer Trust, and as president of both the Palmer Florida Company and the Sarasota-Venice Company. Better than her sons, Adrian Honoré understood Bertha's plans and her leadership style. Adrian, Honoré, and Potter II had now worked together as a team for years managing the Palmer holdings. Their cohesion guaranteed a smooth transition to the post-Bertha Palmer era.[5]

Honoré Palmer. *Courtesy of Gulf Coast Heritage, Inc.*   Potter Palmer II. *Courtesy of Gulf Coast Heritage, Inc.*

These three, as it turned out, found powerful support from Prince Michael Cantacuzene. Cantacuzene had suffered much during the Great War, not only losing his vast lands and wealth to the Bolsheviks, but also suffering serious battle wounds. Even while recuperating in Sarasota, Cantacuzene had campaigned vigorously for the anti-Communist cause in Russia, as did his wife, Princess Julia Grant Cantacuzene. By 1920 the prince likely had concluded that the Communists would not be ousted in the near future, that he was now an exile, and that he needed to make a new life for himself and a living to support his family.

Prince Cantacuzene, a member of the Romanov family. In 1915 he led what was called the last great cavalry charge. In 1899 he married Julia Dent Grant. *By permission of Sarasota County Historical Resources.*

The Princess Julia Dent Grant Cantacuzene, circa 1900. She was Bertha's niece and the granddaughter of Ulysses S. Grant. Julia was born in the White House. *By permission of Sarasota County Historical Resources.*

Working for various Palmer business enterprises seemed an obvious path for him.[6]

Not until December of 1919 did Sarasota and southwest Florida receive any information on the Palmers' future plans. For some reason this news first appeared in the *St. Petersburg Daily Times*. On December 4, the Pinellas County paper announced: "In line with the policy of the late Mrs. Potter Palmer to develop her holdings in Florida into substantial and self-sustaining farms, an organization has been formed to develop and care for the immense holdings belonging to this estate." The news story named R.H. Roberts of New Orleans as the man hired by the Palmer Florida Company to handle the "clearing, development, and planting of the entire tract of some 77,000 acres of land located in Manatee County." The first 16,000 acres would be devoted to citrus and vegetable growing. The land would be cut up into small farms and sold only to those able to work the land. Just as they had at Bee Ridge Farms and Osprey Farms a few years earlier, the Palmers planned to use modern machinery to prepare the land, namely steam-driven stump pullers and tractors. The article concluded with news that Honoré and Potter II would soon be in Florida to direct activities. Only parts of this article proved to be true. However, it was entirely accurate in asserting that the Palmers had legally reorganized their business structure, conceived big ideas for new developments in the Sarasota area, and would soon arrive to begin work.[7]

The reorganization was necessary for several reasons. Bertha's death meant that her sons would take over direct management of the trust fund created for them by their father. Moreover, the sons were also trustees of Bertha's estate. Finally, the successful sale of much of the land developed by the Sarasota-Venice Company made that legal entity less necessary. Indeed, the company sold the last 1,400 acres it controlled in the Venice area in 1925 to Dr. Fred Albee, leaving Osprey Point, Immokalee, and a broad swath of undeveloped land on the south side of Clark Road as the main holdings in the area south of Sarasota.[8]

When the Palmers returned to Sarasota County in 1919 they had two large projects in mind: the Hyde Park grove area and Palmer Farms. Hyde Park stretched east from the present location of the corner of Bee Ridge Road and Tamiami Trail to a point slightly beyond the Venice railway extension. It encompassed 1,200 acres and was located not far from the earlier Bee Ridge Farms project. In 1920 the Palmers successfully petitioned the State of Florida to establish the Hyde Park Drainage District, which had authority to tax residents to fund improvements intended to drain the area and create arable farmland. The original plan seems to have been to repeat the Bee Ridge Farms project by cutting up the acreage into small farms where farmers could grow citrus and vegetables. As they had at Bee Ridge, the Palmers spent a great deal of money on infrastructure, including roads and an irrigation system to go along with the drainage system. In 1922 R. K. Thompson, the chief operations officer of the Palmer Florida Company, decided to lay out a 190-acre orange grove to attract the attention of inventors and show them what they could expect if they settled in Hyde Park. He acquired seedlings for this demonstration grove and had them planted. However, the slow growth rate of the trees disappointed Thompson and cast doubt on the future of citrus growing at Hyde Park. Fortunately, the Palmers had recently hired Ed L. Ayers, a Texan who had served as county agricultural agent for Manatee County. Ayers proved to be an enormous asset at both Hyde Park and Palmer Farms.

After examining the soil at Hyde Park, Ayers urged additional applications of fertilizer that made the citrus trees much healthier.[9]

In 1926 the Palmer Florida Company began aggressively marketing lots in Hyde Park, describing it as a "close in tract" within the Sarasota city limits that had recently but, as it turned out, temporarily been expanded to an astonishing 64 square miles. The principal newspaper ad for land in Hyde Park invited buyers to purchase orange groves for "residential or commercial" purposes. But the timing of the offering was unfortunate for the Palmers, since the great Florida land boom collapsed in late 1926 and early 1927. The results of that dramatic event devastated Florida and Sarasota as the economy contracted and credit dried up. When the city leaders of Sarasota faced plummeting tax income, they quickly reduced the city's size from 64 square miles to a more manageable 17 square miles. Even then, the financial burden proved almost too great. Then, in 1929, the stock market crash followed shortly by the Great Depression left the Florida economy in tatters, as uncounted thousands more lost their investments. Many, if not most, of those who had put money down on Hyde Park property could not make their loan payments and abandoned their investment. The land eventually returned to the Palmers.[10]

By the 1930s the Palmers had decided that running Hyde Park as a company grove and making money through the sale of the fruit and juice maximized their investment return during the worst economic downturn in the nation's history. Prince Cantacuzene took over the active management of the enterprise and demonstrated skill as an administrator. Cantacuzene seemed popular with his 50 or so employees, who appreciated his annual employee picnic. However, one of his less successful innovations involved grazing sheep in the grove to keep down weeds and grass. The sheep obliged, but they also ate the bark off the orange trees and had to be removed. At 1,200 acres, Hyde Park ranked as one of the largest citrus operations in Sarasota. Together with other Palmer groves in the county, the Palmer brothers controlled more than fifty percent of the area's annual citrus production by 1938. In that year the Palmers, in cooperation with the Seaboard Air Line Railroad, erected Sarasota County's only citrus packinghouse next to the Hyde Park grove's station and rail siding along the Venice extension that Bertha Palmer had insisted be built nearly 20 years earlier. The new plant cut production and shipping costs and strengthened the Palmer's dominant position in Sarasota's citrus industry. It also created 100 or so new jobs, a welcome boost to Sarasota's crippled economy. In 1950 the Palmer Florida Company sold Hyde Park to Clinton Foods, Inc., which produced frozen orange juice concentrate under the Snow Crop label. Clinton Foods paid the Palmers one million dollars. In the middle1950s Clinton resold the land to the firm of King & South, which made it part of the South Gate housing development.[11]

The second major project for the Palmers in the 1920s was Palmer Farms, located on a huge block of land due east of Sarasota in the Fruitville area. Palmer Farms encompassed some 8,000 acres, an area comparable in size to the Bee Ridge Farms project a decade earlier. Unlike Bee Ridge, with its relatively high elevation and its dry and sandy soil, Palmer Farms, or at least a portion of it, was located in a swampy area known as Big Camp Sawgrass and always described as "muck lands." For six months of the year during Sarasota's wet season from June to December, water covered the area. Centuries of flooding and plant deterioration had created around 2,000 acres of unusually rich soil. J. H. Lord sensed the possibilities for agriculture in the Camp Sawgrass area early in the century and purchased the property. In turn he sold it to Bertha Palmer shortly after she arrived in Sarasota. While developing Bee Ridge Farms she had experimented with growing celery in the Camp Sawgrass region.[12]

To grasp the physical size of Palmer Farms, it is necessary to describe its dimensions based on today's road system. The northern boundary is present-day Richardson Road (called Old Myakka Road in the 1920s) from where it intersects with Fruitville Road. Richardson then loops northeast and then runs due east parallel with Fruitville Road. Today Richardson abruptly ends at the Tatum Ridge Golf Course, but in the 1920s it continued east to the community of Myakka. About two miles east of Tatum Ridge Road, Old Myakka Road intersected a major canal running south. This canal, which still exists, was part of the Palmer's drainage system and marked the western boundary of Palmer Farms. The line of the canal intersects Bee Ridge Road some three miles south of Fruitville Road. The southern boundary of Palmer Farms extends west along Bee Ridge Road all the way to modern Honoré Avenue. From that intersection, the western boundary runs north three miles to rejoin Fruitville Road. Turning left on Fruitville for a short distance back to Richardson completes the circuit. Today, thousands of people live on what was once Palmer Farms, and Interstate 75 bisects it north and south. Part of the "muck lands" have been restored in recent years, both to aid flood control and to create a large bird sanctuary.

Long before a single settler purchased one of the roughly 10- or 20-acre lots at Palmer Farms, the Palmer brothers, their uncle Adrian Honoré, and their corporate managers engaged in

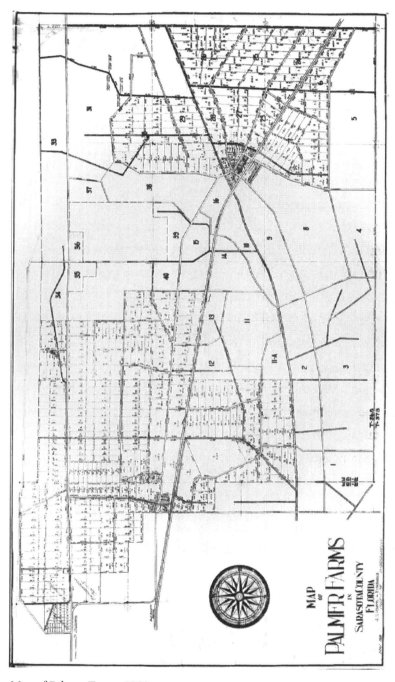

Map of Palmer Farms, 1929. *By permission of the Sarasota County Historical Resources.*

detailed planning for the development of the area. Guided by their earlier experience with Bee Ridge Farms and Osprey Farms, they projected hefty investments in roads as well as irrigation and drainage projects. They intended to create an experimental farm and purchase modern farm equipment. They would set up cooperative organizations to seek out the best scientific advice and to help farmers succeed. In addition, they would saturate the nation in advertisements to attract settlers.

The first steps in establishing Palmer Farms took place in the middle 1920s. In 1924 a second railroad line, the Atlantic Coast Line, extended its reach to Sarasota and immediately built short extensions to Ringling Brothers Circus winter grounds off Beneva Road near Fruitville Road and to the Payne Terminal on Sarasota Bay. Between 1924 and 1926 the Tampa Southern Line, a subsidiary of the Atlantic Coast Line, also completed a 41-mile extension from Sarasota east to Fort Ogden, not far from the town of Arcadia. The railroad and the Palmers must have struck a bargain, because the new extension ran through the site of Palmer Farms. One of its first stops was at Packinghouse Road, where packing plants to process vegetables for shipment would soon be built. At that location the railroad company constructed a system of rail interconnections called Belspur, where long lines of refrigerated boxcars stood beside the packinghouses for loading. Engines then pulled the cars either back to Sarasota and then north to Tampa and beyond, or east to Fort Ogden where the extension joined an Atlantic Coast Line route running south to Fort Myers or north to New York, Philadelphia, and Boston. Either direction brought Palmer Farms produce to the entire eastern half of the United States and even to Canada. Just as Bertha had succeeded in doing with the Seaboard Air Line Railroad, her sons had now assured themselves of easy access to rail transportation and swift delivery of agricultural products to Northern markets.

There was yet more to this railroad deal. The Tampa Southern Line ran southeast through the entire Palmer Farms tract, following the line of Palmer Road. There was even a station planned for a new town, Palmerville, to be located several miles east of Packinghouse Road. Presumably, the Palmer Florida Company intended the town to play the same role as the town of Bee Ridge did for Bee Ridge Farms—a place to serve farmer's needs, act as a civic and social center, and provide accommodations for visitors interested in purchasing Palmer land. However, Palmerville never entirely fulfilled that vision. The Palmers did construct a packinghouse near the site that was even larger and better equipped than the Belspur facility, and the railroad company did erect the Palmerville station. The Palmers also laid out a series of one-acre lots south of the town for celery seedbeds. But only a few farmers appear to have purchased land in Palmerville, and there is little evidence of commercial buildings or a hotel. After leaving Palmer Farms, the Tampa Southern Line crossed the Myakka River and passed through Meadowsweet Pastures, now owned by Adrian C. Honoré. There the railroad built another station called Honoré. This arrangement benefited Adrian by making it easier for him to ship his cattle.[13]

Even as the Palmers worked on transportation issues, they had to confront the drainage problem that affected so much of the proposed Palmer Farms area. In 1923, the Palmers sought state approval for the creation of the Sarasota-Fruitville Drainage District, just as they had already done for the Hyde Park area. The state approved the district in 1925 at the height of the Florida land boom. In Sarasota, as elsewhere in the state at this time, fortunes were made and lost in a few days or weeks as land speculation reached fevered proportions. As the *Cotton States Review* said, Florida was no longer the playground of the idle rich, "but the main objective of thousands of new settlers in the greatest rush for farmlands the World Has Ever Known." The Palmers undoubtedly counted on this land hunger to stimulate sales at Palmer Farms.[14]

The Sarasota-Fruitville Drainage District covered more than just the 8,000-acre Palmer Farms area. In January of 1925 the Palmers announced that the district would include a far larger area of some 26,000 acres. The district officials, almost all Palmer employees, soon hired J. G. Kimmel of Arcadia as chief engineer for the drainage project. After Kimmel completed his evaluation of the topography and soils of the lands in the district, the drainage district board signed a contract with his firm to construct a drainage system at an estimated cost of $789,000. The Palmers expected to complete the work in 20 months. They also predicted that over 10,000 people would move to Palmer Farms, and that new towns would grow up along the railroad line.[15]

The preparation of the land at Palmer Farms was a long process. A vast system of canals and ditches had to be dug. Earlier at Bee Ridge, large groups of black workers handled this task. At Palmer Farms, machinery took over much of the heavy work. The first goal was to excavate a system of main canals that carried great amounts of water away from Palmer Farms and into Philippi Creek during the rainy season. Kimmel's crews had to dredge the creek itself to facilitate the flow. Mechanical shovels did most of the digging. In the Camp Sawgrass area, however, Kimmel mounted the shovels on barges to keep them from sinking into the mud. After finishing the main canals, Kimmel's men began work on a system of secondary or feeder channels that crisscrossed the entire area. Finally, the laborers constructed a system of small canals on every 10- and 20-acre lot that connected to the larger system. These small canals allowed a farmer to regulate the amount of water entering or leaving his property. In the rainy season, the farmer kept his gates open to remove excess water, but in the dry season when water was scarce, the farmer closed the gates to retain water near his fields. However, effective drainage did not guarantee bountiful crops. As the Palmers had learned at Bee Ridge Farms, agriculture could not flourish without an equally effective irrigation system. Once more the Palmers undertook a program of drilling artesian wells strategically located to serve all of Palmer Farms. Thus, as at Bee Ridge Farms and Osprey Farms, farmers at Palmer Farms knew that under reasonably normal conditions they would have neither too much nor too little water to raise their crops.[16]

The most difficult area to work in was the muck lands. Even after being drained, the land was unstable and filled with alligator holes. Thanks to Ed Ayers, adaptations to Ford tractors permitted them to drive across the muck lands without sinking into the soft soil. These were known as "muckmobiles"—tractors modified to use traction belts much like a bulldozer or military tank. The muckmobiles made possible the building of roads and drainage ditches on the rich but very muddy soil. After reviewing the progress as well as what was planned for the future, the newspaper *This Week in Sarasota* called Palmer Farms "the most notable achievement in this county in all history."[17]

By 1926 the Palmer Farms project had made substantial progress. The time had come to implement another idea first tested at Bee Ridge Farms. Ed Ayers, the man who helped secure the success of the Hyde Park grove, launched the Palmer experimental farm. His task was to determine scientifically not only what crops would grow in the different soils of Palmer Farms, but also to evaluate which of those crops would earn the farmers the greatest profit. Since Palmer Farms consisted of two kinds of soils, muck and sandy pine, Ayers divided his 80-acre parcel into two parts, each containing one of the two soil types. The modern location of these tracts is on the northeast and southwest corners of the intersection of Honoré and Fruitville Roads.[18]

As a scientific agricultural man should, Ed Ayers kept careful records on the results of his experiments. In 1930 he published a lengthy report on everything he had done over the prior four years. Ayers' work was important for several reasons. Because of his experiments, those buying land in Palmer Farms knew exactly what crops to grow, when to plant crops, what farm machinery to use, when to harvest crops, what dangers from plant diseases existed, and how much the crop would earn when marketed. This

Muckmobile in use in Palmer Farms.
By permission of the Sarasota County Historical Resources.

was enormously important information for any farmer, particularly one coming from the Northern states and unfamiliar with the peculiarities of agriculture in Florida. For example, Florida land could yield two or three crops a year, while Northern farms could usually count on one. Ayers' work informed newcomers about crop rotation; that is, what sequence of crops you should plant on a piece of land to yield a big profit but not exhaust the soil. Ayers and experts from the University of Florida Extension Service, who also worked at the experimental farm, educated newcomers about fertilizers, seeds, and many other matters essential to success. The experimental farm also served another purpose, as had its predecessor at Bee Ridge: It advertised what could be done with the land. Palmer sales representatives always took potential buyers to the experimental farm first, where they saw 80 acres of celery, tomatoes, potatoes, and many other vegetables, as well as citrus, berries, and grasses. Since these visitors usually came in the wintertime, it is easy to imagine their reac-

Ed L. Ayers, manager of the experimental farm at Palmer Farms, examining celery before shipment. *By permission of the Sarasota County Historical Resources.*

tion to this lush agricultural landscape in comparison to their snow-covered farms in the North.[19]

Ayers tested hundreds of plants at the experimental farm. He soon realized that the lighter soils that made up the bulk of Palmer Farms' land could grow a wide variety of vegetables and citrus. The muck lands, however, were uniquely suited to celery. Celery had been grown at Bee Ridge Farms and even at Bertha's Home Farm, but the soil at Palmer Farms was something special. Ayers compared it to muck soil from the Florida Everglades, which was of similar richness. However, he found that celery plant growth at the experimental farm compared poorly with celery grown in the Everglades. He discovered that the difference between the two soils was acidity. A change in the number of applications as well as type of fertilizer corrected the problem. With that, celery grown at Palmer Farms was on its way to becoming the most important crop cultivated in Sarasota County, even passing citrus in market value. Ayers continued to study celery at the experimental farm. Thanks to him, new farmers knew when to plant the celery seedlings for the two crops each

Entry to experimental farm at Palmer Farms. *By permission of the Sarasota County Historical Resources.*

year, and how to stagger the plantings so that the celery did not all mature at the same time. As a result, Palmer Farms farmers could stretch out the length of time for sales. Perhaps the biggest change made in celery growing at Palmer Farms was the switch from earlier types to Paschal celery, which was far easier to grow and harvest. Paschal seeds, however, had to be purchased abroad and thus were more costly.[20]

As important as Ed Ayers and the experimental farm were to the rise of the celery industry in Sarasota, there was another factor at work. The Palmers, as they had at Bee Ridge Farms, wisely sought help from farmers in the Sanford district of central Florida, which remained the largest celery producing area in the state. Sanford farmers had been growing celery since the 1880s. In 1927 the Palmers persuaded Tom and John Bell, who grew and processed celery for market, to relocate from Sanford to Fruit-

Cutting celery at Palmer experimental farms, 1929.
Photo by Ed L. Ayers. By permission of the Sarasota County Historical Resources.

ville and Palmer Farms. The brothers purchased 100 acres for $13,500 and agreed to build and operate a packinghouse for the Palmers on what is now Packinghouse Road. The idea was that the Bells would process and ship celery crops while the Palmer packinghouse handled the other fruit and vegetable crops grown at Palmer Farms. The Bells' packinghouse boasted the most modern equipment to wash the celery, crate it, and load it on boxcars and trucks. Before celery growing commenced in Fruitville, Florida ranked fourth among the states. Once the 1,400 or so acres of muck land used for celery growing at Palmer Farms became productive, Florida immediately rose to the number three spot.[21]

Other Sanford celery farmers followed the Bells to Palmer Farms, where they shared their knowledge and experience with new farmers who had neither. In time, the Bells expanded their investment by purchasing additional muck land. They also built a packinghouse of their own, located on Palmer Avenue but still

Dasheens, a form of taro, one of the experimental crops grown at Palmer Farms. Photo by Ed. L. Ayers. *By permission of the Sarasota County Historical Resources.*

very close to the railroad facilities at Belspur. Long after the Palmers had phased out their involvement in Palmer Farms, the Bells continued to grow and market celery there.[22]

By 1927 progress had accelerated at Palmer Farms. The infrastructure of railroad connections, road building, the experimental farm, and drainage and irrigation systems had been created. The vast acreage of Palmer Farms had been partially platted, much like a suburban subdivision. The 8,000 acres were divided into five sections, then subdivided into numerous subsections. Within these subsections there were hundreds of 10- and 20-acre farms. Palmerville was situated in the central area of Palmer Farms, with Palmer Road and the train tracks running through it. Here the Palmers laid out town lots for homes, as they did in the extreme northwestern section off Fruitville and Richardson Roads. The idea was that farmers would live in these residential areas and commute each day to work their farms. The Palmers put up for sale initially only 5,000 acres. They designated the remaining 3,000 acres for future development.[23]

With everything in place, the Palmers and R. K. Thompson, the manager of the Palmers' Florida operations, commenced sales activities. It appeared they had picked a very bad time. The collapse of the Florida land boom had already dimmed expectations for developing the Hyde Park tract. Now the Palmers were putting many thousands more acres on the market. There undoubtedly were a few queasy stomachs at the Palmer corporate headquarters on McAnsh Court in downtown Sarasota. However, there were other circumstances that gave the Palmers reason for hope. Nationally, the demand for farmland remained high, and Florida's year-round growing season and wonderful climate were strong attractions. As they had in the past, the Palmers offered generous payment terms and low interest rates. Farmers could pay off their debt from the proceeds of the crops they grew. Moreover, the Palmers had done everything possible to assure the economic success of those who invested in Palmer Farms property. Repeating their experience at Bee Ridge, the Palmers refused to sell to speculators and insisted that those who invested must make a long-term commitment to working the land and being part of the community. The Palmers benefitted from the good reputation the family had developed over the years. They gave good value for what they charged investors. This was important, as the end of the land boom left most Americans with a very low opinion of Florida land dealers, many of who connived to cheat people by every imaginable device.[24]

The Palmers also benefitted from the growing public interest in the huge and complicated project that was transforming 5,000 acres of sawgrass muck land and typical Florida scrubland into one of the great planned agricultural communities in the United States. Tourists in substantial numbers made the short drive from Sarasota to Fruitville to see the steam shovels, muckmobiles, railroad building crews, and tractors that were taming a wilderness. Visitors invariably stopped at the experimental farm to see the remarkable variety of agricultural products Ed Ayers grew. Once the first packinghouse opened, tourists clamored to watch its machinery in operation. When Ayers' men reaped the celery crop at the experimental farm, crowds came to watch them at work as well as the loading of crates of celery aboard the refrigerated rail cars lined up at Belspur along Packinghouse Road. Sarasota Chamber of Commerce publications listed Palmer Farms along with the Ringling Museum and the winter quarters of the circus as the top tourist attractions in the area and

Ad for Palmer Farms. *By permission of the Sarasota County Historical Resources.*

printed maps showing visitors how to get there. Thus, there was already considerable public interest in Palmer Farms even before the first land there went on the market.[25]

The marketing campaign to sell lots and farms at Palmer Farms opened early in 1927 with a major advertising brochure. It characterized the project as "the last word in the development of the famed back country of Florida." It went on to say every vegetable "known to man" could be raised profitably. The brochure mentioned other interesting places to visit in Sarasota including the Edson Keith home, the Stanley Field home, the Ringling Art Museum, and the Acacias, where Prince and Princess Cantacuzene lived. A second advertising brochure put out by the

Sarasota County Board of County Commissioners praised the Palmer Farms as "comprising one of the most complete farming developments in the South." Yet a third marketing piece put out by the Sarasota County Board of Trade asserted that the soil was so rich and productive on each ten-acre farm in Palmer Farms that it was "sufficient to support a family in affluence."[26]

In March of 1927 the Palmer Company began publishing its own ads in newspapers with the headline "Seeking a Farm? – There is one for you at Palmer Farms." The ad asserted that nowhere else could someone find such large crop yields and the highest profits "for the same investment." Moreover, the ad claimed that the soil was unsurpassed, as good as that in the Everglades. This meant that it required only minimum applications of fertilizer. The ad went on to say the tracts could be occupied immediately, and that "prices are reasonable and terms are liberal." It pledged that new farmers could count on expert assistance and aid in selling crops. Now was the time to buy and plant for the early vegetable season. If none of this attracted buyers, the ad concluded by calling to everyone's attention that the Palmers were also selling land in their Hyde Park grove. In St. Petersburg, Florida, the Palmer Company appointed C. M. Yerxa as the local sales representative. On March 16, 1927, Yerxa published a Palmer Farms ad in the *St. Petersburg Times*. He repeated much of what had appeared in the *Sarasota Herald*, but added several points. He stressed the role of the Manatee Growers Association in handling sales of agricultural products grown at Palmer Farms. He also talked about the quality of life. If you bought a small farm at Palmer Farms, you would live in a good home, drive on paved roads, and have access to electricity and telephones, good neighbors, and the many amenities of Sarasota, only four miles away. He offered to drive any interested customers to Sarasota himself to visit Palmer Farms.[27]

Frequent news stories on the progress at Palmer Farms supplemented the drumbeat of paid ads and brochures touting the enterprise. In middle April of 1927 Sarasota learned that the first commercial crops had been harvested, packed, and shipped. Celery grown at the experimental farm filled one and one-half rail cars. Ed Ayers also shipped the first potatoes grown at Palmer Farms. He explained that he got 165 bushels of potatoes per acre by applying 300 pounds of fertilizer. In late May the Palmer Florida Company told local newspapers that Palmer Farms was now shipping melons and tomatoes grown at the experimental farm. The company said it would have shipped carloads of melons sooner, but the local demand was so high that only now did it have a surplus to send north.[28]

In late July, for the first time, the Palmer Florida Company seized on celery as the centerpiece of its marketing strategy. It may be that its earlier small shipment of celery had fared much better in the marketplace than anticipated, but whatever the cause, celery now began to emerge as the featured crop at Palmer Farms. "Celery! Celery! Celery!" screamed the headline of one Palmer ad, adding, "Celery is Scarce and Prices are High!" The ad stressed the high quality of the muck soil at Palmer Farms, the rail connections, and the ability to grow two celery crops a year.[29]

A month later the Palmers stepped up their marketing campaign by inviting city and county officials and representatives of the Chamber of Commerce for a luncheon at Palmer Farms and a tour of the facilities. The reason for this session was to brief these leaders on a huge national advertising campaign to promote land sales but at the same time portray Sarasota as a great place to live.

The company showed the visitors something unusual in advertising at the time: a movie it had produced, covering all aspects of the Palmer Farms operation. The film also featured many scenes of Sarasota attractions. The movie had just been released nationally and already generated numerous inquiries about buying land at Palmer Farms. Later the Palmers re-edited this film to show recent developments. The new version premiered at the Edwards Theater in downtown Sarasota. By the end of the summer the Palmer Company had sold $135,000 worth of land at Palmer Farms. This was a very good start, indeed, for Honoré and Potter Palmer II.[30]

While many investors in property at Palmer Farms had agricultural experience, others possessed little or no knowledge of farming but grasped the chance to own a farm in the Palmer agricultural development. This had been true at Bee Ridge Farms earlier, where the back-to-the-land movement had motivated many purchasers. Similar sentiments may have influenced some Palmer Farms investors, but according to newspaper reports, a great many people simply wanted to acquire choice land at bargain prices while it was still available. William Stockbridge, for example, made $65,000 in 1928 on his first crop of celery grown on 49 acres at Palmer Farms. Stockbridge, a lawyer, visited his sister in Sarasota in 1927 in an effort to improve his health. He and his wife decided to relocate permanently and bought land from the Palmers. He hired an experienced man to work his farm and soon added another 65 acres. His son, a banker in New York, quit his position, moved to Sarasota, and managed his father's agricultural property. He also joined the Palmer Florida Company, working under Ayers at the experimental farm, where he learned about all aspects of farming. He achieved success in both positions. Not all who bought land at Palmer Farms intended to become full-time residents of Sarasota County. Some, like the Amish and Mennonites, were seasonal farmers who came South during the winter to continue their agricultural pursuits while their Northern property was covered in snow.[31]

As at Bee Ridge Farms, the Palmers strongly supported cooperative organizations that enhanced the ability of Palmer Farms growers to pack, ship, and market their crops. Most of these farmers joined the Palmer Farms Growers Association, which replaced the Manatee Growers Association in handling these functions. This organization became the largest farmers' cooperative in Florida at the time. By 1930 the Bell Brothers had split with the Palmers and emerged as the biggest celery producers and shippers at Palmer Farms. They managed their own packinghouse and installed a telegraph line from downtown Sarasota to their office at Belspur, which allowed them in a timely manner to identify the best markets for their celery.[32]

The growth of Palmer Farms in the late 1920s and early 1930s was remarkable. Farmers shipped out over $2 million worth of

Farm workers at Palmer Farms. *By permission of the Sarasota County Historical Resources.*

celery and other vegetables each year, and yet only a portion of Palmer Farms had been cultivated. The *Sarasota Herald* described the agricultural community as a "substantial settlement of happy and prosperous farmers" that "was destined to grow." The muck land section of Palmer Farms where the celery grew attracted the most attention from investors as news spread of the high prices paid in Northern markets. In April of 1929 the Palmer Florida Company announced that only a few hundred acres of the original 2,000 acres of muck land offered for sale remained available. One reason for the high profits earned by Palmer Farms, besides good soil, sophisticated marketing, and the power of cooperative associations, was technology that kept labor costs down. Lutz Johnson, head of the Palmer Farms Growers Association, emphasized this point. Johnson, who had experience growing cotton in Louisiana, cited the importance of spraying and fertilizing machines in achieving both high efficiency and a reduction of labor costs. He quoted Joseph Weld, who said that labor expenses at his Northern farm were double those at his property in Palmer Farms. One great advantage enjoyed by Palmer Farms growers related to the fact that their land rarely lay idle. Muck land celery farmers could count on two crops per year. Once the celery crops shipped, the farmer could raise other vegetables in the same soil. Thanks to Ed Ayers and the experimental farm, the growers knew exactly which vegetable crops would grow best and bring in the highest profit.[33]

The obvious success of Palmer Farms began to draw attention from the leaders of Florida as well as national coverage. In March 1929 Florida Governor Doyle E. Carlton visited Palmer Farms and toured the facilities, proclaiming the area to be "the outstanding agricultural development in America." He praised the Palmers for not acting "precipitously" as had other corporations. They obtained the best engineers to build their irrigation and water management systems. They sought out and used the best scientific information on agriculture, and they spent years planning and preparing before they offered a single acre for sale. This gubernatorial praise undoubtedly helped publicize Palmer Farms. A far more significant endorsement appeared in an article by B. C. Forbes, economics writer for the Hearst newspaper chain and editor of his own magazine on economic news. An influential man with the business and financial communities, Forbes and his opinions appeared in hundreds of papers throughout the United States, reaching an estimated 25 million readers. Forbes had visited Sarasota and singled out Palmer Farms as well as the Ringling Museum for praise. Forbes called the agricultural developments around Sarasota "of most basic importance." He was particularly interested in how the Palmers attracted investors to Palmer Farms by offering easy payment plans. The idea, he noted, was to get "capable farmers" on the land who would pay off their debt from the income earned on the sale of their crops. After a mere two years, "amazing results have been achieved in vegetable production and profits." Forbes' article, plus the national advertising campaign, including the movie, reached most American homes, and the results became evident in increased sales of farms.[34]

Honoré and Potter Palmer II had to be concerned about the events of Black Thursday, October 24, 1929, when a hugely inflated stock market tumbled 16 percent in value in just one day. The bad economic news just kept coming. Within ten weeks, over 50 percent of the value of stocks listed on the New York Stock Exchange had evaporated. The Great Depression would not be far behind. Florida had already gone into its own economic depression in 1927 at the end of the land boom. Now it and the rest of the country plunged into the greatest economic catastrophe in American history, one that would not end for more than a decade and would lead to the greatest war in world history.[35]

Despite the bad economic news in the months just after the stock market crash, the Palmer brothers continued with success to develop Palmer Farms. On December 4, 1930, the Palmers announced that three large groups of farmers interested in purchasing land would soon arrive in Sarasota. The first group of 125 farmers from New England would arrive on January 27 aboard the Seaboard Air Line Railroad. They would be followed on February 9 by 200 farmers from Pennsylvania, also travelling on the Seaboard line. A third group of 150 Indiana farmers planned to arrive on February 5 aboard the Atlantic Coast Railway for a one-day stay. All three groups benefitted from discount tickets provided by the Palmer Florida Company. The first two groups that were staying for several days had similar itineraries. Besides Palmer Farms, the Palmer Florida Company wanted them to see several other attractions in Sarasota, including the Ringling Museum, the circus winter quarters, and Lido Beach. From their Bee Ridge Farms experience, the Palmers had learned that it was far easier to sell farm property inland to people if they found other attractive reasons to become part of the Sarasota community.[36]

Palmer Farms prospered into the 1930s despite the increasingly bleak economic circumstances. By 1935, one fourth of all Floridians relied on some form of welfare. A fruit fly infestation wiped out much of Florida's citrus production in the early 1930s. The epic migration of blacks from the South to the North that gathered momentum in the 1930s reduced the agricultural labor supply. Agriculture ranked as the most important part of the Florida economy, and it suffered greatly in the darkest days of the Depression. Bank collapses and certain federal policies prior to the New Deal reduced the supply of money and credit that farmers needed to operate their farms and pay off their debts and taxes. Farmers and economists both identified low prices for agricultural products as the core of the problem. Farmers tried to accommodate by increasing production and sales of crops. Of course, this strategy merely aggravated the problem of crop surpluses that further depressed prices. Not until Congress passed the Agricultural Adjustment Act of 1933, which offered farmers subsidies in return for reduced production, was any meaningful effort made to rationalize the imbalance between supply and demand.[37]

The Palmers could not escape all the consequences of America's economic collapse, but to a remarkable degree they did avoid serious losses in their Palmer Farms project. They were able to do this for several reasons. First, the Palmers had "deep pockets" and therefore possessed the financial resources to weather hard times. Moreover, their wealth was largely tied up in land rather than stocks and bonds. Another factor was that they often acted in the role of bankers with regard to those who invested in Palmer Farms. Many of the land buyers paid the Palmers a down payment on each acre they purchased and then paid the remainder over seven years. The Palmers offered low interest rates. This system kept financial transactions "in house" and out of the hands of possibly irresponsible or corrupt bankers. When the investors could not repay their debts to the Palmers, the brothers moved legally to reclaim the land. Yet another advantage for the Palmers had to do with the rich muck lands that sustained the main crop, celery. Because of the muck, celery crops at Palmer Farms were much larger than those grown in other types of soils. This efficiency in production increased because of modern machinery, easy access to transportation, and superbly engineered drainage and irrigation systems. The farms at Palmer Farms were incredibly small yet incredibly productive thanks to the Palmers' attention to building infrastructure and the cooperative philosophy that underlay the Palmer Farms operation.[38]

In late January of 1932, the *Sarasota Herald* explained the process of harvesting, processing, and packing celery. By then the thousands of celery seedlings planted a few months earlier had matured. After harvesting, farmers moved the celery quickly to the washing and packinghouse, where machines stripped and washed the stalks. These were then precooled using a system installed a year earlier. Precooling before loading the celery on refrigerated rail cars or trucks lengthened the time the crop could be marketed to consumers, thereby adding 15¢ to the value of every crate of celery shipped north. Each crate earned around $2.60 by the early 1930s. About 1,500 rail cars and uncounted numbers of trailer trucks carried Palmer Farms celery and other agricultural products north each year. In the depth of the Depression, hundreds of men were employed cutting celery, planting a new crop, and laboring in the packinghouse. The payroll for the farm workers alone reached $15,000 a week in harvest season. The Palmer Florida Company and its Palmer Farms operation became the largest employer in Sarasota County.[39]

Palmer Farms in 1932 had also become the second largest celery producer in Florida next to Sanford. Dozens of types of other vegetables also grew at Palmer Farms and profitably sold in the North. Strawberries, too, emerged as an important cash crop. Bertha Palmer had been one of the founders of the Sarasota Strawberry Association, and the fruit had been widely grown in Bee Ridge. With technical improvements in methods of processing and shipping, strawberries now became an increasingly popular crop in Palmer Farms. In the rich soil, growers could raise crops of strawberries that filled 48 crates per acre. Each crate sold for $3.60, and each acre yielded a gross return of $168. After deductions for fertilizer, labor, packing, and shipping, the farmer netted $127.60 per acre, not an insignificant amount in Depression-era America.

However, celery always remained the principal product of Palmer Farms. Indeed, the *Sarasota Herald* headline on page one of the May 18, 1943, issue boasted that Sarasota had shipped 1,777 railroad cars filled with Paschal celery. Of this number, Palmer Farms accounted for 1,179 cars during the winter and spring growing seasons. The story said the Palmer Packinghouse had set a world record by washing, packing, and precooling more cars of celery during a season than any other celery packinghouse anywhere on the globe. The paper added that major shipments of Sarasota celery had gone to Houston, Denver, Duluth, Detroit, Buffalo, and Portland, Maine. Even by the early 1930s, B. W. Powell, who managed all Palmer interests in Sarasota, claimed that Palmer Farms celery reached 90 percent of the nation's population.[40]

Powell also tried to estimate the economic impact of the Palmer Farms' celery operations on Sarasota. He asserted that in 1932, celery growing alone pumped $600,000 annually into the local economy. He chose to discuss the number of small businesses in the area that operated at a profit as a result. His list included ten grocery stores, seven meat markets, four drug stores, three restaurants, three clothing and department stores, four gas and oil stations, one garage, one hardware store, and numerous specialty stores. Further, he asserted that this infusion of cash paid for a large percentage of the costs of the public schools. Powell noted that labor costs at Palmer Farms for the nine-month-long growing season reached $500,000 each year and supported between 600 and 800 workers. Since the total population of Sarasota County was only 12,000 people, the Palmers accounted for a substantial portion of the labor force.[41]

Powell contrasted what private capital had done to sustain Sarasota's economy with what was happening in the rest of the United States:

> From all sides we hear of economic distress, industries in strained circumstances, world-wide unemployment, grain surpluses and low prices, and statesmen advocating many measures of relief. This cannot be said of Sarasota and its farming industry. The farmers of the Palmer Farms development, concentrating on the growing of more and fancier celery and more luscious strawberries, have hit depression for a row of field goats.

Powell identified specialization in growing top-quality products as the chief reason Palmer Farms had flourished. As a result, the farmers themselves earned large profits and the entire community benefitted.[42]

The deteriorating situation in Sarasota in the 1930s underlined the economic importance of Palmer Farms. High unemployment led to a dramatic fall in tax receipts. The city of Sarasota could not even keep the Ringling Causeway, which lead to the barrier islands, in repair, forcing a temporary closure. There was little new building activity and several of the city's most important structures, such as the Mira Mar Hotel, faced foreclosure and auction. John Ringling's own home, Cà d'Zan, was nearly auctioned off. With his death in 1936, the proceedings were halted. Ads in the *Sarasota Herald* begged readers to spend their money in Sarasota for the good of the community. Federal economic recovery funds did help the city when they were used to build the Civic Auditorium and Bayfront Park in 1937–38 and the Lido Beach Casino in 1938. In addition, the Works Progress Administration constructed the Sarasota-Manatee Airport between 1938 and 1940. Together with many smaller projects, the federal money flowing to Sarasota city and county provided hundreds of badly needed jobs. Without Palmer Farms, however, the economic situation in Sarasota County would have been far worse.[43]

The tourism industry also helped sustain Sarasota. Although the numbers of visitors dropped at the beginning of 1932, before long a new wave of sun seekers flooded into Sarasota and the rest of Florida. Many belonged to an organization known as the Tin Can Tourists of America. According to the history on the website of the organization, the name refers to the Model T Fords (Tin Lizzies) they drove, the canned food they brought with them, or the tin cans they hung on the radiator caps of the cars as a distress signal. Tin Can Tourists had first appeared in Sarasota around 1918. They were hardly members of the wealthy elite that Bertha Palmer and Henry Flagler had tried to entice to Florida in an earlier age. They often bunked in their cars or in tents. Rich or not, the Tin Can Tourists made highly desirable guests during the Depression, for they needed goods and services provided by local businesses. Many towns and cities set aside special areas for camping, as did Sarasota along the bayfront. Playgrounds, tennis courts, and other amenities gave the tourists and their children something to do. Since 1927 Palmer Farms had ranked as one of Sarasota's top tourist attractions, along with the circus winter quarters, the John and Mabel Ringling Museum, and area beaches and fishing locales. A lengthy article published by the *Sarasota Herald* in October of 1932 observed that these sites were still the most popular. Tourists, the paper said, could inspect at Palmer Farms seemingly endless plots of land where celery and many other crops grew, see the operations of the packinghouse, and watch the loading of long lines of rail cars that took Palmer Farms produce "to nearly every state in the nation." The story also mentioned that the Hyde Park grove owned by the Palmers was another favorite tourist stop.[44]

A year later, the *Herald* again praised Palmer Farms as a tourist attraction. It asserted that Palmer Farms had fully matured as a commercial operation whose ever-expanding crops of celery, strawberries, and vegetables ultimately made their way to "millions of homes in the United States." Visitors could easily see that the huge scope of agricultural operations at Palmer Farms required considerable organizational skill to supervise the planting of land and the cultivation, cutting, grading washing, and shipping of crops. The most important crop, of course, was celery. The Palmer Farms Growers Cooperative Association principally controlled celery output. Individual farmers owned their own land at Palmer Farms and raised their crops, which they marketed through the growers association or some similar organization. It took capable management to make all the different aspects of raising, processing, selling, and shipping work smoothly and efficiently to produce the highest profits possible. The same was true of the Palmer-controlled Sarasota-Fruitville Drainage District, which had the task of maintaining the sprawling system of canals, ditches, and artesian wells upon which the entire operation depended. Too much or too little water could bring disaster. The paper urged tourists to observe the agricultural, organizational, and engineering triumph that was Palmer Farms, which had propelled Sarasota County into the fifth most important celery-producing county in the entire country.[45]

The Palmers, having sold most of the land in Palmer Farms, withdrew from active leadership of the enterprise during the 1930s, leaving management of the packinghouses they owned to the Palmer Farms Growers Cooperative Association. At its peak in the mid-1940s, Palmer Farms had between 40 and 50 growers raising celery on approximately 1,400 acres of muck land, with each acre producing between 1,000 and 1,200 crates of celery twice a year. Celery remained the most profitable crop in Sarasota County, and many considered the Palmer Farms Growers Cooperative Association the most successful organization of its sort in the state. Nevertheless, circumstances began to change in 1946 and 1947, as many of the largest celery growers quit the original Palmer cooperative and formed their own, the Sarasota Growers and Shippers Cooperative Association, which lasted until 1972. The original Palmer organization ended its existence in 1959. In general, the Florida celery industry went into decline, with fewer and fewer growers but much larger farms. Periods of bad weather, plant diseases, infighting among growers, and stiff competition challenged the celery farmers. In Sarasota, the number of celery farmers fell from between 40 and 50 to only one in 1975. In that year, Florida could identify a mere 18 celery growers in the entire state, most located in the Everglades, south and southeast of Okeechobee. Some celery may have been grown at Palmer Farms as late as 1994.[46]

By the late 1980s and early 1990s Sarasota County identified a need to restore the muck lands at Palmer Farms to their pre-agricultural role as a natural water storage area in order to reduce the danger of flooding along Philippi Creek. Known as the Celery Fields Regional Storm Water Facility Expansion Project, the plan recommended restoring the wetlands, creating passive recreation opportunities, and providing treatment for 3,600 acres of storm water runoff. Before any of that could happen, some 2.3 million cubic yards of soil contaminated by fertilizers containing arsenic had to be relocated. The soil was used to erect a 70-foot-high mound that was then covered with two feet of clean dirt. The whole project, costing $10.8 million, opened in 2013, thus giving Sarasota County a grand new 360-acre park. The Sarasota Audubon Society manages a large bird sanctuary on the site with special provisions for bird watching.[47]

Standing on the top of the man-made mound today, visitors can see much of the 8,000 acres that made up Palmer Farms. At least some of the canals built by the Palmers are still in place and functioning. To the west are the old muck land areas where the celery was grown. Just beyond Interstate 75 is the site of the original packinghouses where Belspur was located, although all the railroad tracks have long since been taken up. To the north and west are farms, many of them appearing to be on 10- or 20-acre lots. To the south and southeast, extending far beyond the line of sight, are hundreds of homes and condominiums. Even today, houses for sale are sometimes located by referring to one of the five subunits of Palmer Farms. The scene is peaceful and gives little hint that this was once one of the most significant agricultural communities in Florida, if not the United States—one that attracted both tourists and new permanent residents, and also generated employment, profits, and advertising that helped keep Sarasota afloat in the depths of the Depression. Once more, the Palmer family had shown itself to be one of the Sarasota's most important assets. As the *Sarasota Herald* commented, the "contribution of the Palmer Estate to the development of Sarasota County is inestimable." And the Palmers were not yet done.[48]

Notes for Chapter Six

1. LaHurd, *Sarasota*, 39; William W. Rogers, "The Paradoxical 1920s," in Michael Gannon (ed.), *The History of Florida* (Gainesville: University Press of Florida, 1996), 299–305; William Frazer and John L. Guthrie, Jr., *The Florida Land Boom: Speculation, Money, and the Banks* (Westport, CT: Quorum Books, 1995), 2–7; Nick Wynne and Richard Moorhead, *Paradise for Sale: Florida's Booms and Busts* (Charleston and London: The History Press, 2010), 50–57.

2. LaHurd, *Sarasota*, 41–45; Weeks, *Ringling*, 81–158; Frazer and Guthrie, *Florida Land Boom*, 97.

3. LaHurd, *Sarasota*, 33–36; *New York Times*, July 7, 1926; Matthews, *Venice: Journey from Horse and Chaise*, 263.

4. Bertha Honoré Palmer's will, Bertha H. Palmer Papers, Vol. V, Sarasota County Historical Resources; Ross, *Silhouette in Diamonds*, 251–252; Pauline Palmer to Mrs. Herman Kohlsaat, July 11, 1920, in Dwight, *Letters of Pauline Palmer*, 170.

5. Matthews, *Venice*, 134; Ross, *Silhouette in Diamonds*, 224; *St. Petersburg Daily News*, Dec. 4, 1919; *New York Times*, July 7, 1926.

6. *New York Times*, March 26, 1955.

7. *St. Petersburg Daily Times*, Dec. 4, 1919.

8. Ibid.

9. Bulletin 67, New Series, Feb., 1931, "Drainage Districts of Florida," compiled by F. E. Bayless Jr., Land Office, Department of Agriculture, State of Florida, 7; Esthus, *History of Agriculture*, 39.

10. *This Week in Sarasota*, June 3, 1926, Sarasota County Historical Resources; LaHurd, *Sarasota*, 39-

11. Esthus, *History of Agriculture*, 39; *Sarasota Herald-Tribune*, October 30, 1938 and November 12, 1939.

12. *This Week in Sarasota*, Jan. 8, 1925.

13. Elmer G. Sulzer, *Ghost Railroads of Sarasota County*, Sarasota County Historical Commission, 1971, 8-19: Esthus, *History of Agriculture*, 151; *Sarasota Herald*, Oct. 2, 1927, and March 29, 1929; *St. Petersburg Times*, Nov. 8, 1925.

14. Bulletin 67, New Series, Feb., 1931, "Drainage Districts of Florida," compiled by F. E. Bayless Jr., Land Officer, Department of Agriculture, State of Florida, 12; Quote from *Cotton States Review* in *This Week in Sarasota*, April 8, 1926.

15. Esthus, *History of Agriculture*, 27; *This Week in Sarasota*, Jan. 8, 1925.

16. *This Week in Sarasota*, Jan. 8, 1925; Ed Ayers, "General Report on Palmer Experimental Farms," typescript, 1930, Sarasota County Historical Resources. Pages unnumbered.

17. Ayers, "General Report"; *This Week in Sarasota*, Oct. 28, 1926.

18. *This Week in Sarasota*, Oct. 28, 1926.

19. Ayers, "General Report."

20. Ibid., *Sarasota Herald*, Dec. 30, 1926.

21. Ayers, "General Report"; *Sarasota Herald*, Aug. 17, 1927; Esthus, *History of Agriculture*, 29, 151.

22. Esthus, *History of Agriculture*, 29, 148; *Sarasota Herald*, Oct. 21, 1927.

23. Map of Palmer Farms, 1929, Sarasota County Historical Resources; Palmer Farms, legal paper describing units 1, 2, and 3 in terms of number of lots and monetary value, Bertha Palmer Family Research Collection, undated, Chicago History Museum.

24. *Sarasota Herald*, Oct. 21, 1927, and March 15, 1928.

25. Ibid., April 10, 1927; Ad brochure, "Sarasota County Florida," issued by Sarasota County Chamber of Commerce, 1927.

26. Ad for Sarasota (1927) put out by Sarasota Board of County Commissioners and distributed by the Chamber of Commerce; Ad brochure (1917) issued by Sarasota County Chamber of Commerce, Sarasota County Historical Resources.

27. *Sarasota Herald*, March 6, 1927; *St. Petersburg Times*, March 16, 1927.

28. *Sarasota Herald*, April 10 and May 25, 1927.

29. *This Week in Sarasota*, July 30, 1927.

30. *Sarasota Herald*, Aug. 8, 19; Oct. 2, 1927; and Feb. 14, 1928.

31. Ibid., Dec. 7, 1937, "Mennonites Have Colony"; *This Week in Sarasota*, April 8, 1926; Ann Shank, Sarasota County Historian, "Amish and Mennonite Communities," reissued in 2015 on the internet site "Sarasota Alive."

32. *St. Petersburg Times*, March 16, 1927; *Sarasota Herald*, March 12, 1929.

33. *Sarasota Herald*, March 12 and March 29, 1929.

34. Ibid., March 12 and 31, 1929.

35. LaHurd, *Sarasota*, 54–55; Grismer, *Story of Sarasota*, 243–245.

36. *Sarasota Herald*, Dec. 4, 1930.

37. Ibid., March 31, 1929; Nick Wynne and Joseph Kneisch, *Florida and the Great Depression; Desperation and Defiance* (Charleston and London: The History Press, 2012), 63–68, 108.

38. William D. Rogers, "The Great Depression," in Michael Gannon (ed.,) *The History of Florida* (Gainesville: University Press of Florida, 1996), 325; *Sarasota Herald*, July 2, 1931.

39. *Sarasota Herald*, Jan. 31, 1932.

40. Ibid., April 5, 1929; March 1, 1931; and Jan. 31, 1932.

41. Ibid., May 1, 1932; in 1931 the Sarasota Chamber of Commerce criticized Palmer Farms for hiring some workers from outside the area. It urged the Palmers to hire only local people. See Ruthmary Bauer, "Sarasota: Hardship and Tourism in the 1930s," *The Florida Historical Quarterly* (Fall, 1997), 139.

42. *Sarasota Herald*, May 8, 1932.

43. LaHurd, *Sarasota*, 53–55; Grismer, *Story of Sarasota*, 243, 249; Weeks, *Ringling*, 231–255; Bauer, "Sarasota," 47.

44. LaHurd, *Sarasota*, 55–76; *Sarasota Herald*, Oct. 29, 1932. Bauer points out that tourism was Sarasota's biggest money generator in the 1930s and provided significant numbers of seasonal jobs. Bauer, "Sarasota," 143–145.

45. *Sarasota Herald*, Dec. 3, 1933.

46. George M. Talbot, "The Rise and Fall of the Florida Celery Industry," *Proceedings of the Florida State Horticultural Society*, Vol. 114, 2001, 278–279; Esthus, *History of Agriculture*, 28; *Sarasota Herald Tribune*, Oct. 15, 1997.

47. Final Project Report for Celery Fields Regional Stormwater Facility Phase 3 Expansion, April 2, 2014. Prepared by Florida Department of Environmental Protection by Stanley Consultants Inc. See Executive Summary.

48. *Sarasota Herald*, March 12, 1929.

CHAPTER SEVEN

The Empire Continues: Oil, a Bank, and Changing Family Fortunes

During the 1920s the Palmers successfully launched their Hyde Park grove and Palmer Farms initiatives. Before the decade ended, Honoré and Potter II expanded their economic horizon by competing in two areas that had little to do with their core business of buying, developing, and selling real estate: oil and banking. In this period some members of the family continued Bertha Palmer's tradition of supporting the community. But as the 1930s and 1940s passed, death and scandal weakened the family's leadership. Even so, the Palmers remained a very important part of the total community and its economy as the nation approached mid-century.

In 1927 Sarasota and its leaders confronted an unpleasant reality: the great Florida land boom had ended. Fueled by easy credit, greed, and a great deal of wishful thinking, the boom encouraged reckless speculation. A few amassed great fortunes in the real estate business, but many more lost everything. Subdivisions and even entire cities seemingly miraculously appeared during this era of excess. Residents abandoned many of these communities in the ensuing economic collapse. Venice, for example, lost most of its population, becoming a virtual ghost town. Sarasota avoided such extreme consequences of the speculative mania, but the city faced many problems. Some of its leading businessmen had taken on large debts to build great mansions, hotels, and resorts, believing that the good times would roll on indefinitely. The Palmer brothers had avoided this speculative trap by not assuming more debt than they could reasonably handle. They grounded their plans for Hyde Park and Palmer Farms in good business principles. The land they offered for sale had real value as agricultural production areas. The Palmers had enhanced that value with infrastructure investments, the implementation of cooperative ideas, and the production and market research carried on at the experimental farm. Moreover, they did not sell to speculators, insisting that investors actually work the land. Still, as it turned out, Honoré and Potter II could not resist the opportunity of making a quick fortune in the oil industry.[1]

Rich men in Sarasota such as Owen Burns, J. H. Lord, and, above all, the circus tycoon John Ringling saw oil production as the next great moneymaking opportunity, a way to rejuvenate their own fortunes as well as the local economy that was reeling from the excesses of land speculation. Ringling was already feeling the effects of rapid economic change that would eventually cost him everything, including the circus he loved so dearly, his art museum, his mansion, Cà d'Zan, and ultimately his health and his life. In 1926 Ringling did not have to look far to see evidence of his declining economic position. One of his greatest initiatives, the massive Ritz Carlton Hotel, located at the south end of Longboat Key, stood unfinished and abandoned. The circus tycoon had no funds to complete the project. Meant to serve the very richest visitors to Sarasota, the hotel never opened and ultimately fell to the wrecking ball. Ringling, therefore, had good reason to roll the dice on oil exploration. If it succeeded, his fortunes would change for the better. Many other entrepreneurs in Sarasota shared this sentiment, as they did not wish to lose all they had gained during the years of the boom.[2]

Oil in commercially exploitable quantities had first been discovered in 1859 in Titusville, Pennsylvania. Oil, and to some extent gas, joined coal in powering the Industrial Revolution in America. By the 1920s, California and Oklahoma led the nation in oil and gas production. The Palmers recognized this trend early in the century and purchased a natural gas drilling facility near Shreveport, Louisiana. Florida and other states where no oil had yet been found wanted to join the oil club and cash in on the energy bonanza. To achieve that goal the Florida state government offered a bounty of $50,000 to the first person or company that discovered commercially significant reserves of oil. As a result, a kind of oil fever gripped the Sunshine State, and in several locales such as Ocala, local investors organized companies to sink test wells.[3]

It is not entirely clear how John Ringling became involved in the great search for oil in Florida, but by late 1926 he decided to commit his energies to the challenge. Ringling actually knew a great deal about the oil business, as he owned several producing wells in Oklahoma. Although most of Ringling's land investments in Sarasota County involved the offshore keys, there was one important exception. He and his brother Charles, who lived in a grand mansion next door to Cà d'Zan, jointly bought

John Ringling, *by permission of the Sarasota County Historical Resources.*

66,000 acres of land southeast of Sarasota. The area was known as the Sugar Bowl for its association with a scheme to grow sugar cane. In January of 1927 the newspapers revealed that Ringling had hired Kenneth Hauer, a Miami oil man and president of the Biscayne Oil Company, to direct the oil project. He also brought in Charles Coulter, a well-known geologist, to examine the Sugar Bowl site and advise on the best plan to drill. Based on these experts' opinions, Ringling came to believe that significant amounts of oil would be found. At this point the circus magnate assembled a group of investors, including the Palmers, who agreed to fund the drilling of test wells.[4]

A few days later, on February 9, 1927, the newspapers announced that Kenneth Hauer would take operational control of the entire drilling project. Ringling, the Palmers, and others soon formed a company, the Community Oil Corporation, in which they held all the stock. The public soon learned that Hauer planned to erect four heavy California-type derricks at four locations selected by Professor Coulter in the Sugar Bowl.[5]

About this time, the publication *Southern Oil and Gas News* let the public know that "Sarasota is to be the scene of the greatest drilling yet seen in Florida." The story asserted that investors had snatched up 100,000 acres of gas and oil leases. The drilling, it said, could go as deep as 6,000 feet. A few days later news broke that Hauer had already shipped in three rail cars full of drilling machinery and that a sawmill had sent lumber to build the derricks, although the site for the first one remained a secret. On March 13, however, Hauer announced a grand event to celebrate the beginning of drilling. The location would be southeast of Sarasota along the new Tamiami Trail, and Rogers Hornsby, the superb second baseman currently in Sarasota for spring training with the New York Giants, would make an appearance. There would also be entertainment, free cigars and candy, and, of course, a few speeches. The event provided all that Ringling promised. He also brought in the Czechoslovak Band, which played at many events in and around Sarasota. Over 5,000 people drove to the site for a festive day. Hornsby broke a bottle of champagne over the drilling machinery, the crowd cheered, and the project was officially launched.[6]

The Community Oil Corporation derrick at Sugar Bowl drilling site.
By permission of Sarasota County Historical Resources.

The drilling went on for months. Citizens could follow the project in the paper or attend nightly briefings in Sarasota that summarized progress. Three crews worked the derrick so that it operated 24 hours a day. Hauer always said publically that oil drilling was a chancy business, but then he would quickly add that experts assured him that oil would be found in the Sugar Bowl area. He frequently placed ads in local papers urging people to invest small or large amounts in partial oil leases. In June, the well passed 1,200 feet and the local paper noted that unnamed gentlemen had come from Oklahoma to see what was happening at the test well. In July, a small quantity of oil "boiled from the well but nothing more." A few weeks later Hauer set off a small explosive charge at the bottom of the well, to no effect. The very last newspaper reference came in the August 4 edition of the *Sarasota Herald*. The drilling had reached 1,400 feet and found promising layers of rock and soil, but no oil. Professor Coulter strongly insisted oil would be found somewhere between 1,400 and 1,800 feet. Hauer said his crews would sink two more test wells shortly. He added that he and his assistants were so confident in eventual success that they were building houses for their families across the road from the first well. And that was that. No further reports appeared, and Hauer never found oil in the Sugar Bowl site. Many years later, in 1943, an oil firm claimed the $50,000 bounty from the state, but even that claim lacked verification. There was never an accounting of how much money the Sarasota investors put into the oil drilling effort, but estimates ranged from $45,000 to $100,000. It is also unknown how much of this cost the Palmers bore, although they could easily afford to pay whatever their portion totaled.[7]

The Palmer brothers' decision to enter the banking industry in Sarasota had far more importance than their dalliance with oil lands speculation. Both Honoré and Potter II had done what amounted to internships in Chicago banks after they graduated from Harvard, so they certainly knew about banking practices. In addition, Potter Palmer II had served for many years as a board member of Chicago's First National Bank. Despite all their experience, the Palmer brothers did not initiate the idea of opening a bank in Sarasota. Rather, Prince Michael Cantacuzene conceived the plan and sold it to the other members of the family. Cantacuzene involved himself in the Sarasota community far more than either Honoré or Potter II. He belonged to several local groups such as the Elks, the American Legion, and the Kiwanis Club, and played an active role each year in staging the Sarasota County Fair. In 1926 and 1927 he served as president of the fair's board of directors. A social man, he knew the businessmen and politicians who ran Sarasota. He lunched at the Plaza Hotel restaurant, where every working day he socialized with the city's leaders. Insiders knew that around Cantacuzene's table men of power discussed matters of civic and economic importance.[8]

Somewhere in his social interactions, the prince conceived the idea of the bank. By 1929 Sarasota had already gone through more than two years of deep recession. Business was slack, the city's existing banks lacked financial strength, and there was insufficient capital available to stimulate economic activity. The Palmers, on the other hand, possessed ample reserves. To at least some extent, the Palmer brothers needed strong local banks able to help some of their investors finance mortgages required to purchase Palmer properties. Cantacuzene would have known that the Ringling family controlled two of the existing banks in the city. John led the board of the Bank of Sarasota, while Charles owned the Ringling Bank and Trust Company. Since John steered mortgage money controlled by the Bank of Sarasota to buyers of property in his Ringling Isles project, Cantacuzene might have reasoned that a new bank owned by the Palmers could give them the same advantage in selling their land at Palmer Farms, Hyde Park grove, and elsewhere. In any case, he knew from his business friends that Sarasota needed a financially strong new bank and that there were profits to be made from its operations. Whatever he said to them, Cantacuzene convinced Honoré and Potter II to support his plan.[9]

Thus, on Saturday, March 20, 1929, a mere seven months before Black Thursday—October 24—and the beginning of the stock market crash, the Palmer National Bank and Trust Company opened its doors. For the moment, the new bank occupied the old quarters of the now defunct American National Bank at Palm Avenue and Main Street. Sarasota warmly welcomed the new institution. Local associations and businesses filled the newspapers with ads saluting the bank. The *Sarasota Herald* published a lengthy editorial on the importance of the Palmers' initiative that said in part:

> Coming at the present time the opening of the bank means much more than the mere addition of another financial institution. It is a further indication of the faith of Potter Palmer and Honoré Palmer in Sarasota and Sarasota County. With their vast holdings in this section and with their development of Palmer Farms they have done a wonderful work for the future of our city and county.

The editorial went on to say that "a great new day is dawning" because "there are now three strong banks" in the city, including John Ringling's Bank of Sarasota and his late brother Charles' Ringling Bank and Trust Company. As events would show, none of this proved to be true. The coming days would be great only in woe as the Ringling banks collapsed in the economic maelstrom. Prince Michael Cantacuzene received much praise from the *Herald* for his role in establishing the Palmer Bank. The editor noted that the Prince's "undaunted spirit, keen business judgement, and organizing ability" were key to the founding of the bank: "Prince Cantacuzene is a leader, a patron saint of Sarasota."[10]

The publication *This Week in Sarasota* also editorialized about the new bank, calling it a "compliment paid to our community by the Palmers" and "a fine expression of faith in the future." The paper saluted the Palmers for "their efficient and concentrated interests in developing their large farm land holdings into modern, up-to-date profitable farms owned and operated by a representative class of farmers who are numbered among our most substantial citizens." Because of the Palmers, Sarasota had taken a "dominant place in the agricultural development of Florida." Like the *Herald*, *This Week in Sarasota* singled out Prince Cantacuzene for praise: "To this versatile man is accorded much of the credit for the new banking enterprise of the Palmer interests." The paper described the prince, although a Russian and a titled aristocrat, "as the spirit of America itself."

In this same edition of *This Week in Sarasota* appeared the first ad for the Palmer National Bank and Trust Company. The ad said the new bank had capital of $100,000 and a $100,000 surplus. The Palmer brothers provided all the money and therefore owned all the stock. They appointed John B. Cleveland, formerly a banker and farmer in Kewanee, Illinois, as the president of the bank. Prince Cantacuzene served as vice president, while Potter Palmer II assumed the role of chairman of the board. Honoré served as one of the directors as did R. K. Thompson, who oversaw all Palmer operations in Florida. Other directors included Cantacuzene and C. P. Hoagland, an accountant and manager of the Sarasota office of the Palmer Florida Company. The bank affiliated itself with the Federal Reserve System. The first person to make a deposit in the bank was an old friend and business partner of the Palmers, J. H. Lord.[11]

Eight months after opening, the Palmer bank purchased Sarasota's first skyscraper, built in 1924 at Five Points, the very center of the city, where the defunct First Bank and Trust had been located. All Palmer operations in Sarasota now occupied space at this location, including Palmer Farms and the land sale office formerly at McAnsh Square. In July of 1930, the Palmer bank issued a report on the first year of operations. It showed that the bank had issued loans to the value of $177,165 and taken in deposits amounting to $765,201.12. Despite the deepening depression, the Palmer bank was doing quite well. At about the same time, the public relations-savvy Palmers published an ad thanking the citizens of Sarasota for supporting the institution. Each year the bank's published balance sheet showed significant increases in profits.[12]

The only time that the Palmer National Bank and Trust closed during the Great Depression was during President Franklin Roosevelt's banking holiday, declared after he took office in 1933. Between March 6 and March 10, the nation's banks closed in an effort to restore public trust in the banking system. The well-funded, competently run Palmer bank easily demonstrated

Palmer First Bank and Trust Company.
By permission of Sarasota County Historical Resources.

its solid financial base. The Ringling banks, however, did not fare as well. Within a year, both Ringling banks closed their doors. In the aftermath of these failures, patrons of John Ringling's Bank of Sarasota received slightly more than 18 cents for every dollar they had deposited. In the case of the Ringling Bank and Trust, Charles Ringling's widow, Edith, protected her husband's reputation by making each depositor financially whole at a personal cost of $200,000. The Palmer Bank was the only bank left operating in Sarasota. The Palmers now were not only the biggest employers in Sarasota County, but also the only local provider of loans and other banking services. Not even Bertha Palmer had been as essential to Sarasota as her two sons had become in the 1930s. The Palmer National Bank and Trust Company remained the oldest and largest banking institution in Sarasota for nearly 50 years, until 1975. It always served as a mainstay of the local economy.[13]

Members of the Palmer family affiliated with the bank throughout most of its history. After Potter II died in 1943, Honoré assumed the chairmanship of the board, a post he held until his death in 1964. Potter's youngest son, Gordon, also served on the board but died the same year as his uncle. Even in the bank's final years, two of the younger family members, Potter Palmer IV and Oakleigh B. Thorne, held appointments on the board. In 1971 the board reorganized the bank and placed it within a holding company, the Palmer Bank Corporation. By now the Palmer banking business had expanded, with new institutions established at St. Armand's Circle and Siesta Key. Prior to 1975 the Palmer Bank Company established other affiliated banking institutions in Naples, Fort Myers, Bradenton, South Gate, and on Beneva Road.

The 1970s proved a difficult time for banks in the United States as they struggled with a recession and soaring mortgage interest rates. The entire banking industry went through a period of mergers, as huge banking corporations bought out smaller community institutions. The Palmer Bank Corporation, now run by professional managers and with no direct leadership from the Palmer family, piled up debt, particularly in its wholly owned Coastal Mortgage Company. To raise funds, the Palmer Bank Corporation in 1972 offered nearly 263,000 shares of common stock for public purchase at $30 per share. However, the fortunes of the eight banks and Coastal Mortgage Company that made up the Palmer Bank Corporation continued to decline. By the middle of 1975 conditions compelled the corporation to take out $13 million dollars in loans from two New York banks, First National City and Bankers Trust. The Federal Deposit Insurance Corporation also advanced $10 million to the company.[14]

Despite these new resources, in late 1975 the Palmer Bank Corporation remained in difficult straits as its net worth declined. Moreover, the press reported that prosecutors had charged two former Palmer bank employees with swindling the institution of $485,000. Palmer Bank Corporation stockholders faced strong pressure from creditors and banking authorities to merge with the far larger Southeast Banking Company of Miami. On December 18, 1975, the stockholders met in Sarasota at the Van Wezel Performing Arts Hall. At that meeting they learned that the Palmer First National Bank and Trust Company had extended less than satisfactory loans that totaled three-and-a-half times its capital. Moreover, the bank had not complied with agreements made with the two New York banks that had extended it loans. The stockholders then approved the merger, which took effect in early 1976. Although the Palmer family had little to do with the bank after Honoré's and Gordon's deaths in 1964, remaining family members could not have been happy with this outcome. It was a sad ending for an institution that for decades had been a central pillar of Sarasota's economy. The bank and its landmark building at Five Points symbolized the power and influence of the Palmer family in Sarasota. In 1999 the old Palmer bank building was torn down.[15]

Between 1918 and 1950, each of the Palmers developed their own personal relationship with Sarasota. For most of them Sarasota remained a winter home. Almost all of them maintained their principal residence in Chicago or, as far as the women in the family were concerned, wherever their husbands pursued their careers. In addition, some of them maintained summer homes in various places across the United States. Potter Palmer II lived at The Oaks when he was in Sarasota, but he spent less and less time there as the years went by, despite the fact that he held the chairmanship of the Palmer bank board. In Chicago Potter was on the board of the First National Bank, with which the various Palmer corporations did extensive business. He also headed the Chicago Art Institute board and belonged to the elite men's clubs in the city, such as the Chicago Club, the Urban League Club, and the University Club. For a time, he and his family lived in the Castle, but they moved to a less ostentatious abode on nearby Astor Place. As a child he had spent many of his summers at Bar Harbor, Maine, and as an adult he and his family maintained a large estate there next to one owned by newspaper magnate Joseph Pulitzer. Potter also served as commodore of the Bar Harbor Yacht Club. When time permitted, he vacationed at his ranch in Santa Barbara, California. Late in his life he established another estate, Shore Acres, in Lake Forest, Illinois, which ultimately became the center of the Palmer family.[16]

Potter II had been involved in the planning and oversight of the many Palmer Florida operations, including the Sarasota-Venice Company, the Palmer Florida Company, Palmer Farms, and the Palmer bank. In 1925 he joined his brother Honoré in making a $5,000 gift to Sarasota Memorial Hospital in memory of their mother. They asked that the funds be used to purchase an x-ray machine. In 1934 Potter II and Honoré gave 9,300 acres of Palmer land near the old Meadowsweet Pastures to the State of Florida as part of a plan to create Myakka River State Park.

They made this gift also in memory of Bertha Palmer. Potter II was an important figure in Sarasota's history for over 35 years, but neither he nor his wife, Pauline Kohlsaat Palmer, developed tight connections to the community. In 1943 Potter died of heart problems at age 67 at Cottage Hospital in Santa Barbara, California. He was buried next to his parents in Graceland Cemetery in Chicago.[17]

Potter II and Pauline had four children. A daughter, named for her grandmother Bertha, married and became Mrs. Oakleigh Thorne. The oldest son, Potter Palmer III, became a decorated intelligence officer during World War II in the Pacific Theater. He was perhaps the most promising of Bertha Palmer's male grandchildren, the one who seemed best equipped to one day assume leadership of the family. After the war he made Sarasota his principal home and moved into The Oaks. He married twice, but in 1946 he died suddenly of heart disease, just as his father had three years earlier. Potter Palmer III's brother, Gordon, then assumed a leadership role in the family. His importance will be described later. Potter Palmer II's youngest daughter, named Pauline after her mother, married Arthur M. Wood, head of Sears, Roebuck and Company. Wood, a major American business leader, later involved himself in Palmer land transactions on behalf of his wife.[18]

Unlike his brother, Honoré's interest in and commitment to Sarasota grew over the years. He had a home in Chicago not far from the Castle. But as the decades went by, his stays at Immokalee lengthened. In part, this deepening connection had to do with Grace Brown Palmer and her sisters. All three Brown sisters married successful Chicago businessmen, and the three couples lived near each other in Sarasota. Immokalee has been torn down, but the Stanley and Sara Field mansion still stands today as the very exclusive Field Club on Sarasota Bay. Not far away Walter and Frances Keith wintered in a mansion that is the centerpiece of Sarasota County's Philippi Estate Park. The three couples stood at the center of the "Chicago Colony," made up of wealthy Chicagoans who followed Bertha Palmer to Sarasota. Beyond family ties, Honoré seemed to relish far more than his brother the Florida lifestyle. He and Grace liked the outdoor life and enjoyed fishing, hunting, boating, and swimming. Eventually, like his mother, Honoré would spend most of his time in Sarasota.[19]

Honoré and Grace had two sons: Potter D'Orsay and Honoré Jr. Both boys had known their grandmother Bertha quite well and had been part of many camping expeditions at Meadowsweet Pastures. They also benefitted from the instruction of Big Bill Ferguson on outdoor skills. Young Honoré, after finishing at Harvard, found that business or banking held little interest and that his real passion was art. He likely acquired that passion growing up among great collections of paintings at Immokalee, The Oaks, and, of course, the Castle in Chicago. He spent much of his adult life in New York working as an artist, but in February of 1938 he died suddenly of a brain hemorrhage.[20]

Potter D'Orsay Palmer, born in 1908, now became the obvious male contender to succeed his father as head of that branch of the family. As a young man D'Orsay sought out a life of adventure, which included two years as a cowpuncher in Oklahoma. By 1926 he was both a fireman and a deputy sheriff in Sarasota. The *Sarasota Herald* told its readers that one day he would be "one of the wealthiest men in the nation," but for now he was leading "a life of pleasure" and living with his parents at Immokalee.

D'Orsay early developed a drinking problem as well as a strong desire for young women. In 1930 at age 22, he worked as a game warden. He also invited female students from Sarasota High School to sail with him on his yacht. On one of these junkets to St. Petersburg he became interested in 16-year-old Eleanor Goldsmith and proposed to her. Honoré and Grace soon heard of their wayward son's plans and arranged to send telegrams to judges in all of Florida's 67 counties asking them not to issue a marriage license to the couple. Nevertheless, D'Orsay found a justice of the peace willing to conduct the ceremony. All of this action took place within two weeks of the yachting party. By 1931, after only 14 months, D'Orsay and Eleanor divorced when Honoré Senior agreed to come up with the cash to fund a settlement.[21]

Within months and with the likely connivance of his parents, D'Orsay married yet again. The new Mrs. Palmer possessed everything that Honoré and Grace could want in a daughter-in-law: wealth, education, beauty, poise, and social connections. Maria Eugenia Martinez de Hoz was from Argentina and the daughter of a wealthy horse breeder. The wedding took place in Paris, and Maria received a warm welcome into the family. For several years things seemed to go well. Maria spent winters with her in-laws at Immokalee. All too soon, however, D'Orsay's penchant for booze and women, now combined with some wife-beating, tore the marriage apart. The couple separated three times, the last occasion in 1934. Huge legal fights over the financial settlement in the divorce case continued for several years. In 1936 D'Orsay was 28 years old, 6′2″ tall, dark-haired, handsome, and sometimes compared in looks to John Barrymore. He also was potentially rich. All of this drew women to him, but he did have a dark side to his personality. While D'Orsay's marital escapades filled the society pages of the national press, only Palmer family members would have known that D'Orsay lacked any ambition or any focus to his life other than personal pleasure. He took no role in the Palmer family businesses or in any business for that matter. His life defined the meaning of playboy: idle, useless, and hedonistic. Above all, he seemingly could not care about anyone other than himself.[22]

As his divorce dragged on, D'Orsay turned his attention to another young woman, Pauline "Polly" Warren of Baltimore, whose family claimed they came to America aboard the Mayflower. For two years he wooed her, but her mother opposed the relationship because he was still a married man. In desperation, D'Orsay persuaded his father to offer Maria de Hoz Palmer $8 million as a settlement if the divorce went through immediately and he could marry Polly. Maria claimed no one had ever made this offer to her, and the matter was dropped. Meanwhile, Polly Warren, caught between her mother and D'Orsay, took to her bed with an apparent nervous breakdown. Eventually, and only temporarily, she left for Baltimore. Even as things went awry with Polly, D'Orsay developed a relationship with Gerry Chapman, "the cutest graduate at the local high school" according to the *Palm Beach Daily News*. The paper also described her as "the curvaceous dream girl of Sarasota High."[23]

Honoré and Grace desperately hoped for a reconciliation between D'Orsay and Maria. In May of 1937, however, D'Orsay reached a new low in his personal behavior. When Maria returned to the United States from a trip abroad, she was questioned by government officials at Ellis Island as a foreign national. They asked how much money she was carrying, which turned out to be very little. They then detained her for lacking adequate means of support. The immigration officials contacted D'Orsay as her husband, but he refused to vouch for her, thus leaving his estranged wife to spend the night at the government facility. Fortunately, Honoré Jr. heard of his sister-in-law's plight and soon arranged for her freedom.[24]

Maria finally signed the divorce papers and accepted a $5 million settlement. At almost the moment that the divorce became final, D'Orsay married Polly Warren, whose nerves had been restored, if not her good sense. In July of 1938 she filed for divorce in Sarasota. The court granted the divorce at the end of November. Thus in little more than a decade D'Orsay Palmer wooed, won, and then lost three wives. He also squandered a huge amount of his father's money getting out of these marriages.[25]

Shortly after the divorce from Polly became final, D'Orsay stopped for a hamburger at the Greyhound Inn located next to the Greyhound racing track in the northwest corner of Sarasota County. There he instantly fell in love with the waitress, Pluma Louise Laurenze Abatiello, an attractive 23-year-old born in Tampa but living with her grandmother in Bradenton. He proposed on the spot, she accepted, and that day the couple drove to Punta Gorda where a county judge married them on December 2, 1938. It was all too much for Grace Palmer. She told a *New York Times* reporter who called her that she did not approve of the wedding and had never heard of Pluma, let alone met her. In fact, Grace and Honoré refused to greet their new daughter-in-law even when D'Orsay brought her to Immokalee. The day after the wedding, apparently stung by the jokes and criticisms made at his expense, D'Orsay returned to the Greyhound Inn and bought it outright. He renamed it the Palmer House, presumably as a way of embarrassing his family. He had become a pathetic laughing stock of Sarasota, and, indeed, the whole country.[26]

The marriage to Pluma followed the well-worn path of the previous three. Alcohol, particularly, made a normal marriage for D'Orsay impossible. Even on the night of his latest wedding, he participated in an all-night gin party. Not surprisingly, Pluma filed for separate maintenance on April 26, a little less than five months after the wedding. She also asked for $300,000 for herself from Honoré Sr. This was the work of Pluma's lawyer, Frank Redd, who hoped to make millions for himself out of the expected divorce proceedings. The county sheriff's deputies searched large areas of the county before they found D'Orsay and served him with the maintenance papers. Part of Redd's justification of asking for $300,000 was that Grace Palmer had characterized Pluma unkindly with such phrases as "curb hopper," "car hopper," "that girl," and "gold digger."[27]

The only thing that prevented a fourth divorce for D'Orsay is that he died. On May 14, 1939, he attended a picnic near Bradenton, picked a fight while drunk, and took at least one hard blow to the head. At the hospital he was in a coma, and both his parents and Pluma stayed in the room to be with him. It was the first time they had met. The next day at around 5:30 P.M., the doctor pronounced him dead and stated that a cerebral hemorrhage had killed him, as it had his brother 15 months earlier. The man who hit him said that he did not know D'Orsay and did not understand why this stranger had attacked him with a bottle. The formal autopsy did not find a hemorrhage or a skull fracture. The coroner said that he actually died of an infection that led to bronchial pneumonia. D'Orsay's death was bad news for Pluma, as he died a poor man who had depended on an allowance from his parents, at least according to the Palmer attorneys. Pluma inherited nothing and eventually settled for a $2,250 payment in 1940 from Honoré Sr. Maria and Polly, wives two and three, also lost out, as D'Orsay's death terminated their legal agreements. Only D'Orsay's first wife, Eleanor Goldsmith, obtained all that she had agreed to, but only because she had already received the payments due her at the time of his death.[28]

Pluma and attorney Redd tried hard to keep her claims to the Palmer fortune alive, but the Palmer lawyers blocked them at every turn. Pluma, needing money, worked as a hostess in Tampa and then took a similar job in Chicago, where she became involved with the son of Bugs Moran, the mobster whose gang had been wiped out by Al Capone's men in the St. Valentine's Day massacre on North Clark Street on February 14, 1929. In 1939 Pluma married Ellsworth Strunk, a factory worker. During World War II she served as a member of the Women's Army Corps. Frank Redd was eventually replaced by the court as Pluma's attorney at her request. He never saw the huge fees he so fervently wanted from the Palmer family. Honoré and Grace Palmer had now lost their two sons, and there was no one left to carry on their branch of the family. It can only be surmised how they felt about their older son, D'Orsay. He produced no heirs and made no contributions to society. He lived a purposeless existence to the very end. Now middle-aged, Honoré and Grace had no choice but to plan a life without grandchildren or great-grandchildren.[29]

The Prince and Princess Cantacuzene also faced marital problems. In the early 1930s the couple still lived at the Acacias, but the princess spent much of the year in Washington, where she emerged as a society leader, particularly among the White Russian emigrés living there after being driven out of their home country by the Bolsheviks. Perhaps the physical distance between

them reflected the growing chasm in their marriage. Cantacuzene, as vice president of the Palmer bank, played an active
role in managing the institution. He noticed one of the tellers,
Jeannette Draper. They began an affair that went on for several years, until the prince and princess agreed to seek a divorce.
In 1934 the princess successfully petitioned the United States
government for the restitution of her United States citizenship,
which she had given up at the time of her wedding, and then
traveled to Sarasota where she filed for divorce in October. She
charged the prince with desertion and "failure to show interest
in matrimonial duties." The prince did not contest the action,
and on October 27 the divorce was granted after a 35-minute
hearing. Julia henceforth was no longer a princess and took the
name Julia Dent Grant Cantacuzene.[30]

The prince soon married Jeannette Draper and they occupied a home at 436 Woodland Drive in Sarasota. The divorce
did not seem to affect his relationship with the Palmer brothers.
He continued to occupy leadership positions in the Palmer bank
and the Hyde Park grove operation. Nor did his standing in the
Sarasota business and political communities suffer. He remained
a key player in putting together deals such as the building of the
Civic Center, which still stands on the bayfront. Although he
never lost his interest in Russia, he did apply to become a natu-
ralized U.S. citizen in 1934, perhaps showing that he had moved
on with his life. He and Jeannette seem to have been quite happy
together, and he was certainly pleased at the success of his son,
Michael, who entered business in Chicago. His daughters married well, one becoming Lady Zenaida Hanbury Williams of Ire-
land, and the other Mrs. Bertha Sieborn of Louisville. He retired
around 1950 and died in 1955 at age 79, an event extensively

reported in the *New York Times* and the Sarasota papers. He and Jeannette are buried side by side in Manatee Memorial Park, a short distance north of Sarasota.[31]

If anything, Julia Dent Grant Cantacuzene led a more exotic life than that of the prince. Born in the White House, granddaughter of President Ulysses S. Grant, presented to the royal courts of Austria and Russia, and surviving a dangerous escape from the Bolsheviks during the Russian Revolution were merely the high points of her life. After World War I she took up writing. Eventually she published three books and many magazine articles. She wrote about events in her interesting life and the people she had known. She even engaged in at least one cross-country book tour in the 1920s. She entertained the rich and powerful at her home in Washington and did what she could to keep alive the White Russian community's ambition of retaking Russia from the Communists. Julia wintered regularly in Sarasota even after the divorce. She continued to live at the Acacias. And she did show interest in the Sarasota community. In 1926, for example, she sought financial support for the still new Sarasota Memorial Hospital. She also served as the first president of the Sarasota YWCA, and was a member of the Sarasota Women's Club. A newspaper story from 1936 mentions that she was a supporter of the George Washington Junior Society at Sarasota High School, a patriotic group, and had sent a telegram to be read at one of their assemblies.[32]

Although these civic involvements in Sarasota were laudable, Julia's interests never strayed far from her commitment to end Communist rule in Russia. Not surprisingly, given her Republican Party heritage, Julia strongly endorsed the party generally and specifically its stand against Communism. In 1919 she gave a public address and sounded much like Senator Joseph McCarthy a generation later when she said she had a list of the top Bolshevik leaders, and claimed all but two were actually Germans. She added that several of these leaders were German Jews, "who had assumed Russian names in order to gain their ends." She charged that Bolsheviks forced many ordinary Russians to fight in the Red Army by holding their families as hostages. A year later New York police provided security for her on one of her visits to the city because of her outspoken attacks on "reds." In 1921 she returned to Chicago, giving speeches to raise $150,000 for Russian relief. There she enjoyed the support of Honoré Palmer and industrialist Cyrus McCormick, among many others. A few months later she "censured" Britain's Lady Astor for accepting an invitation to visit Russia "and finding nothing to criticize there." Julia said that Lady Astor's actions "were humiliating to all women."[33]

The 1932 election and the rise of the Democrats and Franklin D. Roosevelt appalled Julia and spurred her to action. She undertook a nationwide tour for the Republican National Committee, winding up in Chicago giving speeches during the last days of the campaign. After the election and Roosevelt's victory, Julia went on the attack against New Deal policies, arguing that private individuals rather than the government should handle relief efforts. Speaking before the Women's National Republican Club in July of 1936, Julia accused Roosevelt of "autocracy," adding "what has been happening over the last three years is un-American." Julia's extreme rhetoric extended into the 1936 presidential election when she charged that "leaders of communists in Russia have ordered American Communists to vote for Roosevelt's election." The editor of the *Chicago Times* challenged the Republican National Committee to provide proof of Julia's statement. The

Julia Dent Grant Cantacuzene, circa 1925.
By permission of Sarasota County Historical Resources.

editor even offered to pay $3,000 for such proof, but none was forthcoming. Julia remained undeterred in her efforts to defeat the president. Just two weeks before the election she told the Women's National Republican Club of Chicago that the New Deal was comparable to Communist rule in Russia. "Patriotism," she asserted, "no longer resides in the White House." Despite her attacks, Roosevelt won in 1936, 1940, and 1944.[34]

Julia lived a very long life, continuing to write and to shine as an important society hostess in Washington. In her personal life, she looked after her family and visited Sarasota in the winter months. She died at age 99 in October 1975. She had been very much influenced by her aunt, Bertha Palmer, who had treated her as a daughter. In fact, in her many accomplishments, her passion, her intelligence, and her social skills she came closer to Bertha than any other woman in the Palmer and Honoré families. However, she could have used a healthy dose of Bertha's well-known tact and political acumen.[35]

As the 1950s approached, it appeared that age and death had sapped the Palmer family's strength. In 1949 a major reorganization shifted much of the direct management of the remaining Palmer operations to paid professionals. Yet there was still some vigor in the family, and there would be a final flowering of leadership that added to the long list of contributions the Palmers made to Sarasota.[36]

Notes for Chapter Seven

1. LaHurd, *Sarasota*, 39–45; Rogers, "Fortune and Misfortunes," 289–303.

2. Wynne and Moorhead, *Paradise for Sale*, 160; LaHurd *Sarasota*, 50–51; Grismer, *Story of Sarasota*, 51; Weeks, *Ringling*, 139.

3. Weeks, *Ringling*, 139.

4. Ibid., 141; *Sarasota Herald*, Nov. 28, 1926, and Feb. 7, 1927.

5. *Sarasota Herald*, Feb. 9, 1927.

6. Ibid., Feb. 9 and 12, and March 15, 1927; Jeff LaHurd, *Gulf Coast Chronicles: Remembering Sarasota's Past* (Charleston, SC: The History Press, Charleston, 2005,), 63; Weeks, *Ringling*, 142.

7. *Sarasota Herald*, May 227, June 19 and 26, July 12, and Aug. 4, 1927; Weeks, *Ringling*, 137–142.

8. *New York Times*, Sept. 5, 1943; *Sarasota Herald*, April 28, and Oct. 25, 1925, Dec. 29, 1926, Jan. 14 and Feb. 17, 1927, July 21, 1929, Sept. 5, 1943, Jan. 8, 1950, and March 26, 1955.

9. *Sarasota Herald*, July 21, 1929; Weeks, *Ringling*, 79, 153; *This Week in Sarasota*, July 25, 1929.

10. *Sarasota Herald*, July 21, 1929.

11. Ibid.

12. *Sarasota Herald*, July 2, 1930.

13. *Sarasota Herald Tribune*, June 2, 1999.

14. Ibid., Oct. 5, 1971, and July 30, 1972; *New York Times*, Nov. 14, 1975.

15. *Sarasota Herald Tribune*, May 8 and Oct. 5, 1971; June 30, July 30, and Dec. 20, 1972; Dec. 2, 1973; June 18 and Dec. 1, 1975; Articles on Palmer Bank, Bertha Palmer and Family Research Collection, Box 3, Chicago History Museum.

16. *Sarasota Herald Tribune*, Sept. 5, 1943; *New York Times*, Sept. 5, 1943; *Chicago Sun Times*, July 8, 1956, in Bertha Honoré Palmer Research Collection, Box 3, Chicago History Museum.

17. *Sarasota Herald* Tribune, Sept. 5, 1943; *New York Times*, Sept. 5, 1943, and Sept. 15, 1945.

18. *New York Times*, June 22, 2006; *Chicago Tribune*, Oct. 4, 1946; *Sarasota Herald*, Oct. 3, 1946.

19. Albert N. Marquis (ed.), *The Book of Chicagoans: A Biographical Dictionary of the Leading Living Men and Women of the City of Chicago* (Chicago: A. N. Marquis Co., 1917), 522.

20. Dwight, *Letters of Pauline Palmer*, 273; *Chicago Tribune*, Feb. 8, 1938.

21. *Sarasota Herald*, Aug. 22, 1926 and April 4, 1930; *Palm Beach Daily Times*, Feb. 20, 1938.

22. *Sarasota Herald*, Jan. 22, 1936.

23. *Palm Beach Daily Times*, Feb.11, 20, and March 11, 1937; *Sarasota Herald*, Feb. 23 and 25, and March 3, 1937.

24. *Palm Beach Daily Times*, May 13, 1936; *Sarasota Herald*, May 13, 1937.

25. *Palm Beach Daily Times*, Aug. 7, 1938; *Sarasota Herald Tribune*, Aug. 3, 1938; *Miami Times*, Oct. 30, 1938.

26. *Tampa Times*, Dec. 3, 1938; *Sarasota News*, Dec. 6. 1938.

27. *Sarasota Herald Tribune*, April 30, May 1, 1939; *Tampa Times*, Dec. 3, 1938.

28. *New York Times*, Feb. 8 and May 19, 1939; *Sarasota Herald Tribune*, Feb. 20, 1938; April 26 and 29; and May 15 and 16, 1939.

29. *Sarasota Herald Tribune*, Aug. 7, Nov. 14, 1939; Jan 3, May 29, June 15, July 16, Sept. 27, Oct. `15, 1940; June 11, 1941; Sept. 5, 1943.

30. *Gettysburg Times*, Oct. 17, 1934; *New York Times*, Oct. 19, 1934; *Chicago Tribune*, Oct. 28, 1934; Bertha Palmer and Family Research Collection, Box 1, Chicago History Museum.

31. *Sarasota Herald Tribune*, Nov. 11, 1949, and March 26, 1955; *New York Times*, March 26, 1955.

32. *This Week in Sarasota*, April 29, 1926; *Sarasota Herald Tribune*, March 21, 1936; Nov. 20, 1949.

33. Princess Cantacuzene, Speech to Chicago Women's Club, Nov. 3, 1919, Bertha Palmer and Family Research Collection, Box 1, Chicago History Museum; *Chicago Tribune*, Nov. 14, 1919; May 1, 1920; Feb. 21 and Oct. 26, 1921; *Chicago Journal*, Nov. 13,1919.

34. *New York Times* Oct. 7 1975; *Chicago Tribune*, Nov. 9, 1932; July 15, and Oct. 22, 1936; *Chicago Times*, Sept. 22, 1936; Bertha Palmer and Family Research Collection, Box 3, 1934, Chicago History Museum.

35. *New York Times*, Oct. 7, 1975.

36. *Sarasota Herald Tribune*, April 29, 1949.

CHAPTER EIGHT

Sunset of Empire

In 1950 Honoré Palmer celebrated his 76th birthday. He and
Grace continued to live at Immokalee, leading a still active
life that included hunting and horseback riding. Honoré remained president of the Palmer bank board of directors and the
most important figure in the Palmer Florida Company and its
parent, the Palmer Corporation, which controlled Palmer investments across the nation. Despite age and large responsibilities,
Honoré and Grace announced in 1950 that they intended to enter the field of beef ranching, just as Bertha had done some forty
years earlier. The Palmer Estate still controlled large amounts
of land south of Sarasota, and Honoré selected a 6,000-acre site
south of present-day Clark Road, east of the Tamiami Trail and
west of the Seaboard Air Line Railroad extension to Venice. He
ordered 2,000 acres cleared of pines and palmettos. In this area
he planned a system of roads and fences as well as drainage and
irrigation. The remaining 4,000 acres he intended to use for range

and pasture land planted with a variety of grasses. As part of his scheme, Honoré set aside 120 acres of his Immokalee estate where he hoped to develop a herd of 500 purebred cattle. Honoré named Charles Dempsey as manager of the ranch and Reuben Lanier of Okeechobee as the herdsman. Lanier was particularly valuable to the enterprise, as he had studied Brahman cattle in India during World War II.[1]

Honoré and Grace named their new enterprise Meadow-sweet Pastures Ranch, in honor of Bertha. They wasted no time in putting their plans in motion. They spent a small fortune to purchase three Brahman bulls and a heifer at a sale in Ocala, Florida, and before long their basic herd of cattle exceeded 325. Within six months, the Palmers added an additional 9,500 acres to Meadowsweet Pastures Ranch by absorbing the adjacent Rocking Chair Ranch, located mostly on the east side of the railroad. This acreage already belonged to the Palmers, but had been leased. Honoré also purchased 500 head of cattle from the Rocking Chair Ranch. At almost the same time, the couple acquired a herd of 50 Santa Gertrudis cattle, the only pure breed of American cattle, to go along with their growing herd of Brahmans. These were the earliest examples of this breed brought to Florida's west coast. Honoré and Grace were so impressed with the Santa Gertrudis cattle that they purchased two bulls from the King Ranch in Texas, one costing $8,500 and the other $6,750. On the same trip, they purchased 40 Santa Gertrudis cows and a five-year-old bull from the Brownlee Ranch, also in Texas. By the end of 1951 the Palmer's Santa Gertrudis herd numbered 250 head.[2]

Thanks in part to Honoré and Grace and their rapid expansion of Meadowsweet Pastures Ranch and its herds, Sarasota began to attract attention as one of the fastest growing cattle production areas in Florida. They were credited with, among other things, having one of the largest Santa Gertrudis herds in the state in 1952. The quality of the purebred cattle at the Palmer ranch was recognized at the 1953 Manatee County Fair where Santa Gertrudis cattle from Meadowsweet Pastures Ranch won all eight awards given to that breed. Like his mother, Honoré had helped lift the quality and economic impact of cattle raising in the Sarasota area. Like her, his motives for entering that industry appear to have been personal rather than out of a simple desire to make money. Unfortunately, both mother and son died before they could fully develop their cattle raising strategies.[3]

Honoré Palmer passed away at Immokalee on March 14, 1964, at age 90. More than any other Palmer he had been closely associated with the city and county of Sarasota. He had spent every winter since 1910 in Sarasota, jointly built Immokalee with his brother, served as an officer in the Sarasota-Venice Company and the Palmer Florida Company, helped lead the development of all the major Palmer business initiatives including Palmer Farms, the Hyde Park grove, and the Palmer bank, of which he was a founder and long-time chairman. He had made signal contributions to many aspects of Sarasota's economic progress, even in his final years as he initiated and built Meadowsweet Pastures Ranch. He also sought to make Sarasota a better place in other ways, such as his contribution to Sarasota Memorial Hospital and the donation of land to establish Myakka River State Park, both made jointly with Potter II. In 1962 he and Grace had made a personal gift of $1 million to support the establishment of New College in Sarasota, an innovative private liberal arts and sciences college that is now an autonomous campus within the University of Florida system.[4] New College is an important contributor to Sarasota's vibrant cultural and intellectual life

Honoré, unlike his parents and brother and other Palmer family members, was not buried in Chicago. Rather, he and Grace, who died of cancer a few years later, were interred in Westchester, New York. Honoré's estate sold Immokalee with its 26 buildings situated on 216 acres to the United States Home Corporation. The acreage minus the buildings became an exclusive housing subdivision known today as The Landings. The Meadowsweet Pastures Ranch was placed in a trust, but given the rapid growth of Sarasota in this period, it seemed obvious it would soon be targeted for development. In 1973 the 13,000-acre ranch sold for $12,250,000 to Hugh F. Culverhouse and Sheldon Morris of Jacksonville, Florida. It was the largest undeveloped tract in Sarasota at the time. Called Palmer Ranch today, the vast area is divided into many planned residential communities and home to thousands of people.[5]

The last of Bertha Palmer's male grandchildren was Gordon, youngest son of Potter Palmer Jr., and his wife, Pauline. Born in 1915, Gordon likely had little memory of his grandmother Bertha. Like his father, uncle, and most other male Palmers, Gordon attended St. Mark's Preparatory School in Massachusetts and graduated from Harvard University. During World War II he served with the U. S. Navy as a lieutenant commander in Washington, D.C., and was discharged in 1946. In June of 1949 he married Janis Hardage of Atlanta in New York City. A year later he brought his bride to Sarasota to Bertha Palmer's great estate, Osprey Point. However, he did not occupy The Oaks itself, which had last been used by his brother, Potter Palmer III. Instead, he and Janis lived in a quaint white cottage on the grounds of the estate built before Bertha bought the property.[6]

Gordon Palmer, grandson of Bertha Palmer, and the last Palmer to reside at
Osprey Point. *Courtesy of Gulf Coast Heritage, Inc.*

An energetic man, Gordon threw himself into work related
to Palmer family investments. He became president of the Palmer Florida Company and took a director's seat on the boards of
the Palmer banks in Sarasota and St. Armand's Circle. In the
tradition of Prince Cantacuzene, he became the public face of
the Palmers as a leader of the Members Council of the Ringling
Museum of Art, the Field Club where he served as commodore,
the Red Cross, the Harvard Club, and the New College board. In
1953 he opened a new business, Palmer Nurseries, on the grounds
of Osprey Point. This would likely have pleased Bertha to have at
least one of her grandchildren take a deep interest in gardening.
Gordon and his staff laid out gardens and tended them as well,
although his newspaper ads made clear the company did not cut
grass in people's yards. Bertha had planted a lychee grove not far
from The Oaks, and lychee trees and their fruit fascinated Gor-

don. He joined the Florida Lychee Growers Association, serving as president for two years and secretary/treasurer for three years.[7]

Gordon seemed to understand that as the owner of Osprey Point he had a special responsibility as well as an extraordinary opportunity to educate new generations about the role and historical importance of his grandmother. One relatively easy way to do this involved opening The Oaks to the public. The house and its contents were little changed from 1918. Even many of Bertha's paintings remained on display. And so in November 1958, Gordon announced that the gardens and three rooms in the house would open for tours on four consecutive Sundays as an experiment. If public interest in the 11 acres of lawns and 31-room mansion proved sufficient, then the estate might be kept open for a fee of $1.50 per tourist. The newspapers discussed some of the sights, such as grand oak trees ranging in age from 300 to 400 years, a jungle trail built over an immense Indian midden, and a large fishpond. The three rooms opened for public inspection included the living and dining rooms and Bertha's bedroom. The experiment clearly worked, for by February 1959, newspaper ads said the entire estate would be opened to visitors every Sunday. The ads noted that Osprey Point had been "created by a fabulous woman."[8]

The tide of tourists stimulated local interest in Bertha. The November 22, 1959, edition of the *Sarasota Herald Tribune* said, "An estate virtually undisturbed since 1918 is proving one of the currently most popular points of interest in Sarasota County." The article reviewed what Bertha had created at Osprey Point, such as the gardens, summer houses, scenic walks, drives, pools, dock, ornamental plants, and an artificial brook. It particularly advised visitors to view the valuable collection of Impressionist and post-Impressionist paintings inside The Oaks. In early 1960 the Palmer estate opened daily to visitors, testifying to the popularity of the site and the woman who created it. Perhaps a high point for the publicly rediscovered estate was in late February of 1960 when the papers announced a Pioneer Day tea with Gordon Palmer to be held at The Oaks and sponsored by the Sarasota County Historical Society. The event celebrated the fiftieth anniversary of Bertha's arrival in Sarasota. Guests included A.B. Edwards, who greeted her on that long-ago day; Albert E. Blackburn, who had worked for her; Dr. Joseph Halton, whom she knew; Mrs. C. V. S. Wilson, former editor of the *Sarasota Times*, who had chronicled Bertha's every move; and Charles Webb, grandson of the man who founded the town of Osprey. The stories told that day were undoubtedly fascinating.[9]

Besides opening The Oaks to the public, Gordon made the great art collection at the home available to a far larger audience. In 1959 he loaned the paintings to the Chicago Art Institute for six months. He then sent thirty of the art works to the Florida State Fair in Tampa. Additionally, he put some paintings on display at the Palmer Garden Center where he conducted business at Osprey Point. Gordon also took an interest in the evidence of prehistoric Native American habitation of the Spanish Point area. He likely knew that Bertha had also been fascinated with the mounds and middens throughout her estate, particularly at the south end. She had carefully avoided destroying or seriously damaging these remains of past inhabitants. Gordon went further. He set out to explore them scientifically.[10]

In the late summer of 1956, Gordon contacted George W. Dekle, head of the Florida State Plant Board, concerning a possible cooperative archaeological investigation of the extensive prehistoric remains present at Osprey Point. Gordon proposed that the two sponsoring entities for this project be the Florida State Museum in Tallahassee and Palmer Nurseries. For his part, Gordon pledged to provide laborers and to house the researchers. Dekle, in turn, approached Arnold B. Grobman, Director, and Ripley P. Bullen, Curator of Social Sciences, at the state museum. They reached an agreement, and Bullen together with his spouse, Adelaide, led a team of researchers to Osprey Point in 1959, 1960, and 1962. Bullen released some of his findings to the press, but he did not publish the full report until 1976 when it appeared in a publication put out by the Florida Anthropological Society.[11]

The Bullens identified four significant prehistorical sites around Osprey Point. The oldest was a shell midden below Hill Cottage. Middens are piles of shells discarded by the prehistoric inhabitants usually over a very long period. Middens often contain buried human remains, pottery shards, broken tools, and religious relics. Humans created the Hill Cottage Midden between 2100 B. C. and 1000 A. D. The Bullens reported that this midden contained a great array of artifacts. It was, in fact, the oldest of the four sites. Two other shell middens identified were located along the southern shoreline of Spanish Point. The westernmost of these jutted out into Little Sarasota Bay and was associated with people living there in the centuries just before and after the Christian era began. The more easterly midden had also been established in this period. Just to the north of this midden stood a burial mound that the Bullens excavated, finding over 400 human interments. They also discovered the remains of an alligator decorated with religious symbols. The Bullens believed that Indian people lived in the area as late as 1300 A. D.[12]

The report reflected the elation of the Bullens at their discoveries. The couple pointed out that modern development along the coastline of western Florida had destroyed many middens and other evidence of prehistoric occupation of the area. The Palmer site was virtually intact and provided a wealth of information on the evolving native cultures that continuously occupied the area for three millennia. The Bullens called Osprey Point the only sizeable prehistoric village on the Gulf coast south of Crystal River and north of Fort Myers that had remained largely undisturbed. For this important opportunity to research and gather information on these predecessor groups, the Bullens thanked Bertha Palmer in their report for her foresight and sensitivity in not damaging these prehistoric remains when she built The Oaks and developed her estate at Osprey Point. As for Gordon Palmer, the man who proposed and helped fund the archaeological research program, the Bullens dedicated their entire report to his memory.[13]

Gordon had not lived long enough to see the Bullens' published report. In February 1964, he died at age 49 at Sarasota Memorial Hospital and was buried near his grandmother Bertha and his parents at Graceland Cemetery. The extensive obituaries published at the time show that he was not only a prominent businessman and citizen of the community, but genuinely well liked. As the *Sarasota Journal* said, he was "one of the kindest persons this community has ever known." The near-simultaneous deaths of Honoré and Gordon in 1964 significantly weakened the Palmer family influence in Sarasota, as there was really no one left capable of organizing and directing the great works that had characterized the previous fifty years.[14]

Without Gordon, who had loved and looked after his grandmother's great mansion, the grand structure fell on hard times.

Vandals broke the windows and destroyed the interior while wind and water caused general decay. The house became an eyesore and a potential danger. In January 1969, wrecking crews destroyed The Oaks, but not before some souvenir hunters carried away a few mementos. As the *Sarasota Herald Tribune* observed, "the mansion was the victim of a growing community, vandals, and the unrelenting force of sea and storm."[15]

Before Gordon's death but after he was made aware of Ripley Bullen's preliminary findings on the importance of the Indian sites at Osprey Point, Gordon and his spouse, Janice, began a process that would ultimately provide Sarasota County with one of its outstanding attractions. In 1960 he pledged to give 30 acres of Osprey Point to the Gulf Coast Heritage Association in order to preserve the historical and prehistorical treasures located there, including many of his grandmother's gardens and the archaeological sites identified by the Bullens. The association was a private volunteer group of citizens. This was an important and generous act on Gordon's and Janice's part, but challenges lay ahead that had to be overcome before what is now known as Historic Spanish Point became truly safe from development.[16]

In the 1970s Janis Hardage Palmer, Potter Palmer IV, and other family members encouraged the nomination of the 30-acre site to the National Register of Historic Places. When approved in 1976, Spanish Point became the first such designated location in Sarasota County. The area now had some protection, but its future appeared clouded. The small historical area was only a part of Bertha's huge estate, which included the mainland portion of 350 acres as well as 93 acres of Bird Key in Little Sarasota Bay, 13 acres at the northern tip of Casey Key, and 24 acres at the south end of Siesta Key. The last two sites, a short distance over the water from The Oaks, constituted the shores of Midnight Pass, one of the few waterways linking the Gulf of Mexico to Little Sarasota Bay. The two keys had long been havens for wealthy people seeking escape from Northern winters. They had built great estates, valued their privacy, and did not want more neighbors. At the same time, powerful environmental groups had come into existence, aiming to protect the ecologically sensitive areas along the coastline. Chief among these was the Save Our Bays Association (SOBA), a large, well-funded, and politically connected organization. Concerned citizens originally formed SOBA in the 1960s to block the Arvida Corporation's plans to dredge parts of Sarasota Bay to create additional land that could then be developed and sold.[17]

In 1973 the Palmer family proposed to sell off Osprey Point, Bertha's old estate. Their plan called for building over 1,800 units of housing on the mainland. The family did not intend to oversee this development, preferring to sell the property to a Canadian firm. The Palmer lawyers asked the Sarasota Board of County Commissioners to make necessary changes in zoning regulations, which that body refused to do. The Palmers then sued the county, and a seven-year-long battle commenced, which involved SOBA, other environmental groups, a protest march, demands that the State of Florida purchase the land and protect it, and many court hearings. At least one Sarasota County Board of Commissioners' meeting degenerated into a shouting match with a commissioner yelling at an environmental leader to shut "his god damned mouth."[18]

Despite high tempers and vacillating public opinion, the Board of County Commissioners found its legal position weak in respect to the Palmer lawsuit and was forced to negotiate an out-of-court settlement. The public learned the provisions of that settlement in February of 1980. The Palmers agreed to cut the number of proposed housing units on Bertha's old estate to 541. They also agreed that all these units would be single-family dwellings and that no condominium towers would be erected. The Palmers pledged to deed the 93-acre area called Bird Island as well as a few acres on Casey Key to the county for a nature preserve. In addition, the county obtained easements through Palmer property on Siesta Key so that workers could, when needed, address problems in Midnight Pass. The Palmers would be free to sell their remaining lands on the two keys. Finally, the agreement specified that the Palmers would deed the 30-acre National Historic Site to a local volunteer group.[19]

There was much more to come in this confrontation, as SOBA tried unsuccessfully to overturn the Board of County Commissioner's decision to accept the negotiated deal in the courts. In the end, the bargain stood for better or worse. The various parties signed the final settlement on August 2, 1980. That same day the Palmer heirs sold much of Bertha's estate to the Canadian developer Vroom, Inc., and officially deeded the 30-acre historical site. Nearly two years later, in April 1982, crowds gathered at the invitation of the Gulf Coast Heritage Association for a ceremony dedicating Sarasota's newest historical and cultural center, Historic Spanish Point. Lillian Burns, head of the association and daughter of one of Sarasota's most influential pioneers, Owen Burns, spoke about the new endeavor and the ambitious plans for restoration work. Janis Hardage Palmer, widow of Gordon, also addressed the audience. The event brought the story of the Palmers in Sarasota to a fitting end and did so at the place that story began 72 years earlier when Bertha paid

$11,000 for the initial 13 acres of her estate. Palmers would continue to live in Sarasota for many years, and some, like Janis Palmer, would maintain Bertha's commitment to philanthropy. However, the real basis of Palmer power and influence in Sarasota was land, and that had now largely been sold.[20]

The Palmer family and Sarasota were closely connected for over seven decades. The relationship was certainly beneficial for the Palmers, whose real estate profits were many times greater than the sum Bertha paid to purchase 140,000 acres. But what was the impact of the Palmers on Sarasota? Certainly their legacy includes such things as Historic Spanish Point as well as Myakka River State Park in the eastern portion of Sarasota County where Bertha's Meadowsweet Pastures once flourished. Both are open to the public. A third site, Eagle Point Camp in Venice, still retains much of its 1917 appearance, but is located on private property. Unfortunately, most other physical sites associated with the Palmers have long since disappeared, among them The Oaks, the Acacias, and Immokalee, as well as the Palmer bank building at Five Points in downtown Sarasota. The Palmer presence in Sarasota endures in street signs such as Honoré, Cattlemen, Palmer, D'Orsay, Potter, MacIntosh, and several others. Historical markers put up by the Sarasota County Historical Commission at key locations preserve at least some of the Palmer history in the area. Sarasota County's Historical Resources Division houses a large number of manuscripts, photographs, and artifacts pertaining to the family.

While these remains are significant, they hardly begin to explain the many and important ways that Bertha and her family shaped Sarasota over 70 years. To uncover the entire story requires a journey into newspaper archives, manuscript collections, and government records. For example, one of Bertha's most significant gifts to Sarasota was to use her wealth, fame, and access to the press to make the area known from coast to coast and in Europe as well. Before February of 1910, Sarasota and its 900 citizens were virtually invisible. When Mrs. Potter Palmer announced she was making her winter home there, everything changed. New energy and resources she provided through land purchases quickly transformed Sarasota into a booming town filled with new stores, paved streets, electric power, and a growing number of other rich Northerners attracted by Bertha's cachet as an international figure accepted into the royal courts of Europe.

Bertha played on her fame to boost Sarasota. Reporters journeyed to her estate to hear all the reasons she thought Sarasota was so wonderful. When she traveled she never missed an opportunity to praise the town and county. Her comment that Sarasota Bay was as beautiful as the Bay of Naples became Sarasota's most effective endorsement. There can be no question that Bertha very much liked the locale of her winter home. But it can be surmised that her public enthusiasm had much to do with persuading a great many Northerners to come to Sarasota and buy some of the 140,000 acres she owned. Bertha proved to be a one-woman public relations agency. She made Sarasota something of a household name and succeeded in bringing great numbers of tourists and wealthy investors to her part of Florida. Both during her life and for decades after, the Palmer family maintained a huge national sales campaign to persuade people to buy Palmer property. Palmer ads appeared in every major newspaper and many magazines and often offered discounted railroad tickets to encourage potential buyers to come to Sarasota. Thus, even after Bertha died, the family, for business reasons, continued to boost the

Sarasota area. At times the several Palmer corporations seemed indistinguishable from the Sarasota Board of Trade or the county Chamber of Commerce. Palmer executives often served as board officers of these organizations, and the Palmer companies paid to produce their literature for distribution nationally trumpeting Sarasota's many assets and, of course, the benefits of purchasing Palmer lands.[21]

Another way the Palmers helped Sarasota County was to improve transportation to and from the area as well as within it. Transportation was absolutely key to the Palmers. They had to move potential buyers to see their sites, and they needed transportation to carry agricultural products to markets in the north. The Palmer family and their corporate structures strongly supported railroad construction. Their first project was the Seaboard Air Line Railroad extension from Fruitville to Venice, which ran across their lands, thus increasing their value. Later they worked with the Atlantic Coast Line to extend its rail line from Sarasota through Palmer Farms and Meadowsweet Pastures to connect with a north-south line just below Arcadia. These two extensions opened up the Palmer lands south and east of Sarasota to development. But railroads were only part of the transportation challenge. Hard-topped roads that connected Fruitville, Bee Ridge, Bayonne, Venice, and Bradenton were essential as automobile travel became common. Moreover, commercial trucks were beginning to compete with railroads in delivering bulk products. The Palmers strongly backed the Good Roads movement that swept Florida and the nation in the 1910s and 1920s. The Tamiami Trail linking Tampa and Miami was of particular interest to them.

Water-borne commerce also attracted the Palmers, who

owned miles of coastal property. They lobbied hard and success-fully to have the federal government dredge deeper channels in Sarasota Bay to accommodate larger vessels. Their intent was to create a viable transportation alternative to railroads in order to keep those companies from charging exorbitant rates. In the Venice area, the Palmers privately financed dredging that opened better water connections between Venice and Sarasota. Although all of these improvements benefitted the Palmers, they also helped build a solid infrastructure to sustain Sarasota Coun-ty growth and development.[22]

Closely related to building a modern transportation system was the Palmers' recognition of the fact that the people they aimed to attract to purchase their lands, whether rich or middle class, desired the kind of social and cultural opportunities they enjoyed where they now lived. This led the Palmers to invest con-siderable amounts of money in hotels, golf courses, post offices, and more sophisticated-looking railroad stations. They even built or at least intended to build towns like Bee Ridge, Bayonne, and Palmerville within their planned agricultural communities in part to offer farmers and their families the social benefits of churches, schools, women's clubs, and parks. It was all part of a strategy to make Palmer lands more attractive. Palmer self-inter-est blended nicely with civic progress. Both Venice and Sarasota benefitted as well, since the Palmers owned large amounts of land in both places, and they were anxious to make those communi-ties as attractive and socially inviting as possible, particularly to wealthy investors.[23]

Yet another way the Palmers helped Sarasota was by promot-ing tourism. They did this in part through their transportation improvement activities as well as by their marketing and public relations programs. Tourists meant dollars for hotels, restaurants, and many other businesses. They also were targets of real estate developers such as the Palmer family. In the late 1920s and 1930s, the Palmers took advantage of public fascination with their mammoth Palmer Farms operation to make it one of the area's top tourist attractions, on a par with the Ringling Museum and the winter quarters of the Ringling Brothers and Barnum and Bailey Circus. Thousands drove out Fruitville Road to see the verdant fields, the experimental farm, and the modern packinghouse operation. In the 1950s Gordon Palmer opened The Oaks to the public for a small fee, and it soon became one of Sarasota's major tourist attractions. Historic Spanish Point carries on that tradition today.

One of the most profound contributions of the Palmer family was to change the topography of thousands of acres of Sarasota County land. Because much of the land Bertha originally purchased could not sustain agriculture in its natural state, the Palmers found it necessary to undertake huge and complex engineering projects on a scale far greater than seen before in that part of Florida. They remade 8,000 acres of Bee Ridge Farms and the 5,000 acres of Osprey Farms by constructing a system of canals to remove excess water and another system of channels and artesian wells to provide water when and where needed. These engineering projects together with the use of modern machines to clear the land made this acreage prime agricultural lands and later as sites for sprawling housing developments. Palmer Farms and the Hyde Park grove utilized similar techniques and technologies. However, unlike their earlier planned agricultural communities, the Palmers spread the cost to others besides themselves. Under a 1913 state law the residents of an area could petition for the establishment of a water drainage district that had the power to tax all landowners benefitting from improvements made by the district's elected governing board. Since the Palmers owned most of the land in both districts, they paid the great bulk of the taxes and controlled elections of board members. The boards had the authority to hire engineers to design and to build water control systems as happened at both Palmer Farms and Hyde Park grove. The Sarasota-Fruitville Drainage District, often praised as one of the best-run operations of its type in Florida, did succeed in making 8,000 more acres of Palmer land marketable as farmland. But by obliterating vast amounts of wetlands and changing drainage patterns, the drainage district created future flooding problems, particularly along Philippi Creek. Nevertheless, tens of thousands of people live on former Palmer farmland that exists only because of the family's enterprise and willingness to take on large engineering projects.[24]

Little remains today of Bee Ridge Farms, Osprey Farms, Palmer Farms, or Hyde Park grove. Yet these were at the time major achievements. The Palmers thought big and acted decisively. Their key insight was to treat big tracts of land as a unitary whole. They planned to sell off farms in lots of 10 and 20 acres, but in fact each small farm was connected to a complex infrastructure. Water drainage and irrigation systems composed major parts of this infrastructure, but so too did experimental farms, roads, packinghouses, farmers' cooperatives, small towns, railroad connections, and stores selling needed supplies at a discount. This was farming on an industrial scale but geared to the needs of small farmers. These were planned agricultural communities, the likes of which had never been seen before on the west coast of Florida or, for that matter, in very few places in the nation.

The settlement of these 22,000 acres brought thousands of people to Sarasota not as visitors, but as residents. Their farming activities pumped huge amounts of money into the Sarasota County economy. These new residents needed houses, railroad connections, stores of every variety, churches, and much more to live a modern life; and they had the funds to pay the bills. The Palmers' farming communities provided a solid basis to Sarasota County's economy at a time of great turmoil.

Just as they transformed farming in Sarasota, the Palmers completely changed cattle and hog raising and made those enterprises bigger contributors to the local economy. At Meadowsweet Pastures Bertha confronted a local cattle industry mired in ignorance. Despite sometimes violent local opposition, she built dipping pens to fight the Texas tick, fenced in her pastures, grew some of her own cattle feed, and imported Brahman bulls from Texas as well as other breeds to improve the runty Florida cattle. Then she did the same thing with hogs. In the 1950s her son Honoré picked up her mantle of leadership by developing Meadowsweet Pastures Ranch. He and Grace took the lead in breeding Santa Gertrudis cattle. And like Bertha, they also won prizes at fairs for the quality of their cattle.[25]

The Palmers played a very special role in helping Sarasota survive the Great Depression. As the economy contracted, capital disappeared and jobs evaporated. Palmer Farms and the Hyde Park grove made the Palmer family the largest employer in Sarasota, as it had been when Bertha still lived. The importance of Palmer Farms as a tourist magnet has already been noted. Along with jobs, the Palmers provided investment capital to the community through the Palmer bank. As the only bank in town after 1934, it was an indispensable engine of economic progress for the entire county. Prince Cantacuzene has already been profiled regarding his business and civic leadership in the hard days of the 1930s.

The answer to the question of what Sarasota gained from its association with the Palmers is, emphatically, a great deal. The family had profited handsomely, but it gave a lot back in return. Indeed, it is hard to find another such relationship where an outside family had such a profound and long-lasting impact on a city's development. In Sarasota's history only John and Charles Ringling might be considered rivals of the Palmers; but both were dead by the end of the 1930s, and John's fortune did not survive the Depression.[26]

The Palmers were Chicagoans, first and foremost. That is where most of them lived when not in Sarasota, that was the society they found most comfortable, and when they died, most were buried at Graceland Cemetery next to Bertha and Potter or across a narrow cemetery road in the Honoré plot. They willed a substantial amount of their great fortune and much of their spectacular art collections to Chicago institutions. Yet many of the family members, including Bertha, Honoré and Grace, Prince and Princess Cantacuzene, Adrian C. Honoré, and Gordon and Janis, developed a real fondness for and commitment to Sarasota County and its people. The Palmers and Honorés came to Sarasota aiming to do well for themselves economically and ended up helping to create one of Florida's most attractive communities. Thus the citizens of both Chicago and Sarasota owe a great deal to this remarkable family and therefore share a common historical bond.

Notes to Chapter Eight

1. *Sarasota Herald Tribune*, July 3, 1950; *Chicago Tribune*, undated (1940s), Vertical File, Sarasota County Historical Resources.

2. *Sarasota Herald Tribune*, Jan 5 and Nov. 25, 1951.

3. Ibid., Nov. 16, 1952, and Feb. 1, 1953.

4. Ibid., March 15, 1964; Dwight, *Letters of Pauline Palmer*, 273; Notice to Creditors, handwritten note, undated, in folder marked Bertha Honoré Palmer and Sarasota, Bertha Palmer and Family Research Collection, Chicago History Museum.

5. Bertha Honoré Palmer and Sarasota, folder of clippings and manuscript materials located in the Bertha Palmer and Family Research Collection, Chicago History Museum; *Sarasota Herald Tribune*, March 3, 1984, and Feb. 28, 2005.

6. *Sarasota Herald Tribune*, Feb. 17, 1964; *Sarasota Herald*, June 8, 1949.

7. *Sarasota Herald Tribune*, Jan. 23, May 15, and Nov. 15, 1955; Feb. 17, 1964.

8. Ibid., Nov. 15, 1958; *Sarasota Journal*, Nov. 14, 1958.

9. *Sarasota Herald Tribune*, Nov. 22, 1959, and Feb. 12, 1960; *Chicago Tribune*, Feb. 28, 1960.

10. *Sarasota Journal*, Jan. 27, 1959.

11. Ripley P. and Adelaide K. Bullen, "The Palmer Site," *The Florida Anthropologist*, Vol. 29, No. 2., Part 2, 1–52; Ripley Bullen to Mrs. Ralph F. Davis, Feb. 7, 1966, Vertical File, Sarasota County Historical Resources; *Sarasota Herald Tribune*, May 18, 1962.

12. Bullen and Bullen, "The Palmer Site," 1–52.

13. Ibid., 1–2.

14. *Sarasota Herald Tribune*, Feb. 17, 1964; *Sarasota Journal*, Feb. 18, 1964.

15. *Sarasota Herald Tribune*, Jan. 17, 1969.

16. Ibid., Oct. 30, 1960.

17. *Sarasota Journal*, Nov. 7, 1973, and March 28, 1975.

18. Ibid., Nov. 7, 1973, and Feb. 21, 1980; *Sarasota Herald Tribune*, July 2, 1980.

19. *Siesta Key Pelican*, Feb. 21, and March 6, 1980.

20. *Sarasota Herald Tribune*, March 8 and 12, July 11, and Aug. 2 and 27, 1980; April 18, 1982; *St. Petersburg Times*, Oct. 19, 1981.

21. Charles E. Horner, "The Promoters," *Florida Trend*, June, 1972, Vertical File, Sarasota County Historical Resources.

22. Ibid.

23. Ibid.

24. *The Sarasota Independent*, May 28–June 3, 1992, Vertical File, Sarasota County Historical Resources.

25. Ibid.

26. Janet Snyder Matthews, *Sarasota Over My Shoulder* (Sarasota, Sarasota County Historical Resources, 1998), 10–11; *Sarasota Herald Tribune*, Nov. 8, 1940.

BIBLIOGRAPHY

Books and Articles

Addams, Jane. *Twenty Years at Hull House*. New York: Macmillan Co., 1949.

Amory, Cleveland. *The Last Resorts*. New York: Harper & Brothers, 1952.

Bauer, Ruthmary. "Sarasota: Hardship and Tourism in the 1930s," *The Florida Historical Quarterly*, Vol. 72, No. 2, Fall 1997, 135–151.

Benshoff, P. J. *Myakka*. Sarasota: Pineapple Press, 2002.

Bickel, Karl. *The Mangrove Coast*. New York: Coward-McAnn, 1942.

Black, Hope L. "Mounted on a Pedestal, Bertha Honoré Palmer." M.A. Thesis, 2007, University of South Florida.

Brolin, Dona. *Back to the Land: The Enduring Dream of Self-Sufficiency in Modern America*. Madison, WI: University of Wisconsin Press, 2011.

Breuning, Margaret. *Mary Cassatt*. New York: Hyperion Press, 1944.

Bullen, Ripley P., and Adelaide K. Bullen. "The Palmer Site," in *The Florida Anthropologist*, Vol. 29, No. 2, Part 2, 1–52.

Burroughs, Lana, Tim Lancaster, and Grant Rimbey. *Images of America: Temple Terrace*. Charleston, SC: Arcadia Publishing, 2010.

Cantacuzene, Princess Julia. *My Life Here and There*. New York: Charles Scribner's Sons, 1921.

———. *Revolutionary Days*. Edited by Terence Emmons. Chicago: The Lakeside Press, 1999.

Cassell, Frank A. "A Confusion of Voices: Reform Movements and the World's Columbian Exposition of 1893," in Alan D. Corré, *The Quest for Social Justice II: The Morris Fromkin Memorial Lectures, 1981–1990*. Milwaukee, WI: The Golda Meir Library of the University of Wisconsin-Milwaukee, 1992, 59–76.

Cassell, Frank A., and Marguerite Cassell, "The White City in Peril: Leadership and the World's Columbian Exposition," *Chicago History*, XII, Fall, 1983, 10–27.

Chandler, David Leon. *Henry Flagler: The Astonishing Life and Times of the Visionary Robber Baron Who Founded Florida*. New York: Macmillan Publishing Company, 1986.

Dedmon, Emmett, *Fabulous Chicago*. New York: Random House, 1953.

Edwards, A. B. "History," *The Look-Out*: April 1, 1960.

Esthus, George I. "Pete." *A History of Agriculture of Sarasota County, Florida*. Sarasota: Sarasota County Fair Association and the Sarasota County Historical Commission, 1976.

Frazer, William, and John L. Guthrie, Jr. *The Florida Land Boom: Speculation, Money, and the Banks*. Westport, CT and London: Quorum Books, 1995.

Gannon, Michael, ed. *History of Florida*. Gainesville: University Press of Florida, 2013.

———. *The New History of Florida*. Gainesville: University Press of Florida, 1996.

Ginger, Ray, *Altgeld's America*. New York: Funk & Wagnall's Company, 1958.

Graham, Thomas. "The First Developers," in Michael Gannon, ed. *The New History of Florida*. Gainesville: University Press of Florida, 1996, 276–295.

Grismer, Karl H. *The Story of Sarasota*. Sarasota: M. F. Russell, 1946.

Harner, Charles E. "First a Panic and Then a Lady: Mrs. Potter Palmer," in *Florida's Promoter's: The Men Who Made it Big*. Tampa: Trend House, 1973.

Harrison, Carter H. *Stormy Years: The Autobiography of Carter H. Harrison*. Indianapolis: The Bobbs Merrill Company, 1935.

Harvey, John. *The Sarasota School of Architecture, 1941–1966*. Boston: MIT Press, 1997.

Hibbert, Christopher. *Edward VII: The Last Victorian King*. London: Palgrave Macmillan, 2007.

Hines, Thomas S. *Burnham of Chicago: Architect and Planner*. Chicago: University of Chicago Press, 1974.

Hobbs, Margo. "Bertha Honoré Palmer's Philanthropy in the Arts." M.A. Thesis, 1992, School of the Art Institute, Chicago.

Hoffman, Glenn. *A History of the Atlantic Coast Line Railroad Company*. CSX Corporate Communications and Public Affairs, 1995.

Kalmbach, Sally Sexton. *The Jewel of the Gold Coast, Mrs. Potter Palmer's Chicago*. Chicago: Ampersand, 2009.

Korwek, Dorothy and Carl Shriver. *John Nolen Plan of Venice, Florida*. Venice: Triangle Inn Association, 2011.

LaHurd, Jeff. *Owen Burns: The Man Who Bought and Built Sarasota*. Friends of the Sarasota County History Center, 2011.

———. *John Hamilton Gillespie: The Scot Who Saved Sarasota*. Sarasota. Friends of the Sarasota County History Center, 2011.

———. *Sarasota: A History*. Charleston, SC: The History Press, 2006.

Logan, Mrs. John A. *Reminiscences of a Soldier's Wife*. New York: Scribner's Sons, 1913.

Long, Timothy A. *Bertha Honoré Palmer*. Chicago: Historical Society of Chicago, 2009.

McCarthy, Kathleen D. *Women's Culture, American Philanthropy and Art, 1830–1930*. Chicago and London: University of Chicago Press, 1991.

———. *Noblesse Oblige, Charity and Philanthropy in Chicago, 1849–1929*. Chicago and London: University of Chicago Press, 1982.

Marquis, Albert N. *The Book of Chicagoans: A Biographical Directory of the Leading Living Men and Women of the City of Chicago*. Chicago: A. N. Marquis Co., 1917.

Marth, Del. *Yesterday's Sarasota, Including Sarasota County*. Miami: A. E. Seaman Publishing, 1973.

Marx, Leo. *The Machine in the Garden*. New York: Oxford University Press, 1964.

Matthews, Janet Snyder. *Sarasota Over My Shoulder*. Sarasota: Sarasota County Historical Resources, 1998.

———. *Edge of Wilderness: A Settlement History of Manatee River and Sarasota Bay*. Sarasota: Coastal Press, 1983.

———. *Venice: Journey from Horse and Chaise: A History of Venice, Florida*: Sarasota, Florida: Pine Level Press, Inc., 1989.

———. *Journey to Centennial: Sarasota.* Rev. ed. Sarasota: Sesquicentennial Productions, Inc., 1997.

Matthews, Janet Snyder, and Linda W. Mansperger. *Mrs. Potter Palmer, Legendary Lady of Sarasota.* Osprey, FL: Gulf Coast Heritage Association, 1999.

Mormino, Gary. "World War II," in Michael Gannon (ed.). *The History of Florida.* Gainesville: University Press of Florida, 2013, 332–352.

———. *Land of Sunshine, Land of Dreams: A Social History of Modern Florida.* Gainesville: University Press of Florida, 2005.

Ottewill, David. *The Edwardian Garden.* New Haven: Yale University Press, 1989.

Pierce, Bessie Louse. A *History of Chicago.* 2 Vols. New York: Alfred K. Knopf, 1940.

Poole, Ernest. *Giants Gone.* New York: McGraw-Hill Company, 1943.

Prince, Richard E. *Seaboard Air Line Railroad.* Bloomington, IN: Indiana University Press, 1967.

Raban, Johnathan. *Bad Land: An American Romance.* New York: Parthenon, 1996.

Robie, Virginia. "The Oaks, Osprey on Little Sarasota Bay," in *The House Beautiful*, LXVII, No. 1, Jan. 1920, 34–58.

Rogers, William D. "The Great Depression," in Michael Gannon, (ed.). *The History of Florida.* Gainesville: University Press of Florida, 2013, 313–331.

———."Fortune and Misfortune: The Paradoxical 1920s," in Michael Gannon (ed.). *The History of Florida.* Gainesville: University Press of Florida, 2013, 296–312.

Ross, Ishbel. *Silhouette in Diamonds: The Life of Mrs. Potter Palmer.* New York: Harper & Brothers, 1960.

Sarinen, Aline B. *The Proud Possessors: The Lives, Times and Tastes of Some Adventurous American Art Collectors.* New York: Random House, 1958.

Smith, Mark D. "A Look Back, The Meadowsweet Pastures," in *Sarasota Herald Tribune*, 3/17/1999.

Stronge, William B. *The Sunshine Economy: An Economic History of Florida Since the Civil War.* Gainesville: University Press of Florida, 2008.

Sulzer, Elmer G. *Ghost Railroads of Sarasota County.* Sarasota County Historical Commission, 1971.

Talbot, George M. "The Rise and Fall of the Florida Celery Industry, 1895–1995," in *Proceedings of the Florida State Horticultural Society.* Vol. 114, 2001, 278–279.

Tebeau, Charlton W. *A History of Florida.* Coral Gables: University of Miami Press, 1971.

Warner, Joe G. *Biscuits and Taters: A History of Cattle Ranching in Manatee County.* St. Petersburg, FL: Great Outdoors Printing Company, 1980.

Weeks, David C. *Ringling: The Florida Years, 1911–1936.* Gainesville: Florida: University Press of Florida, 1993.

Weimann, Jeanne Madeline. *The Fair Women.* Chicago: Academy, 1981.

Wynne, Nick, and Joseph Koretsch. *Florida in the Great Depression: Desperation and Defiance.* Charleston and London: The History Press, 2012.

Wynne, Nick, and Richard Moorhead. *Paradise for Sale: Florida's Booms and Busts.* Charleston and London: The History Press, 2010.

Joe G. Warner, *Biscuits and 'Taters: A History of Cattle Ranching in Manatee County.* St. Petersburg, FL: Great Outdoors Press, 1980.

Youngberg, George E. Sr., and W. Earl Aumann. *Venice and the Venice Area.* Venice, Florida: Sunshine Press, 1969.

Ziegler, Louis W., and Herbert S. Wolfe. *Citrus Growing in Florida.* Gainesville, Florida: University of Florida Press, 1961.

Manuscripts

Chicago History Museum

Bertha Honoré Palmer Papers
Potter Palmer and Palmer Estate Papers
Bertha Palmer and Palmer Family Research Collection
World's Columbian Exposition Records
World's Columbian Exposition, Board of Lady Managers Records
Palmer Photographs

Manatee Historical Records Library
Bertha Palmer Folder
General Index to Deeds
Plat Books

Sarasota County Historical Records Library
Bertha H. Palmer Papers
Map of Palmer Farms (1929)
A. B. Edwards Papers
Lillian G. Burns Collection
Alexander Browning, Memoirs
Joan Berry Dickenman, "The Homesteaders; Early Settlers at Nokomis and
     Laurel," typescript, 1987
A. B. Edwards, Interview by County Historian Dottie Davis
Vertical File
Sarasota County Plat Books
Map Collection
Photograph Collection
Helen C. Gruters, unpublished analysis of Sarasota's 1916 population
Ed Ayers, "General Report on Palmer Experimental Farms," 1930

Historic Spanish Point Archives
Webb Papers
Map of Osprey Point Estate
Master Plan for "Spanish Point at the Oaks," Shepard Associates, 1982
Materials for Training Historic Spanish Point Tour Guides
List of Seed Planted at The Oaks, 1917
Department of Environmental Protection. Palmer Ranch: An Interview with
     Buck Hawkins, a Cattle Rancher. Also interviews with Walter and Ron
     Sweeting who lived at Meadowsweet Pastures
Daily Reports of William F. Prentice to Bertha Palmer Through March 1917
Research Paper on works of art at The Oaks.

Printed Primary Sources

Dwight, Eleanor, ed. *The Letters of Pauline Palmer, 1908–1926: A Great Lady of Chicago's First Family*. MTT Scala Books, 2006.

Howe, Julia Ward. *Reminiscences, 1819–1899*. Boston: Houghton Mifflin & Company, 1899.

Eagle, Mary Kavanagh Oldham, ed. *The Congress of Women Held in the Women's Building, World's Columbian Exposition*. Chicago: Monarch Book Company, 1894.

Palmer, Bertha Honoré. *Addresses and Reports of Mrs. Potter Palmer: President of the Board of Lady Managers, World's Columbian Exposition*. Chicago: Board of Lady Managers, 1893.

Newspapers

Chicago American
Chicago Daily News
Chicago Examiner
Chicago Herald
Chicago Herald and Examiner
Chicago Inter Ocean
Chicago Sun Times
Chicago Tribune
Jacksonville (Florida) Metropolis
Miami Times
New York Times
Palm Beach Daily Times
Sarasota Herald
Sarasota Herald Tribune
Sarasota Independent
Sarasota Journal
Sarasota Times
This Week in Sarasota
St. Petersburg Daily Times
Tampa Times
Tampa Tribune

INDEX

For more books from Pineapple Press, visit our website at www.pineapplepress.com. There you can find author pages, discover new and upcoming books, and search our list for books that might interest you. Look for our weekly posts and giveaways, and be sure to sign up for our mailing list.

Myakka by Paula Benshoff. Discover the story of the land of Myakka in southwest Florida This book takes you into shady hammocks of twisted oaks and up into aerial gardens, down the wild and scenic river, and across a variegated canvas of prairies, piney woods, and wetlands, all located in Myakka River State Park, the largest state park in Florida.

Florida's Past: People and Events That Shaped the State by Gene Burnett. Virtually every month for fourteen years, Gene Burnett wrote a history piece under the title "Florida's Past" for *Florida Trend*. Collected in three volumes.

The Florida Chronicles by Stuart B. McIver. Florida's past is full of people — from the most influential to the most nefarious, follow Stuart McIver on a fascinating trip through the history of the people of the state. This collection of essays is divided into three volumes. Volume 1: *Dreamers, Schemers, and Scalawags*. Volume 2: *Murder in the Tropics*. Volume 3: *Touched by the Sun*.

Historic Homes of Florida by Laura Stewart. Houses tell the human side of history. In this survey of restored residences, their stories are intertwined with those of their owners in a domestic history of Florida from the days of Spanish occupation to the Rawlings House in Cross Creek, Vizcaya in Miami, and President Harry S. Truman's "Little White House" in Key West.

A Land Remembered by Patrick Smith. Ranked #1 Best Florida Book eight times, *A Land Remembered* tells the story of three generations of the MacIveys, a Florida family who battle the hardships of the frontier to rise from a dirt-poor Cracker life to the wealth and standing of real estate tycoons. Love and tenderness are here too: the hopes and passions of each new generation, friendships with the persecuted blacks and Indians, and respect for the land and its wildlife.

Marjory Stoneman Douglas: Voice of the River by Marjory Stoneman Douglas. The voice that emerges in this autobiography is a voice from the past and a voice from the future, a voice of conviction and common sense with a sense of humor, a voice so many audiences have heard over the years—tough words in a genteel accent emerging from a tiny woman in a floppy hat—which has truly become the voice of the Everglades, which she famously named the "river of grass."